Irish Questions and Jewish Questions

Irish Studies

Kathleen Costello-Sullivan, *Series Editor*

SELECT TITLES IN IRISH STUDIES

IRISH
Questions and
JEWISH
Questions

CROSSOVERS IN CULTURE

Edited by
Aidan Beatty *and* Dan O'Brien

SYRACUSE UNIVERSITY PRESS

First Edition 2018
19 20 21 22 23   6 5 4 3 2

∞ The paper used in this publication meets the minimum requirements of the
American National Standard for Information Sciences—Permanence of Paper for
Printed Library Materials, ANSI Z39.48-1992.

For a listing of books published and distributed by Syracuse University Press,
visit www.SyracuseUniversityPress.syr.edu.

ISBN: 978-0-8156-3561-1 (hardcover)   978-0-8156-3579-6 (paperback)
      978-0-8156-5426-1 (e-book)

Library of Congress Cataloging-in-Publication Control Number: 2018020650

Manufactured in the United States of America

Contents

Part Three. **Migrations**

Part Four. **Promised Lands**

Irish Questions and Jewish Questions

Introduction

Irish Questions and Jewish Questions

AIDAN BEATTY AND DAN O'BRIEN

This book is about Irish Jewish history. First, this volume concerns the history of Jews in Ireland and the ways in which Irish Jews have interacted with mainstream Irish society. Second, it concerns the ways in which Irish history and Jewish history have often crossed paths, not only in Ireland but throughout the world.

Irish Jewish history has a definite starting date. In the year 1079, according to the *Annals of Inisfallen*, a medieval chronicle, the first Jews to ever set foot in Ireland arrived from overseas, bearing gifts for their new hosts: "Five Jews came from over sea with gifts to Tairdelbach [an Irish king], and they were sent back again over sea." It is very telling, for the later course of Irish Jewish history, that they were promptly relieved of their gifts and then ordered to leave Ireland.

There is a subtle paradox at work in this seemingly simple sentence. No one in Ireland had ever seen a Jewish person prior to this incident, yet the visitors are unambiguously described as "five Jews" (*coicer Iudaide*) and the Irish people already have a word for Jews, *Iudaide*, a medieval Gaelic word that clearly has its roots in the languages of classical antiquity. But more than that paradox, there is also a certain kind of cultural knowledge at work here. The medieval Irish who gave such short shrift to these Jewish guests "know" some things about Jews, or more accurately they think some things about Jews: they "know" that Jews are not trustworthy, that Jews bearing gifts are not to be taken into one's care. And Jews are not suitable for residence in Ireland—they should be expelled from the country. It is quite telling that the medieval chroniclers of the *Annals of Inisfallen* did not feel the need to explain any of this knowledge: a contemporary reader would presumably have readily agreed with the underlying assumptions here about Jewish perfidy and untrustworthiness.[1]

In this one short sentence, there are two quite different histories at work. First, there is a conventional social history: five Jews, presumably seeking a better life, arrived in Ireland hoping to find refuge there. It was refused to them, and they were promptly expelled from the country. And second, there is a kind of cultural history, or what is sometimes called the history of ideas, in this case, ideas about Jews and Jewishness. This book is interested in both strands. It will focus on the actual social lives of actual flesh-and-blood Jews in Ireland, mainly focusing on the modern era. And it will also look at the Irish history of ideas of Jewishness: what Irish people thought of Jews, which is partly a history of antisemitism, as well as the history of how various people for various reasons have claimed that the Irish shared something essential with the Jews.

The Jews of Ireland

The documentary evidence for the history of the Jews in Ireland in the Middle Ages, like the one sentence in the *Annals of Inisfallen*, is brief and elusive. There are various references in medieval sources to Jewish traders active in Ireland and to property owned by Jews in Dublin. Some of these Jewish merchants may have come in the aftermath of the Anglo-Norman invasion of Ireland in 1169, and indeed, for the medieval period in general, whatever Jewish community existed in Ireland would have been a satellite of the English Jewish community. Probably the only medieval Irish Jew of which there is any definite information is Aaron de Hibernia, Judaeus (Aaron from Ireland, a Jew). Aaron, apparently, was something of a rogue. He was jailed in Bristol Castle in England in 1283 for a number of crimes, including debasing currency. In any case, Jews were barred from England by royal decree on July 18, 1290, and it is almost certain that whatever organized Jewish communities may have existed in Ireland shared their fate and were also expelled.

Nonetheless, there are a number of names that pop up in Irish medieval sources that do suggest that some Jews did remain in Ireland: presumably Jewish names such as William Jew and David Abraham feature in medieval Irish historical sources. And some Marranos, Spanish Jews who had converted to Christianity, also appear to have moved to Ireland after the expulsion of the Jews from Spain in 1492. One particular Marrano, William Annayas, was elected mayor of Youghal, in Cork, in the later sixteenth century. His sons were also prominent figures. In general, though, the Jewish population of Ireland in the later Middle Ages was practically nonexistent; aside from the continued ban on open expression of Judaism, Ireland in the sixteenth century was an impoverished and not all that peaceful place— not the kind of place to be attractive to outsiders.

This situation changed somewhat in the seventeenth century when Oliver Cromwell decreed that Jews would be allowed to again live in England, a ruling that extended to include Ireland. Shortly after the formal return of Jews to England in 1656, there was again a formal Jewish presence in Ireland. But as with the earlier Jewish community in Ireland, this group was initially little more than a small satellite of the English Jewish community. And like their English cousins, the Irish Jewish community in the seventeenth and eighteenth centuries tended to be merchants involved in international trade—the jewelry trade particularly—and they tended to be Dutch Sephardim, the descendants of Jews expelled from Spain and Portugal who ended up in the Netherlands before being invited to settle in the British Isles by Cromwell. It was with the growth of this community that the first synagogue in Ireland came into existence in the early 1700s, on Crane Lane in Dublin, said to have been in the house of a merchant called Phillips. As a sign of the community's growth, the first Jewish cemetery in Ireland was built in Ballybough—then a rural area just outside Dublin, today a suburb of the city. Prior to the building of this cemetery, deceased members of the Irish Jewish community had been buried in Britain. For all that progress, though, the Jewish population in Ireland remained quite small, even negligible, into the eighteenth and early nineteenth centuries.

But starting in the later nineteenth century, the Irish Jewish community grew, owing to a small but noticeable inward migration, mainly from Lithuania. Dublin had a Jewish population of 350 in 1880, most of whom worked as craftsmen—gold and silversmiths, watchmakers, and picture-frame makers.

Cork already had a small Jewish community in the middle of the eighteenth century, mainly involved in the export trade from the city, and was large enough to support a full-time *shochet*, or kosher butcher. As early as 1725 there was a Jewish cemetery in Cork, although it has since been built over. The Cork Jewish community was in a period of decline in the early nineteenth century but was revitalized by the arrival of immigrants from eastern Europe in the later nineteenth century. This revitalization in fact took place across the entire Irish Jewish community. According to the 1881 census, the Jewish community across all of Ireland numbered only 472 persons. By 1891 this figure had reached 1,779, and a decade later it was just under 4,000; the Jewish communities in Cork, Dublin, and Belfast all grew, and new communities emerged in Dundalk, Derry, Waterford, and Limerick. The arrival of relatively large numbers of immigrants, mainly coming from Lithuania, then part of the Russian Empire, fomented something of an intracommunal struggle within the Jewish community, with the Ashkenazi Jews eventually wresting control of Jewish institutions from what they termed the "English" element, predominantly Sephardic Jews with roots going back in Ireland a number of centuries. The Lithuanian Jews also tended to be fairly poor, mostly finding work in Ireland as peddlers or petty traders. As some gained a foothold in the grocery business, there were some early tensions with Irish-born traders. The Limerick Boycott of 1904 remains perhaps the most famous manifestation of this tension.

Another example of this kind of tension can be seen in the anti-semitic advertisements that regularly appeared in Irish nationalist publications at the start of the twentieth century. Similar accusations—that Jews were an alien presence in the Irish economy—are apparent in the mid-1920s, when the Irish Republican Army started a campaign against moneylenders in Dublin. As several historians have pointed out, IRA raids on the offices and homes of moneylenders exclusively targeted Jewish moneylenders. And when a Moneylenders Act was passed by the Dáil Éireann in 1930, there were coded references about Jewish moneylenders in the parliamentary debate. The first Jewish member of the Dáil, Robert Briscoe, was elected in the 1920s for Eamon de Valera's Fianna Fáil party, notwithstanding this background noise of persistent anti-Jewish sentiment.

Where there was something far more sinister was in Irish government policy regarding refugees before, during, and after the Second World War. Already in 1938, when Franklin D. Roosevelt had called a conference to deal with the international question of Jewish refugees fleeing Nazi Germany, Ireland had quietly refused to accept any refugees. This rejection was partly an unwillingness to allow foreigners to move to Ireland, but there were also specifically anti-Jewish elements at work here. Charles Bewley, the Irish ambassador to Nazi Germany in the years leading up to the war, sent openly antisemitic messages back to the Irish government, warning them of the danger of admitting Jewish refugees into Ireland. His various diplomatic communiqués also repeated a number of common Nazi accusations about Jews controlling the German media or causing Germany's defeat in World War I. Unsurprisingly, Bewley was unwilling to issue Irish visas to Jewish refugees seeking to leave Germany. Other government bureaucrats refused to issue visas for Jews because they claimed they wanted to avoid the danger of antisemitism and argued that an increased Jewish presence in Ireland would be seized upon by antisemites. In a small number of cases, though, the Jewish Dáil deputy Robert Briscoe and Chief Rabbi of Ireland Isaac Herzog were able to use their political connections to gain residency visas for Jewish refugees.

In the years since 1945, the Irish Jewish community has been in slow decline. Numbering about 4,000 in 1946, the community had dropped to 1,581 in 1991, though it has since risen to 1,984, in 2011.[2] Nonetheless, when compared with the 45,000 Orthodox Christians, 50,000 Muslims, or 10,000 Hindus in Ireland, it is apparent that the

Irish Jewish community is today a tiny minority, albeit a community that has become fairly well assimilated into Irish society.

Irish Questions, Jewish Questions

Israeli scholar of Irish history and memory Guy Beiner notes the irony that while the Jewish population of Ireland continues to dwindle, "'Jewish Ireland' has emerged as a flourishing academic topic."[3] Beginning with Dermot Keogh's *Jews in Twentieth Century Ireland* (1998), there has been a steady publication of Irish Jewish books in the fields of memoir, history, economics, sociology, and literature. This edited collection is unique in drawing together these disparate elements in one book. It is also timely, coming out amid a decade of commemoration in both Ireland, North and South, and Israel-Palestine. The former reflects on events such as the 1916 Rebellion one hundred years on, leading on to the centenary of the foundation of the Irish Free State in 1922, while the latter looks back at the 1917 Balfour Declaration through to the British Mandate for Palestine in 1922. We are also approaching seventy years since the creation of the State of Israel in 1948 and the declaration of an Irish Republic in 1949. It is almost a half century since the beginning of the Troubles in Northern Ireland and fifty years too since the 1967 Arab-Israeli War. Indeed, a coterie of Irish authors, led by Eimear McBride and Colm Tóibín, have recently traveled to Israel and Palestine—along with Jewish American novelists such as Michael Chabon—to write about the region five decades on from the Six-Day War. Closer to home, in the same year that the Cork synagogue closed its doors after more than a hundred years, Ruth Gilligan's novel *Nine Folds Make a Paper Swan* (2016) and Simon Lewis's poetry collection *Jewtown* (2016) artistically resurrect the now disappeared Cork Jewish community. These books will form the most modern elements of Ulster University's recently launched "Representations of Jews in Irish Literature" project, which seeks to create an online database of every depiction of Jews and Jewishness in Irish texts dating back to antiquity.

The Irish and the Jews are two of the classic outliers of modern Europe. Both struggled with their lack of formal political sovereignty in nineteenth-century Europe. Simultaneously European and not European, both endured a bifurcated status, perceived as racially inferior yet also seen as a natural part of the European landscape. Both sought to deal with their subaltern status through nationalism, and their nationalist movements had some remarkable similarities; both emerged in a new form after the First World War; both had a tangled, ambiguous, and sometimes violent relationship with Britain and the British Empire; diasporas played a major role in both movements; both sought to revive ancient languages as part of their drive to create a new identity; and leading figures of both movements, such as Michael Davitt, Arthur Griffith, Ze'ev Jabotinsky, and Avraham Stern, had an active interest in the successes, and failures, of the other. The career of Irish politician Robert Briscoe and the travails of Leopold Bloom, the central figure of Joyce's *Ulysses* (1922), are just two examples of the delicate balancing of Irish and Jewish identities in the first half of the twentieth century.

These links and parallels are the central theme of this collection, which aims to bring the Jewish Questions of the modern world into conversation with some Irish Questions. As prominent Jewish historian Derek Penslar has said, the "Jewish Question" (or "Jewish Problem") of nineteenth-century Europe shared a similar "taxonomy of dysfunction" with British society's contemporary "Irish Question." Penslar observes, "A hegemonic or dominant majority group that discriminated against a subaltern or minority group called the latter a 'problem,' suggesting that the members of the group were themselves mainly responsible for its disabilities."[4]

Clustered under the part headings "Representations," "Realities," "Migrations," and "Promised Lands," this volume seeks to understand the shared history of the Jewish and Irish Questions (in Europe, Israel-Palestine, and North America), the perceptions of Jews in Irish popular culture, and the ways in which Irish nationalists have used Jewishness as a means of understanding their own minority status. In addition, the volume adds to the critically understudied field of Irish Jewish social history.

As well as being of obvious interest to students of modern Irish and Jewish history and culture, this volume will hopefully appeal to scholars of British imperial history, nationalism, diasporas, migration, whiteness studies, and race and ethnicity. Together, the assembled chapters provide a broad overview of Irish and Jewish history.

Representations

In her chapter, "British Israelites, Irish Israelites, and the Ends of an Analogy," Abby Bender traces the political and literary uses of the Irish Israelite analogy from its origins in medieval genealogy through its role in Irish Jewish relations at the beginning of the twentieth century. Moving through Irish history, she considers Israelite genealogies in early Christian Ireland, the emergence of a typological imagination in the seventeenth century, and the increasing nationalization of the analogy in the eighteenth and nineteenth centuries. The chapter begins at its chronological endpoint, by examining a remarkable incarnation of the biblical Exodus story in 1902, when the imperialist British Israelites attempted to excavate the Ark of the Covenant at Tara in County Meath. Through this example and others, Bender explores the irony by which both colonial and anticolonial rhetoric has enlisted the same biblical tropes and analogies for opposite ends: by the twentieth century, the disenfranchised Irish and the English settlers had spent hundreds of years viewing themselves as Israelites looking for a promised land.

R. M. Douglas's chapter, "'Not So Different after All': Irish and Continental European Antisemitism in Comparative Perspective," counteracts the general perception that antisemitism in twentieth-century Ireland has been mild, sharing little in common with the more virulent forms visible in continental Europe during the same period. Whether attributed to the negligible Jewish presence in the country or to the Irish people's supposed fixation on more parochial concerns (especially the "national question"), such assessments all too typically ignore the substantial degree of evidence to the contrary, Douglas argues. They also leave unhistoricized the alarming levels of antisemitic prejudice existing in contemporary Ireland. Douglas contends that a highly visible strain of antisemitism can be found in Irish political discourse throughout the twentieth century and that it shares many characteristics and correlates with its counterparts in mainland Europe. The chapter offers possible reasons for the failure of scholars and political commentators alike to accord expressions of Irish antisemitism the prominence in the country's political narrative that, based on their prevalence, they deserve.

Douglas's contribution is followed by Peter Hession's chapter, "'New Jerusalem': Constructing Jewish Space in Ireland, 1880–1914." Hession shows how Jewish migrants to Ireland in the later nineteenth century responded to widespread antisemitism and unpacks the roles that Zionism and "spatial legitimacy" played in this response. Hession breaks major new methodological ground in his original approach to the study of Jewish Irish life.

In "Irish Representations of Jews and Jewish Responses/Jewish Representations of Jews and Irish Responses," Natalie Wynn shows that Irish attitudes toward the Jews remain a hotly contested topic. Traditional interpretations of Irish Jewish history claim that Ireland has exhibited relatively little anti-Jewish prejudice since the surge in Jewish settlement in the late nineteenth and early twentieth centuries. According to this version of events, Jews have experienced a comparatively smooth and unhindered integration into Irish society, making a contribution to many fields of Irish life that has been disproportionate to their modest numbers. Uncomfortable episodes such as the Limerick Boycott of 1904 have been glossed over in both scholarly and anecdotal histories as a form of historical aberration. Attempts to challenge such views have been sidelined in the efforts of the communal and scholarly establishment to maintain the standard, relatively uncontentious, and harmonious version of events that has been presented as the virtual "last word" in Irish Jewish history. The polarized historical narrative that has resulted does little to advance our understanding of anti-Jewish prejudice as manifested in the Irish context. This chapter argues the need for a balanced and objective debate on anti-Jewish prejudice in Ireland. Traditional understandings of the Irish reception of the Jews and the Jewish relationship with Ireland and the Irish are reexamined by Wynn through the lens of contemporary critical analysis. In particular, the insights of contemporary Jewish historiography, hitherto virtually absent, are introduced. Wynn contends that negative popular stereotypes and anti-Jewish prejudice have played a significant role in molding the frequently cautious approach to Irish Jewish history that has prevailed among scholars and nonprofessional historians, Jews and non-Jews, alike.

Realities

Sander L. Gilman's chapter, "From Richard Lalor Sheil to Leon Pinsker: The Jewish Question, the Irish Question, and a Genealogy of Hebrewphobia," reexamines an often-overlooked moment in Irish history, when Richard Lalor Sheil, a supporter of Daniel O'Connell, spoke in favor of the Jews Relief Act of 1848, which removed previous barriers to Jews in Great Britain. In so doing, Lalor Sheil coined the term *Hebrewphobia*, one of the earliest incidents of the relabeling of anti-Jewish sentiment (only later in the century to be again relabeled as antisemitism) as a "phobia," suggesting a form of mental illness. This chapter examines the speech and its specific context in Irish and European political history, while also focusing on the evocation of "prejudice" as a mental illness and its repercussions within Jewish self-awareness in the later nineteenth century.

In "Rebellious Jews on the Edge of Empire: The Judæo-Irish Home Rule Association," Heather Miller Rubens looks at this short-lived association, set up by members of Dublin's Jewish community in 1908. The launch of this organization by Irish Jews who supported Irish national aspirations prompted a contentious public exchange in Jewish communal newspapers, highlighting the complexity of Jewish political and religious identities in Ireland at the beginning of the twentieth century. Members of the British Jewish community, in both Dublin and London, strenuously objected to the formation of this group and called for these Irish Jews to not involve their Jewishness in Home Rule politics. In this chapter, Rubens traces the newsprint narrative surrounding the foundation of the association, discussing how public Jewish identity was contested within an Irish context at the beginning of the twentieth century.

In her chapter, "Rethinking Irish Protectionism: Jewish Refugee Factories and the Pursuit of an Irish Ireland for Industry," Trisha Oakley Kessler explores specific cases of Jewish migration to Ireland in the lead-up to World War II. As a solution to high unemployment and emigration, Fianna Fáil's protectionist policy, post-1932, promised an Irish industry that would serve the Irish people, yet this policy was ridden with contradictions. In response to a dearth of native industrial investment and manufacturing skills, the Department of Industry and Commerce accepted proposals from foreign industrialists. In particular, a number of Jewish refugee businessmen offered skills that were of use to Fianna Fáil's industrial drive, and factories were established in provincial towns across Ireland. To assure the public that any foreign presence in Irish industry was there purely to serve the nation, Sean Lemass, Kessler argues, developed a narrative of functionality within which he placed foreign industrialists as conduits of industrial processes. The question of how the imposition of such a rigid identity impacted Jewish refugee businessmen is examined here with particular reference to the challenges each industrialist faced as their own personal circumstances changed during their time in Ireland. This chapter explores the complexities of identity and encounter within communities that had to negotiate a politically charged nationalist industrial narrative alongside the acceptance of nonnative industrialists as local employers and neighbors.

Migrations

In his reflective autobiographical essay, "Irish, Jewish, or Both: Hybrid Identities of David Marcus, Stanley Price, and Myself," George Bornstein continues the great tradition of Irish Jewish memoir of David Marcus. Here Bornstein tracks the growth and awareness of his own interest in Jewish Irish relations. It began with his interest in romantic and modern poetry, which resulted in first a doctoral dissertation and then in 1970 his first book, *Yeats and Shelley*. Bornstein discovers a more personal connection to Ireland in the autobiography of his distant relative Jewish Irish writer Stanley Price, which contains an account of his ancestor coming to Ireland in the 1890s. Bornstein's ongoing work on W. B. Yeats, and friendship with his children, Michael and Anne, kept him aware not just of Yeats's involvement in Irish politics and culture but also his signing of a newspaper ad in America supporting the Zionist cause. Irish and Jewish culture came together with much else in his book *The Colors of Zion: Blacks, Jews, and Irish* (2011), a seminal work in the field of Irish Jewish literary criticism and the study of popular culture.

Dan Lainer-Vos's chapter is titled "The Irish Victory Fund and the United Jewish Appeal as Nation-Building Projects." Drawing on his recent book *Sinews of the Nation*, Lainer-Vos shows how sacrifice and self-denial in the homeland were used to justify demands for financial generosity from Irish Americans and Jewish Americans. His contribution shows that an exchange of blood and money connected multitudes of people in America to Ireland and Israel through bonds of obligation and solidarity.

In his chapter, "The Discourses of Irish Jewish Studies: Bernard Shaw, Max Nordau, and the Evocations of the Cosmopolitan," Stephen Watt takes a look at one specific Irish Jewish literary dispute. In 1895 George Bernard Shaw reviewed Dr. Max Nordau's book *Degeneration* (1893), a vastly influential work about the decline of fin de siècle culture. Shaw eventually damned the book as "manifest nonsense" and suggested the *Degeneration* "boom" was now totally "exhausted." This chapter shows how Shaw would continue to attack the book in later work and in doing so made several assertions of relevance to our understanding of Irish Jewishness, which for him is construed not as a national, demographic, or hereditary fact but as a cultural construction within which identity is inevitably hybridized.

Promised Lands

Muiris Ó Laoire's chapter is titled "The Historical Revitalization of Hebrew as a Model for the Revitalization of Irish?" In a sixty-year period that straddled the end of the nineteenth and the beginning of the twentieth centuries, Hebrew was revitalized and reintroduced in Palestine, becoming a full-fledged vernacular of some Jews living there. Later it was to become an official language of the State of Israel. Ó Laoire examines the sociolinguistic settings and conditions in the revitalization of Hebrew and offers comparable and contrastive insights to the restoration of Irish in Ireland during the same historical period.

Finally, Seán William Gannon's chapter, "'From the Isle of Saints to the Holy Land': Irish Encounters with Zionism in the Palestine Mandate," looks at the role played by Irishmen in the British colonial project in Palestine. As they did throughout the empire, many Irish served in the Mandate civil service, judiciary, and police until the foundation of the State of Israel in 1948. As Gannon argues, "For the great majority of these Irishmen, their posting to Palestine constituted their first encounter with Jews or Jewish nationalism (or both). Occasionally friendly, but more frequently fraught, this encounter, in many cases, defined their views of Israel and Zionism for the rest of their lives."

Collectively, these twelve chapters represent a major revision of Irish Jewish history and an attempt to bring two interdisciplinary scholarly fields—Irish studies and Jewish studies—into a productive conversation with each other.

PART ONE | **Representations**

I

British Israelites, Irish Israelites, and the Ends of an Analogy

ABBY BENDER

From the seventeenth century through the twentieth, a common strain of Irish lament involved the analogy with the Jews. Ireland's preeminent bard of the nineteenth century, Thomas Moore, described the two nations similarly, "conquer'd and broken," in his poem "The Parallel," and even James Joyce, with his knowing and deflating irony, would invoke their comparative struggles in *Ulysses*, his "epic of two races (Israel-Ireland)." From poetry to politics, the widespread belief that both the Irish and the Jews had suffered more than other people persisted into the twentieth century, when George Bernard Shaw suggested, somewhat less morosely than others had, that "Jews . . . just like Irishmen . . . languish in their own country, and flourish in every other."[1] But beyond the gloomy note of comparative affliction, the Irish had compared themselves to Jews (or their biblical predecessors, Israelites) not only to mourn the past but also to look forward and imagine how Ireland might become a modern, independent nation. Indeed, for most of Irish history, the Jewish experience, particularly the narratives of the Hebrew Bible, provided powerful protonational and nationalist narratives for the Irish.

But it was not only the Irish: many other groups also found these biblical narratives compelling as analogies, typologies, and genealogies. By the twentieth century, the disenfranchised Irish had been sharing the Israelite trope with English settlers—who also saw themselves as

17

oppressed Israelites looking for a promised land—for hundreds of years. Colonial (English) and anticolonial (Irish) discourse enlisted that same story of the biblical Exodus from Egyptian slavery for opposite ends, one of many paradoxes and complications that would eventually combine with other cultural and political shifts in Irish life to make the Irish Jewish analogy obsolete. If the Irish-as-Jew motif was so common as to be seen as a banal cliché by the Dubliners of *Ulysses* in 1904, by the time that novel was published in 1922 (also the year of the birth of the Free State), Joyce's representation of the analogy was already history. Only recently have we begun to unearth the remarkable literal and figurative Irish Jewish connections that revolutionary Catholic Ireland buried under its new discourse in the mid-twentieth century.

One moment in particular—the story of an attempted excavation of another sort—offers a useful vantage point on how this analogy disappeared from Irish life. On June 24, 1902, a distinguished company of Dublin literati—W. B. Yeats, Douglas Hyde, George Moore, and Arthur Griffith—set out from the city to an amateur excavation under way at the Hill of Tara, the site where Ireland's high kings had been crowned centuries earlier. Yeats and company were on a mission to protect both the hill itself and any Irish antiquities that lay within it, for indeed the English diggers were working to disinter a singularly momentous artifact (although not, in fact, an Irish one). These excavators, members of a British Israelite sect who believed themselves to be descendants of the lost tribes of Israel, were convinced that the biblical Ark of the Covenant was buried beneath that hill in County Meath.

This unconventional theory of the Ark's secret resting place in the Irish countryside was authorized, as Mairéad Carew writes in her book on the bizarre episode, by a "strange mixture of early Irish history, genealogy and Old Testament rhetoric." In a more immediate sense, the British Israelites were motivated by an understanding of themselves as God's chosen people, true inheritors of all that the Hebrew Bible had promised. They would use their pseudoarchaeological and biblical evidence to prove that this promised land—Ireland—truly belonged to them. According to nationalist revolutionary Maud

Gonne, who initiated the campaign to save Tara from the unsightly excavations, the diggers planned to present the Ark to Edward VII;[2] in doing so, they would reconfirm the colonial relationship between England and Ireland and the imperial power from which their project had sprung.

Meanwhile, Irish writers, politicians, and cultural nationalists, including those individuals who journeyed to Tara on June 24, were already invested in the metaphor, if not the reality, that *they* were the chosen people, the Israelites of Old Testament enslavement and liberation. Although we might have expected Yeats and his colleagues to embrace any archaeological evidence that would literalize their metaphor, in this case they rejected it, since it came entangled with the offensive imperialism of the British Israelites. (And needless to say, no evidence of the Ark was recovered.) Literary Anglo-Irish Protestants (and Yeats and Hyde especially) were particularly trying to disassociate themselves from the taint of their colonial past, as they faced Irish Ireland nationalists (including their Tara companion Griffith) who rejected them as non-Catholic and nonnative. Yeats and his friends had traveled to Tara to condemn the excavation; at Gonne's urging, and rather astonishingly equipped with a shotgun, they meant to shut it down. Any association with English fundamentalists was to be sedulously avoided.

Upon their return from Tara, the writers composed an angry letter to the *Times* protesting the excavation's desecration of their Irish national heritage. The letter, published on June 27, 1902, and signed by Yeats, Hyde, and Moore (and apparently typed by Lady Gregory), exposes and attacks the ideological core of the British Israelite project: the Hill of Tara, "probably the most consecrated spot in Ireland," where Irish kings once ruled the autonomous Irish nation, was being ruthlessly torn up by the English in yet another act of cultural appropriation. Later that summer, in the poem "In the Seven Woods," Yeats would try to put the distressing event out of mind:

> I have forgot awhile
> Tara uprooted, and new commonness
> Upon the throne and crying about the streets.[3]

The British Israelite mythology, downgraded from ancient genealogy to "new commonness," is quickly dispensed with, but Yeats, like his poem, was clearly troubled by it. That the English should find the biblical Ark, that through their manipulation of Irish pseudohistories *they* should be the "chosen," and thus the rightful, people of Ireland, was an appalling notion for nationalists looking to prove exactly the opposite point.

While trying to fend off someone else's arrival in their promised land, Yeats, Hyde, Moore, and Gregory nevertheless retained the biblical Exodus as a narrative of Irish national liberation. Writing in the *United Irishman* in 1903, Yeats would reaffirm the value of the Ark, as if to clarify that in rejecting the excavations at Tara, he was not rejecting the metaphoric potential of the Exodus story: "To me it seems that ideas, and beauty and knowledge are precisely those sacred things, an Ark of the Covenant as it were, that a nation must value even more than victory."[4] Refusing to abdicate the biblical trope to his opponents (or, indeed, to address the critique from other Irish revivalists that biblical genealogies were highly questionable, convoluted "spurious Celto-Hebraic mythology"),[5] Yeats held on to the centuries-long Irish investment in the Israelites as both literal and metaphoric ancestors. Indeed, Tara's association with the Israelites was not a British invention but an Irish one, and it is just one example of the rhetorical power and persistence of the Israelite motif in Ireland. By the start of the twentieth century, negotiating the English appropriation of "their" Israelite story was something that Irish writers had been managing for years.

The Exodus story, in particular, had long been important to Gaelic Irish imaginings of national struggle and provided what Breandán Ó Buachalla describes as "the central literary metaphor" of early modern Ireland—one that was "invoked incessantly."[6] Indeed, the primacy of Exodus seems almost inevitable when we consider that the Gaelic literati were surrounded, as it were, with biblical material from all sides of Irish life. There were the early Mosaic genealogies in the histories of Keating and his predecessors, and there was the Bible itself, circulated and read widely in Ireland in the 1600s—in Irish as well as English and Latin.[7] Also circulating through the culture were the Exodus themes ubiquitous in English and European discourse that the Gaelic Irish would have encountered both in exile abroad and at home. These biblical stories irresistibly mirrored Irish oppression and exile.

Irish "Israelites" found their trope embattled, however, once Cromwell arrived, figuring the English as Israelites and the Catholic Irish as Canaanites or Egyptians.[8] The surplus of biblical analogies was by no means unusual; "scriptural politics" was the norm, as David S. Katz notes of the English case, and for good reason: "A partial biblical phrase, a sanctified word or two, served the dual purpose of conveying a synecdochic message . . . and ratifying it with the stamp of divine authority."[9] Thus, Christians everywhere used narratives from the Hebrew Bible—and chiefly Exodus—as types for their own struggles.[10] New promised lands became particularly compelling during the epochs of imperial expansion and the rise of the European nation-state. From England to Ireland to South Africa to the Americas, biblical rhetoric circulated.[11] Tom Garvin has remarked that "a central feature of a good myth is how easy it is to transfer it to new soil and to new political purposes," and Exodus seemed always to take root.[12]

The seventeenth century had been, as Katz explains, the high point of "scriptural politics" in England, when the Bible was a "cultural common denominator." English cultural approaches to sacred texts would change, however, along with Enlightenment critiques of the Hebrew Bible's literal truth and Mosaic authorship. But whereas scriptural politics waned demonstrably in England, the Israelite trope remained an important presence—if a changing one—in the Irish context. Genealogical links between the Irish and the Israelites, for example, experienced a renewal in the eighteenth century in both Irish and English sources. Biblical and Gaelic genealogies were reintroduced in works like historian Charles O'Conor's popular *Dissertations on the History of Ireland* (1753), in which the Irish are described as "a kind of ethnic Hebrews."[13] But most influentially, renowned antiquarian and philologist Charles Vallancey, cofounder of the Royal Irish Academy, established a new mode of connecting the Irish and the Israelites through his work on ancient linguistics, linking the Irish and Hebrew languages.[14] Vallancey's scholarship would serve a range of political uses—including, eventually, the British Israelite theory about the Ark of the Covenant. But Vallancey was also influential in Ireland, where his work provided modern evidence for the biblical ancestry described in much earlier Irish texts. William Sampson was most likely drawing on Vallancey when he wrote of the Irish language that "it has been traced by its affinities to that in which the word of God was delivered by Moses and the prophets."[15]

By the nineteenth century, an obsession with biblical genealogies was widespread in Europe and the United States. For the British Israelites who would eventually dig at Tara, typological thinking of the sort that had buoyed Cromwell, combined with a literal genealogy reaching from Queen Victoria back to the lost tribes, was deployed to indicate modern British imperialism's biblical mandate.[16] British Israelites read genealogies as racial histories; as Colin Kidd points out, in their hands, "the message of the Bible seemed to be reducible to a kind of ethnology." This racialism was particularly clear as the group's beliefs related to Ireland. American Reverend Thomas Rosling Howlett comments, in his book *Anglo-Israel* (1892), that "the difference between [the inhabitants of the North of Ireland and the Scots] and those of the south of Ireland lies, not in their religion, but in their origin. They sprang from different races." Howlett insists that if the native Irish—modern Canaanites—are not driven out of the land, then in Moses's words, "it shall come to pass that those which ye let remain of them shall be pricks in your eyes and thorns in your sides, and shall vex you in the land wherein ye dwell." "This," writes Howlett, "is the 'Irish Question.'"[17]

Other British Israelites answered the Irish Question with the same potentially genocidal proposal and used the same biblical evidence from Exodus: that, as Canaanites, the (Catholic) Irish must be expropriated, if not eradicated. Edward Hine, author of *Forty-Seven Identifications of the Anglo Saxons with the Lost Ten Tribes of Israel Founded upon Five Hundred Scripture Proofs* (1874), repeatedly decries "these Irish Canaanites"; they must, he insists, "come under the dying out process." Hine's argument illustrates the profound danger of Exodus as a colonial narrative—a danger that in the late twentieth century

Edward Said warned of—particularly when he makes the startling claim that "we have literally fulfilled Israel's mission by pushing the aborigines of our colonies to the ends of what was once their own country." Moreover, British Israelism was anti-Irish not only in racial but also in political terms: "Ireland is one of our many possessions fairly won by conquest and it is absolutely impossible for England to lose any of her rightful Possessions without doing violence to Scripture. . . . Therefore the notion of repeal becomes nonsense agitation."[18] Irish nationalist interests, such as repeal of the Union, are rendered biblically forbidden by British Israelite belief. And while the British Israelites were not quite mainstream, their politics essentially gathered up genealogical evidence in support of already widely held views on the subject of Ireland.

In contrast to the divisive racial categorizing of the British Israelites, in the nineteenth century Irish Catholics and Protestants used biblical analogies and genealogies as a way of overcoming perceived differences in ethnicity (and real differences of religion and class) across Irish society, thus developing a powerful nationalist discourse through the analogy with the Jews. While most nineteenth-century Irish would not have considered themselves literal descendants of the Israelites, or felt they were typologically fulfilling the Bible, they were generally amenable to the analogical link with the chosen people. The metaphor served, indeed, to designate all Irish people as chosen—making them a unified nation. By the close of the eighteenth century, after all, it was not only the Catholic Irish who were invested in Irish independence, and analogical forms of thinking helped to integrate the various groups of Irish nationalists who were struggling for political and religious freedoms. At the forefront of the United Irishmen movement were members of the Protestant Ascendancy, enlisted by Theobald Wolfe Tone "to unite the whole people of Ireland, to abolish the memory of all past dissensions, and to substitute the common name of Irishman in place of the denominations of Protestant, Catholic and Dissenter."[19] In keeping with this inclusiveness, the Israelite analogy in this period became nonsectarian as it became explicitly nationalist; it allowed a diverse nation to (at least rhetorically) figure itself as cohesive. Helpfully, both the Israelite analogy and scriptural politics more generally were native to all three communities that made up the United Irishmen: Catholics, Protestants, and the Presbyterian Scots for whom political typologies were even more explicitly prescriptive.[20] Exodus, with such universal appeal, would for now retain its status as an important national—and increasingly anticolonial—trope. Not until the 1880s would various factors begin to contribute to a newly sectarian understanding of Exodus, one that would eventually become inextricably linked to Protestant Parnellite constitutionalists and would finally be disowned by most Catholic nationalists.

Until the first decades of the twentieth century, then, *Exodus* would serve as shorthand for national aspirations and serve equally Catholic and Protestant Ireland. James Clarence Mangan's iconic translation of William Heffernan's eighteenth-century poem "Kathleen Ni Houlahan," which was hugely popular across the spectrum of nationalist ideology in the decades following the Union, offers a fine example of the trope's potential for wide appeal. Its providential mode in which the people "wait the Young Deliverer" accommodates a passive longing for freedom, while the percussive rhythm and strong rhyme, along with the invocation of the Aisling figure, Kathleen, suggest more militant human action:

> He, who over sands and waves led Israel along—
> He, who fed, with heavenly bread, that chosen tribe and throng—
> He, who stood by Moses, when his foes were fierce and strong—
> May He show forth His might in saving Kathleen-Ni-Houlahan.[21]

Lady Wilde (mother of Oscar) also helped to solidify the imaginative place of the Exodus narrative in nineteenth-century Ireland.[22] Wilde's poems, published under the name Speranza in the widely read journal the *Nation*, epitomize the turn toward more aggressively nationalist literature. Of the poems she collects in her 1871 volume, at least eight allude to Exodus, and the two that bookend the collection take the trope as their central theme. Opening the volume is the poem "Dedication: To Ireland," in which Wilde calls out to God,

To come in Sinai thunders down,
And, with His mystic radiance, crown
Some Prophet-Leader, with command
To break the strength of Egypt's band,
And set thee free,
Loved Ireland![23]

While God and some Moses figure will do the liberating, Lady Wilde relishes the task of stirring her country into action. She invokes the figure of Moses's sister, Miriam, who, after passing through the Red Sea, "flung her triumphs to the stars / In glorious chants for freedom won." The vigor of Wilde's poems suggests that she thrives by imagining the liberation yet to come. But Wilde is not unreservedly optimistic, and her poems claim that both sectarianism and a slave mentality inhibit Irish freedom. Wilde implies that the people must have more than faith; they will be freed only through human work and human change. In acknowledging that the population is ambivalent about liberation, Wilde anticipates the work of twentieth-century writers—especially Lady Gregory and James Joyce—for whom this element was what made Exodus both truth telling and productive as a literary, cultural, and political trope.

Toward the end of the century, it was Home Rule party leader Charles Stewart Parnell who finally emerged as the Moses that Wilde and other nationalist poets had been seeking; he embodied the Israelite deliverer to a degree that seemed to confirm the metaphor definitively. Like Moses, Parnell was both an heir of the elite ruling class and one of the people, imbued with their revolutionary spirit. Parnell himself would entreat his party, in 1890, "I should like . . . that I should come within sight of the Promised Land."[24] Yet just as Parnell was to be denied continued leadership of his party after the revelation of his affair with the married Katherine O'Shea, Parnell's embodiment of Moses also functioned to undermine the appeal of the Israelite analogy for an increasingly empowered Catholic Ireland, for whom the idea of an Anglo-Irish leader was ever less appealing. Parnell's Protestant Ascendancy background, like his relationship with the

English O'Shea, appeared to threaten national purity in an increasingly Catholic-identified country. Although Yeats, Gregory, and Joyce would all continue to imagine Parnell as Moses in their literary works and essays, after his death in 1891 the Israelite analogy would, in the years approaching the Easter Rising, lose its rhetorical power.

Jewish immigration to Ireland also contributed to the decline of the Israelite analogy. Poets and politicians who took up the Exodus narrative as a model for liberation could not have anticipated that their metaphoric Israelites would soon be arriving, literally, on Irish shores. The new Jewish population would complicate the ways in which both Exodus and the Israelite Irish analogy more broadly were used in cultural and political discourse in Ireland. A land of extreme emigration from the nineteenth century until the end of the twentieth, Ireland's largest foreign-born population from outside of the United Kingdom and the United States (whose emigrants were mostly of Irish ancestry) was, until the Celtic Tiger of the 1990s, composed of Jews from Lithuania who arrived in the greatest numbers between the 1870s and 1910s.[25] Israelites had been in Ireland's imagination for centuries, but living Jews presented different challenges from ancient and metaphoric ones. As Elizabeth Cullingford notes, "When the Other with whom the Irish choose to identify is a long-dead civilization this practice of retro-empathy may bolster native pride, but it requires no exertion in the present."[26] "Exertion in the present" was precisely what was now at stake as the Irish confronted a once rhetorical parallel face-to-face.

The Irish Jewish analogy becomes troubled in this period of immigration, and, as Andrew Gibson writes, "in certain nationalist quarters . . . the Irish-Jewish identification traditional within the culture breaks down." Gibson further notes that Jews—even the impoverished peddlers arriving from Lithuania—were seen by some Catholic nationalists as colonizers: "They threaten to 'plant their heels' on the people's necks and impose a worse 'slavery' than did Cromwell." In making this link between Jewish and Protestant settlers, these nationalists ironically shore up the Unionist mythology of British chosenness. Consequently, amid this reanimation of Cromwellian (and

British Israelite) rhetoric, nationalists become either antisemites or supporters of both literal Jews and the Israelite analogy.[27] The ideological function of the Israelite analogy, so recently used to promote unity within the nationalist movement, splits down sectarian lines.

The fracture was catalyzed by the Limerick Pogrom of 1904, in which a Redemptorist preacher initiated a hateful boycott against Jewish businesses, fueled by both racism and economic jealousy.[28] Members of Father Creagh's church badly beat several Jewish men, and Jewish families with businesses were eventually forced to move from the city. Arthur Griffith responded with his own antisemitic rant on the front page of the *United Irishman*, calling Jews "usurers and parasites."[29] Along with his increasing antisemitism, Griffith developed a resistance to the Israelite analogy, arguing for not only racial but aesthetic national purity as well. In 1904, some months after the Limerick incident, he explicitly disavowed Exodus as an Irish narrative. At the national Feis Ceoil (Irish Musical Festival) of that year, the prizewinning cantata was "The Exodus: A Sacred Cantata," with words by poet (and future Easter Rising martyr) Thomas MacDonagh and music by Benedetto Palmieri.[30] The libretto—which, as MacDonagh's biographer Johann Norstedt notes, has been ignored by musical and literary critics—is a straightforward exposition of the biblical text, with solos for Moses, Aaron, Pharaoh, and Miriam. But set amid the cultural nationalism of the revival, the subject was hardly innocuous. Opening with a chorus of Hebrew women calling on God, the libretto echoed the recent surfeit of Exodus-themed nationalist poetry that had only increased after the death of Parnell, and it sounds not unlike Wilde: "Long in bondage and chains we have suffered. . . . We implore Thee in humble subjection, / The fair land of our fathers restore." The one extended review of the performance was published in Griffith's *United Irishman*, and, as Norstedt points out, it "attacked the cantata on the grounds that neither . . . its music, lyrics, nor general subject had . . . anything to do with Ireland." According to this review, "The Exodus," "despite its disingenuous claim on our reverence for things sacred, must . . . be called foreign." As Norstedt suggests, MacDonagh "must have been considerably annoyed by such criticism; and it is incredible—whether or not MacDonagh had this in mind—that so strident a nationalist newspaper as the *United Irishman* could not see the similarity in the plight of the ancient people of Israel and that of the modern Irish."[31] Griffith, who almost certainly wrote the review himself, was as aware of the analogy as anyone—in fact, he had used it himself in his comparative study of Irish and Hungarian nationalism, published in the same year.[32] Thus, rather than an oversight, this criticism is a conscious snub, a pointed attempt to now reject Exodus as "foreign" in a way it had not been perceived before.

Although Griffith did not speak for the entire Catholic community, it was mostly Protestant writers (at least until Joyce) who continued to identify with both ancient and modern Jews. Yeats, in 1901, imagined himself as Moses, and Lady Gregory recycled the Exodus story as an Irish allegory throughout her life, most directly in her Parnell play *The Deliverer*. Douglas Hyde repeatedly invoked the Jews—contemporary Jews—as models for national linguistic renewal, and Standish O'Grady would denounce the persecution of Jews, "brothers in a common struggle." Most famously, however, it was the Catholic Michael Davitt who wrote a series of rebuttals to Griffith and the Limerick incident.[33] Upon his death, Davitt was honored with a funeral wreath from the Jewish community of Dublin, "in grateful remembrance of Davitt's efforts on behalf of the one race which has suffered more than the Irish," as Francis Sheehy-Skeffington wrote in 1908. Sheehy-Skeffington described Davitt as "the prophet who had led [the people of Mayo] out of the wilderness,"[34] a trope possibly borrowed from those individuals who had used it of Parnell, but also originating in Fanny Parnell's poem "Michael Davitt," published in the *Boston Pilot* in 1880:

> Out of the slime and the squalor,
> Out of the slough of despond,
> Out of the yoke of Egypt,
> Out of the gyve and bond[35]

Fanny Parnell was writing before her brother Charles Stewart became, for the Irish people, the unequivocal Moses, yet the trope rings prophetic as well for Davitt, who would devote so much energy not only to Irish liberation but also to Jewish rights and freedoms.

A decade before the events in Limerick, Davitt had made the following speech, published in the *Freeman's Journal*: "The Jews have never to my knowledge done any injury to Ireland. Like our own race, they have endured a persecution the records of which will for ever [*sic*] remain a reproach to the 'Christian' nations of Europe. Ireland has no share in this black record. Our country has this proud distinction—freely acknowledged by Jewish writers—of never having resorted to this un-Christian and barbarous treatment of an unfortunate people." Davitt was echoing the chief rabbi of the British Empire, Dr. S. Hermann Adler, who had made similar comments when he consecrated the headquarters of the Dublin Hebrew Congregation in 1892, telling the community, "You have come here, my foreign brethren, from a country like unto Egypt of old to a land which offers you hospitable shelter. It is said that Ireland is the only country in the world which cannot be charged with persecuting the Jews." Adler, in turn, was echoing Daniel O'Connell, who had famously supported the Jewish emancipation bill in Britain, writing in 1828, "Ireland has claims on your ancient race, as it is the only Christian Country that I know of unsullied by any act of persecution against the Jews."[36] This transmission of transnational sympathy has been remarked upon, but perhaps even before O'Connell expressed it, the idea was already circulating in Ireland. In a letter written in 1820 and reprinted that year in the *Jewish Expositor and Friend of Israel*, we find much the same conceit expounded by the Reverend L. Way. He writes, "The Scotch have *heads*, the English *hands*, but the *Irish hearts*, and *their desire* is, that Israel may be saved:—this triple cord, bound with love, will not easily break.—The Irish *never persecuted* the Jews, and now they *are blessing them*."[37] The *Jewish Expositor*, it should be noted, proffered an ideology profoundly at odds with anything that could be acceptable to either Irish nationalists or Jews; it was published by the London Society for Promoting Christianity amongst the Jews, and the "triple cord" was meant to bind Ireland into the British Empire, while the "blessing" of Jews meant their conversion. Irish nonpersecution of Jews, then, was a theme apparently shared by British evangelical imperialists, Irish Jews, and Irish nationalists alike.

The same trope of Irish Jewish solidarity circulates, finally, into Joyce's *Ulysses*, in which the headmaster, Mr. Deasy, jokes that Ireland never oppressed the Jews because she never let them in.[38] Deasy's anti-semitism reverses the sympathetic rhetoric that had become part of the conventional wisdom about Jews in Ireland, and Joyce seems to ominously acknowledge that the Irish-Jewish connection central to *Ulysses* is easily reversible in the wrong hands. Indeed, in 1901, with the excavations at Tara under way, Griffith's paper had found an opportunity to attack simultaneously both Jews and British Israelite Unionists: "Instead of thanking Providence for the disappearance of ten of the twelve tribes of Jewry, a number of people in different ages had been striving to find them out and inflict them on a world suffering from the villainy of the remaining two."[39] Whether the remark originated with Griffith himself or not, it has the same repeatable quality as Deasy's wisecrack, and it is not surprising that we hear a version of this joke again, a decade later, in a review of Irish novelist George Birmingham's *The Lost Tribes* (a romance whose titular "tribes" function principally as a prelude to a conventional marriage plot).[40] But by the time Birmingham's novel appeared in 1914, the British Israelites seem to have been forgotten in Ireland: no Irish or English reviews of the novel (of which there were many) make any mention of the group, whose name is evoked in the book's title. While the British Israelite excavation at Tara had been a real political controversy at the turn of the century, it had now passed into the realm of the farcical. Moreover, by 1914 the Israelite analogy had become increasingly irrelevant in Ireland. Moore's "The Parallel" was a tired cliché, Parnell-Moses was long dead, and a new narrative of Irish liberation, based on the New Testament and blood sacrifice and shepherded by Patrick Pearse, was ascendant—and soon to be reified by the Easter Rising. The Israelite analogy, so recently worthy of bitter debate in the pages of a nationalist newspaper, and soon to be explored in all its rich complexities and ironies by Joyce, had been buried and covered over with new language, new images, new analogies. We excavate it now, though, with renewed appreciation.

2

"Not So Different after All"

Irish and Continental European Antisemitism in Comparative Perspective

R. M. DOUGLAS

For most of the twentieth century and a depressing proportion of the twenty-first, historians of modern Ireland have been strongly resistant to placing the experience of the independent Irish state and society into any kind of comparative framework.[1] Joe Lee, in his enormously stimulating survey *Ireland, 1912–1985*, was one of the first to do so in any sustained way.[2] But that work appeared more than three decades ago, and he has had few followers since then. Even the most prominent representatives of the younger generation of Irish historians have retreated into the comfort of an unarticulated *Sonderweg* thesis for modern Ireland, reassuring themselves that nothing that happened on the European continent need disturb the tranquility of their scholarly lives.

This reluctance to engage the history of the continent of which Ireland, in however semidetached a fashion, remains a part is especially unfortunate when it comes to the study of antisemitism in its Hibernian manifestations. Some authors, to be sure, maintain that there is little to be said upon the subject: because Ireland had a tiny Jewish population—probably never more than five thousand for the entire island—antisemitism must have been on a similarly negligible scale. Such was the conclusion of economic historian Cormac Ó Gráda, who argued in a 2006 book that "Irish anti-Semitism existed . . . but it was of a relatively mild variety." For Ó Gráda, whose glass in this respect is a good deal more than half full, hostility toward Jews reached its peak with the so-called Limerick Pogrom of 1904 and quickly dwindled into relative insignificance. Thereafter, he says, Jews "never encountered more than mild prejudice in Ireland." Eunan O'Halpin of Trinity College, Dublin, in a knowing nod to James Joyce, likewise holds that "the relative rarity of virulent anti-Semitism in interwar Ireland was attributable mainly to the scarcity of Jews." Joe Lee himself goes so far as to assert that "despite considerable potential for antisemitism, Ireland had no Jewish question."[3]

Whether this agreeable picture accurately reflects the Jewish experience in modern Ireland depends above all on what meaning one attaches to the various qualifiers introduced by these authors. One man's or woman's "mild" prejudice may well be another's "virulent anti-Semitism," depending on whether the frame of reference is, say, Germany of the 1930s or the United States today. Certainly, one would suppose that we know too much about the phenomenon of "antisemitism without Jews," in countries with as little in common with each other as Romania and Malaysia, to find entirely persuasive the notion that there is a direct correlation between the size of a society's Jewish population and its proclivity for intolerance.[4] In the specific context of Irish nationalism, moreover, a social scientist knowing nothing of the country's history might reasonably conclude that twentieth-century Ireland would be unlikely to present a favorable assimilative environment for those Jewish residents it did possess. Too many of what were widely perceived to be the correlates of Jewish life stood in opposition to the image of the national community that Irish leaders of public opinion were busily constructing for themselves: agrarian rather than urban, "racy of the soil" rather than cosmopolitan, autarkic rather than entrepreneurial, romantic rather than intellectual.

Unquestionably, there were some points of overlap also. As Michael Davitt, one of Ireland's relatively few philo-Semites, liked to mention, the Irish and the Jews shared a history of foreign domination, a common experience of exile, and a commitment to the revival of their respective languages and the creation of a new nation-state in their ancestral homelands. Unfortunately, those similarities pointed in the direction not of coexistence, nor even of assimilation, but of physical separation—which is one of the reasons that Sinn Féin founder Arthur Griffith, like many other European antisemites of his generation, always had kind words to say for Zionism.

This point is not to contend, in contrast to those individuals who consider Irish antisemitism trivial, that the character of Irish nationalism made it inevitable. But by the same token, there seems to be no very persuasive reason for seeking to explain the phenomenon in wholly different terms from those terms applicable to the rest of the European continent. To be sure, some important differences do exist between Ireland's modern history and the experience of the mainland. Although Ireland participated in the Great War—and although, even today, it is too often forgotten that the number of casualties it incurred as a result greatly exceeded the number caused by all other manifestations of political violence during the rest of the twentieth century put together—it was not left, in comparison, to other European combatant countries, with a very large cohort of disillusioned and disruptive former servicemen, radicalized by their experience of that conflict, to try to reintegrate into peacetime society. Despite the overheated imaginings of Catholic clergy and conservative politicians like the former minister of defense Desmond Fitzgerald, who expressed his apprehension in a letter to Jacques Maritain in March 1933 that "the country may go Bolshevist," no real threat existed from either the parliamentary or the extraparliamentary Left.[5] But independent Ireland confronted stresses of its own: a modernization crisis, albeit on a modest scale; a political system from which, in the aftermath of the Irish Civil War, a strong minority remained disaffected to a greater or lesser degree; and, most important of all, a pervasive sense of disillusionment when an incomplete national revolution, and an aborted social and economic one, disappointed the utopian expectations that had been bound up with the achievement of self-government.

It would be altogether too simple, though, to see Irish antisemitism as driven solely by a quest for scapegoats. The new political order in independent Ireland produced winners as well as losers, and those who benefited most from the opportunities it generated were often prone freely to express attitudes toward Jews that ranged from the prejudicial to the conspiratorial. In this context, it is especially noteworthy that open expressions of antisemitic sentiment were to be found not only on the fringes but across the mainstream political spectrum, from Cumann na nGaedheal on the Right all the way to the Labour Party on the moderate Left. The sheer volume of antisemitic rhetoric present in the political and intellectual discourse of independent Ireland before 1945 is striking and can readily be observed by anyone with an afternoon to spare leafing through the provincial press of the first half of the twentieth century—or, for that matter, the debates of the Oireachtas. In 1942, indeed, the High Court dismissed a lawsuit brought by a dentist who sued a landlady who refused to rent a house to him because of his Jewishness precisely on the ground that antisemitism, as the Court explained, was so "prevalent as an attitude of mind" in Ireland that those individuals subscribing to it could not be accused of acting out of "caprice" or "mere prejudice."[6]

An equally significant fact is that despite the relative absence of antisemitic inspiration from overseas—no Irish edition of the *Protocols of the Elders of Zion* was ever published—remarkable similarities are to be found between not only the ideas but even the modes of expression of leading Irish and continental antisemites. Writing in *Scènes et doctrines du nationalisme*, for example, Maurice Barrès maintained that Jews could never become fully French because, "for us, the *patrie* is the soil and our ancestors; for them, it is the place where they find the greatest personal interest."[7] In like fashion, Michael Donnellan, head of the farmers' party Clann na Talmhan, argued in 1941 that Irish Jews remained not just theologically but ontologically different from the Christian majority. "Why," he rhetorically inquired, "should we leave our land to be peopled by Jews and aliens—aliens to our form of life, foreign to our spiritual outlook, foreign to our Gaelic culture, seeking not only to come in but to control the land of St Patrick?" Jews would, he said, "ever be strangers to the real interests of Ireland. They will be concerned only with that which affects their pockets."[8] Such sentiments, which Donnellan seemed compelled to ventilate from virtually every public platform upon which he ever stood, did not impede his rise to become a junior minister seven years later in the First Inter-Party Government. In the same vein, there is little even in phraseology to distinguish the claim of Abbé Théodore Garnier of the antisemitic *Union Nationale* that Jews have "always cherished [the dream] of dominating the world and subjugating the Christian nations," with Dominican Father Benedict O'Sullivan's announcement at the Pro-Cathedral in Dublin that communism's hidden agenda consisted of "the placing of the Jews in possession of supreme power over the whole world."[9]

If we cannot, therefore, acquit Irish political and religious figures of harboring antisemitic sentiments, at least we can hold them guiltless of any taint of originality in the way in which they conceived them. The prejudices that Irish commentators freely expressed about Jews were derivative and imitative to the highest possible degree, stereotypes obtained off the peg from elsewhere and applied to the Irish situation with apparently no modifications or local variations of any kind. What, then, were the vectors or routes of transmission of antisemitic ideas in Ireland during the first half of the twentieth century? Unoriginal if not positively clichéd though it may be to drag the much-abused figures of the Christian churches in general, and the Catholic Church in particular, back into the dock on yet another charge, the evidence seems incontrovertible that as in France under the interwar Third Republic, the lands of the former Austro-Hungarian Empire in the same period, and above all, perhaps, Poland under the Sanacja, clergymen played a crucial role, especially in the interwar years, in disseminating and lending their credibility to Judeophobic ideas.[10] However, the implication of Joe Lee and many others that religious antisemitism in Ireland was confined to a handful of rogue priests such as the obsessive Father Denis Fahey of the Holy Ghost Fathers is not one that stands up to close examination.[11]

It is impossible to discern any significant difference, even in emphasis, between Fahey's conspiratorial ravings and the notions about the Jews that were publicly advertised by some of the country's leading Catholic clergymen. The equation of Judaism and communism, which was already tirelessly broadcast by a wide variety of religious and secular commentators elsewhere in Europe, was no less a staple of clerical discourses in Ireland.[12] Thus, the dean of Cork, Monsignor Sexton, declared at a public meeting in 1936 that a "gang of renegade Jews in Moscow" was responsible for the spread of communist doctrines elsewhere, notably in Spain.[13] Dr. John Dignan, bishop of Clonfert, took a more traditional stance, using one of his Lenten pastorals to accuse "monied-vested interests chiefly in the hands of Jews" for the sins of the capitalist system.[14] Dr. Thomas Cummins of the Diocese of Elphin, fulminating against Dublin Corporation's licensing of a kosher abattoir, looked forward to the day when the city's municipal authorities would "call in the services of an Irish Hitler to do for Dublin what the *Führer* did for Berlin."[15]

Probably the most comprehensive public airing of Judeophobic fantasies, though, came in a Passion Sunday lecture by one of the country's leading Catholic intellectuals in 1932. In an address lasting more than two hours, the speaker worked his way methodically through very nearly the entire canon of antisemitic conspiracy theories, of the reality of which, he reminded his audience, he had documentary proof. Commencing with the Bavarian Illuminati and concluding with the modern-day Rotary Clubs—both of which were identified as nothing more than fronts for the centuries-long Jewish scheme of world domination—the exposé described how the Jewish-owned Warburg bank "gave Lenin and Trotsky 6 millions to finance the second Russian Revolution." That these facts were not as well known as they should be was the consequence of "the Press of the world [being] largely controlled by Jew-enemies of Our Saviour." Likewise, Hollywood danced to the tune of "the powerful Masonic and Jewish group, the Benai Berith [*sic*]," while the Great Depression was "the deliberate work of a few Jew financiers." The ultimate objective of all these devious Semitic schemes, the speaker concluded, was to bring the world completely under the sway of what he described as the "Jew-controlled League of Nations."[16] The orator in question was the president of Blackrock College, Dr. John Charles McQuaid; eight years later, he would become archbishop of Dublin and the country's most influential Catholic clergyman for more than three decades.[17]

The scale and significance of these clerical effusions—many more examples of which could be cited—have been persistently overlooked or understated by historians of modern Ireland. In part, that oversight is the result of the prevalent habit in Irish historical scholarship of regarding so-called religious antisemitism as being in some way less serious, or less meaningful, than its "racial" counterpart. This belief is a mistake in two respects. In the first place, it is not at all true that racial antisemitism was unknown in Ireland. For example, Senator Oliver St. John Gogarty, one of several members of the Oireachtas with a monomania about Jews, advised the *Irish Independent* in 1937, "There is no such thing as a Jewish nation. There is a Jewish race." In the second, as Vicki Caron has pointed out in the context of France, Catholic antisemitism "did not simply provide the groundwork for modern antisemitism. Nor was it merely ancillary to it. Rather . . . it was a central component of the new modern antisemitic movements linked to the rise of nationalism. Ultimately," she argues, "any distinction between [religious] anti-Judaism and antisemitism falls by the wayside."[18]

The clearest illustration of the accuracy of this assessment in the Irish context is to be found in the rise in the 1930s of a galaxy of right-wing leagues, in many respects paralleling the similar appearance of organizations such as Charles Maurras's Action française, Pierre Taittinger's Jeunesses patriotes, or François de la Rocque's Croix de feu in interwar France. When one speaks of militant rightist movements in Ireland during this period, the example of General Eoin O'Duffy's Blueshirts comes immediately to mind. So many investigations of this movement, however, have been carried out at both national and local levels that it can be said with a high degree of confidence that there was less to the Blueshirts than met the eye and that they are better regarded, in Mike Cronin's wry and accurate summation, as "the drunken uncle of Fine Gael" than as a coterie of Hibernian Hitlerites.[19] The arguably excessive attention paid to the Blueshirts, though, has overshadowed a network of groups existing at the same time that collectively are no less significant. Some of them, like Aontas Gaedheal (Union of the Gaels) or An Córas Gaedhealach (the Gaelic Network), were small-scale organizations more notable for their extremism than their popular appeal. Others, such as St. Patrick's Anti-Communist League and, the largest of them all, the Irish Christian Front, were capable of drawing crowds of many thousands, or even tens of thousands, to their public meetings.[20]

As yet far too little is known about the membership and activities of these leagues. Unlike the Blueshirts, though, it is clear that antisemitism was not merely a decorative feature but rather a foundational component of their respective Weltanschauungen. Aontas Gaedheal, to take one example, stood for the exclusion of Jews from the country's commercial life; its newspaper, in the familiar language of dehumanization, spoke of exposing "the malignant Semitic growth" and the "eradication" of "this cancer" in the Irish body politic. Indicating its concern with race mixing, the paper threatened to publish the names and addresses of Christian girls who associated with Jewish men. Other leagues proceeded from rhetorical to actual menace, in the form of street hooliganism and physical attacks—some of them on a substantial scale—against those individuals who were perceived as internal enemies. In general, these attacks were directed against targets identified as communists rather than Jews as such. Irish historians, though, may wish to reconsider the degree to which these assaults may have been motivated by antisemitic as well as antileftist prejudice. Father Thomas Mahon of the Irish Christian Front was one of many spokesmen for the right-wing leagues to assert that "Jewery [*sic*], which was behind Communism, was Anti-Christian and had been Anti-Christian since the time of Our Lord."[21] To break up communist (or supposedly communist) meetings, to beat up communist (or supposedly communist) speakers, and to lay siege to communist (or supposedly communist) premises was thus also a means of combating the Jewish menace, of which communism was only a visible symptom. It would be optimistic to assume that this equation never occurred to the young men and women of St. Patrick's Anti-Communist League or the Catholic Young Men's Society as they went about their violent work in the 1930s, with the blessing and at times at the direct instigation of members of the Irish episcopacy.[22]

Contemporary scholarship on Irish social and political life has not yet featured a sustained engagement with the specific component of violence to be found across the range of Irish antisemitic practices or any analysis of the complex dynamic between "moral and physical force" comparable to L. P. Curtis Jr.'s insightful examination of this theme in Irish nationalist discourse of the nineteenth century.[23] Indeed, the literature on Irish antisemitism has tended persistently to underestimate, or altogether to ignore, the degree of violence, whether physical or "merely" rhetorical and intimidatory, embedded in it. There is, to be sure, some excuse for this lacuna, bearing in mind the readiness of many leaders of the Irish Jewish community themselves to downplay the significance of their own experience of prejudice. What is more surprising, however, is the reluctance of commentators to consider the possibility that this stance of theirs may have been—as, on the evidence, it all too clearly was—a survival strategy rather than a reflection of lived experience.[24]

The motivation behind Irish Jews' efforts to minimize their vulnerability by these means, for which numerous parallels can be found elsewhere on the European continent, is obvious. Michael Davitt's optimistic but unfounded claim that alone among the European nations Ireland had never given way to antisemitism offered the Jewish community a means of deploying Irish nationalism as a shield against popular Judeophobia.[25] The assertion of the country's supposed uniqueness in this respect could be represented as one of the markers of Irish cultural distinctiveness upon which the claim to self-government was based, as well as the Jewish minority's accepted place within the national community as a symbol of that distinctiveness. Such a stance could be maintained, however, only by denying that the all too evident manifestations of anti-Jewish sentiment were either typical or of any importance.

The Irish example thus presents the paradox of leading Jewish figures and organizations vigorously acquitting their Gentile countrymen and women of antisemitism, even as the latter frankly admitted it. In 1944, for example, the Jewish Representative Council of Ireland denounced as "false, irresponsible and mischievous" the suggestion that there was "any organised anti-Semitic movement in Éire." The chief rabbi, Isaac Herzog, went still further two years later in professing that he had "found no anti-Semitism either in Ireland or Britain." Had he chosen to do so, Rabbi Herzog need not have looked far for counterexamples. As his own son, the future president of Israel Chaim Herzog, recalled of his childhood in Ireland, "Many times we [Jewish children] were stoned in the street by urchins, many times. This was quite normal at the time." It was telling of what had by then become an entrenched exculpatory stance on the part of the Irish Jewish community that even the younger Herzog went on to deny that the repeated attacks on him and his coreligionists were actuated by "anti-Semitism as such. I would call it religious fanaticism."[26]

The proposition that Ireland had been miraculously preserved from the taint of anti-Jewish attitudes became so prevalent as a result of denials of this kind that *Variety* attributed the Irish commercial failure of the film *Gentleman's Agreement*, a fictional exposé of anti-Jewish prejudice starring Gregory Peck that went on to win the Academy Award for Best Picture in 1947, to the proposition that the "pic lacked interest for Ireland where there is virtually no anti-Semitism, and [the] problem merely puzzles [the] average filmgoer." There is, however, no reason for historians today to take such claims at face value, especially as others, closer to home, were better informed. Colonel Dan Bryan, the shrewd and efficient head of the Irish military intelligence service, G2, reported in 1945 that "the extent to which Dublin has become what may be described as Jew-conscious is frequently coming to the notice of this Branch."[27] His impression was endorsed by the Church of Ireland dean of Cashel, R. Wyse Jackson, who warned in 1948 that "there is undoubtedly a growing bitterness against the Jewish people," and by a political commentator in the general election of the same year, who observed among aspirants to office from Fine Gael and Clann na Poblachta "the raising of the racial issue by more than one candidate. The Jews are being denounced as Jews." It ought, therefore, to come as little surprise that the secretary of the Department of Justice, Peter Berry, should have recorded in 1953 "a fairly strong anti-Semitic feeling throughout the country based, perhaps, on . . . the fact that the Jews . . . have not permitted themselves to be assimilated, and that for their numbers they appear to have disproportionate wealth and influence."[28]

The ability of anxieties about Jews and Jewishness to unite Gentile Irish citizens who were otherwise divided by ideology or sect has, in more recent times, been paralleled by the virtual national consensus—contested only by dyed-in-the-wool contrarians like Conor Cruise O'Brien—over the particular criminality of the new State of Israel, in its most extreme forms depicted as either being unprecedented or, at most, having only a single precedent. It is unnecessary for our purposes to enter into a discussion of the vexed question of where the line is to be drawn between opposition to Israeli policy as such, on the one hand, and attacks on Israel motivated by anti-Jewish animus, on the other. Such controversies lie beyond the scope of this chapter. More relevant is the unawareness, or indifference, of Irish commentators to the connection noted by Bernard Harrison to "the revival of antisemitism through the reanimation of the traditional antisemitic stereotype of the Jews as a people whose depravity exceeds that of all other nations. . . . [I]f it were really true that the Jews of Israel . . . are 'the new Nazis,' or 'worse than the Nazis,' it would follow rigorously that the Nazis were, in effect, right about the Jews, who thus resume their traditional role as perpetrators of a degree of wickedness so extreme as virtually to exonerate everyone else."[29]

Considerations of this kind were very far from the minds of mainstream Irish politicians who, from the beginning of the 1980s, were early adopters of the trope that Israel was a genocidal state, filling the niche in contemporary history that had previously been occupied by Nazi Germany. A week after the invasion of southern Lebanon in June 1982, Garret FitzGerald, in the brief interregnum between his first and second terms as Taoiseach, declared that descriptions of Israeli actions in the region as constituting "genocide" were "increasingly difficult to resist." His front-bench colleague Austin Deasy, Fine Gael's spokesman on foreign affairs who would become minister of agriculture some months later, agreed that Israel appeared bent on "attempted wholesale genocide of the Palestinian people in Lebanon." Proinsias de Rossa of the Workers' Party, later minister for social welfare in the Rainbow Coalition government of the mid-1990s, described Tel Aviv as being engaged in a "holocaust" whose "merciless and systematic" aim was "to wipe out the Palestinian people." Independent member of Dáil Éireann Tony Gregory likewise drew attention to what he regarded as the irony that a people who had themselves experienced genocide should themselves be carrying out "a genocidal war" against the Palestinians.[30]

Such rhetoric conveyed obvious dangers for Jews, in Ireland as elsewhere in Europe. Almost from the moment of the creation of the State of Israel, Irish Jews had been put on notice that certain of their Christian compatriots were willing to hold them personally responsible for the Israeli government's actions or inactions. Archbishop McQuaid, for example, wrote to Chief Rabbi Immanuel Jakobovits in May 1949 to warn him that if Christian access to the holy places in Jerusalem were not protected, "innocent people of your community" might be made to suffer in retaliation for "the attitudes and actions of irreligious members [*sic*] of Israeli people." The chief rabbi later recorded his outrage that Irish Jews were thus being "treated as hostages" and "being held accountable and threatened with reprisals for the actions of an independent country, thousands of miles away, for whose policies this community is not responsible and in whose affairs it has no say." The archbishop, for his part, made clear in a subsequent report on the matter to the Papal Nuncio that he saw nothing morally problematical in using as a weapon "that which most worries a Jew: the fear of reprisals."[31]

Neither, in the aftermath of the Israeli incursion into Lebanon in 1982, did others. One correspondent in the *Irish Times*, a former University College Dublin lecturer, again bridged the conceptual gap between the Israeli government's policy and Jews' personal answerability for it when he demanded that "Jewish communities the world over . . . formally and publicly dissociate themselves from what has become the sole source of terrorism, an epitome of barbarism in the Middle East."[32] The disturbing implication that any Jews failing to do so had thereby associated themselves with Israeli foreign policy and could be considered accountable for it went uncommented upon by other writers.[33] But the acts of violence and intimidation against Jewish persons and properties that followed indicated that some members of the majority community had indeed proceeded to the conclusion that Irish Jews as such might be regarded as legitimate targets for those individuals angered by events in the Middle East. Already the chief rabbi had complained of the emergence of "an atmosphere when Jews here probably felt more uncomfortable than at any time since the war," arising out of attacks on the Jewish community following the killing in 1980 of two Irish soldiers serving with the UN peacekeeping contingent in Lebanon.[34] Now, the Cork synagogue was firebombed, and death threats were made by telephone to Gerald Goldberg, briefly the Fianna Fáil lord mayor of Cork in the late 1970s and one of the country's most high-profile Jewish figures. The episode marked the beginning of a pattern of assaults, extending over the following three decades, in which Israeli actions were immediately followed by, or made the excuse for, crimes against the Irish Jewish population.

The logic of this linkage was set forth by Raymond Deane, head of the Ireland Palestine Solidarity Campaign, in 2004. "Overt anti-Semitism," he asserted, was "a rare aberration in Europe, subject to occasional surges (which usually coincide with particularly criminal operations of the Israeli Occupying Forces)." In his explication of the relationship between the two, Israel's existence was "the cause, rather than the effect, of occasional violence against Jews emanating from Islamic and other forces."[35] It followed that the targeting of Jews locally was a natural and expected consequence of Israel's continuation as a state and that only the latter's elimination—rather than acceptance, and enforcement, of the proposition that religious minorities were not to be treated as proxies for foreign governments—could reduce the physical danger in which Irish Jews stood.

That this danger was all too real has been demonstrated by the long series of attacks directed against Irish Jews, their property, and their sacred sites, especially from the mid-1990s until the present day. In 1994 thirty-six headstones marked with the Star of David in the Progressive Jewish cemetery in Rathfarnham, County Dublin, were smashed. The offenders were not detected, and the Garda Síochána offered no explanation for its counterintuitive conclusion that the desecration may not have been "specifically antisemitic." Jewish burial grounds, however, were to prove an especially attractive target, with graves in the Belfast City Cemetery being vandalized in 2004. An even more determined assault was carried out in August 2016, by a mob using "hammers and blocks to break up the headstones while a larger mob looked on encouraging their actions." The *Belfast Telegraph* found "clear evidence" of "forward planning," noting that the action had been carried out in broad daylight against Jewish grave markers alone and that those persons responsible had "even more unforgivably attempted to gain entry to the graves."[36]

Other prominent Jewish sites, religious and secular, have experienced frequent onslaughts. In a series of sustained attacks in Dublin between November 2004 and May 2005, the Central Synagogue, the Jewish Museum, the Jewish Old Age Pensioners' Home, and the gates of two Jewish cemeteries were damaged, some repeatedly. A fresh wave of violence erupted in 2014, with the windows of the Belfast synagogue being smashed twice in twenty-four hours. Chaim Herzog's birthplace on Cliftonville Avenue, Belfast, marked with a blue plaque, was defaced with swastikas and SS symbols, marking the beginning of so sustained a campaign of vandalism that the Ulster Historical Society removed the plaque because of the danger to which those workers inside the building were exposed.[37] A local councillor, Brian Kingston, described the decision as "a shocking indication of the level of tension and anti-Semitism which currently exists in part of Belfast."[38] The city's rabbi, David Singer, found it necessary in August 2016 to warn his flock that "after services they should not congregate outside the synagogue, that if they want to talk to their friends, they should do it inside."[39]

Individuals no less than institutions have likewise been exposed to intimidation and threats. An Italian Jewish resident of Tuam, County Galway, was the target of another sustained campaign in 2008, his parked car twice being set on fire and his house spray-painted with swastikas and the message "Go Home Jew." Tommy McGuigan, a Gaelic Athletic Association intercounty footballer, more recently urged any of his social media followers who "know or work with a Jew" to punch them in retaliation for Israeli policy in Gaza.[40] The affinity of antisemites to those individuals in political life has been particularly marked, in some cases resulting in threats to the lives of politicians merely (and mistakenly) suspected of being Jewish.[41] Gerald Goldberg received so many death threats that for a time, he contemplated emigrating from Ireland.[42] In recent times, the country's most prominent Jewish politician, Alan Shatter, has been singled out for a sustained barrage of threatening criminal acts, including the sending on two separate occasions of suspect packages containing white powder accompanied by anti-Jewish material, an obscene and explicitly antisemitic harassment campaign conducted by a Dublin council worker over a five-week period that was ended only by the latter's arrest and ultimate conviction, and the display of posters in Limerick depicting Shatter as the agent of "Jewish influence" in Ireland.[43]

To be Jewish in Ireland during the past century, therefore, has been to live in an atmosphere whose element of menace has been more overt at some times than at others, but never wholly absent. There is little to indicate that this situation will change significantly even as Ireland joins other European countries whose Jewish communities have become extinct, or virtually so. The "Jewish era" in Irish history is now visibly drawing to a close, as older members of the community reach the end of their lives and younger ones seek greater personal opportunity and, perhaps, a less hostile environment in which to live their lives as Jews. By 2002 the population had shrunk to such an extent that the option of recording one's religion as "Jewish" was no longer included on census forms.[44] Services at the Cork synagogue were discontinued because a quorum of ten adult or teenage males could not be mustered. The building was put up for sale in 2016.[45] The Republic's Jewish population is now fewer than 2,000 and marked by an age profile positioning it for near-term demographic collapse. In Northern Ireland, similarly, the Jewish community by 2016 was estimated at a mere 350, most of them elderly.[46]

Paradoxically, however, the elimination of Jews and Jewry from Irish life is unlikely to have much effect on the prevalence of antisemitism among the majority population. In 2007–8, 12 percent of respondents in a national survey believed that Jews should be ineligible for Irish citizenship, and barely half were willing to accept an Israeli as kin through marriage, even though the likelihood of any of those Irish people polled ever having met, or being likely to meet, a member of either of these categories in the flesh was small.[47] Significantly, anti-Jewish prejudice was most intense among the youngest cohorts of the population. All current indications, then, are that the phenomenon of "antisemitism without Jews" will prove to be as viable in Ireland as in other parts of Europe that have, by one means or another, been rendered constructively Jew-free.

In all this, though, there is little that has been unique to Ireland. Local particularities have not been such as to require the application of different categories of analysis in explaining either the nature or the popularity of antisemitism in its Irish context. Wherever it has appeared, as it has done much more often than is typically acknowledged, it has taken markedly similar forms, served the same purposes, and manifested itself as an expression of the same social and cultural pathologies, as elsewhere in Europe. As with so many other aspects of Ireland's recent history, an explicitly comparative approach, rather than an exceptionalist (or denialist) one, offers by far the most effective means of revealing and representing it in its true proportions.

3

"New Jerusalem"

Constructing Jewish Space in Ireland, 1880–1914

PETER HESSION

Recent scholarship has helped to transform our understanding of perceptions of Jewishness in modern Irish society. Explorations of "Irish Orientalism" have emphasized the deep roots of the "Irish Israelite" analogy, an ethnosymbolic trope evident in both Gaelic Catholic and Protestant "new English" protonationalism from the sixteenth century onward.[1] The notion that the pre-Celtic "Milesian race" represented a lost tribe of Israel was later developed by eighteenth-century antiquarians Charles Vallancey and Francis Crawford.[2] And in the age of nineteenth-century "print capitalism," imagined renderings of Daniel O'Connell and Charles Stewart Parnell as biblical "deliverers" became commonplace in the nationalist press; by the turn of century, as Abby Bender has recently put it, "Moses was perhaps as ubiquitous as Kathleen Ní Houlihan" in revivalist rhetoric.[3] Indeed, for Irish cultural nationalists, favorable comparisons with the incipient Zionist project represented only the latest phase in a long litany of inventive comparisons.[4]

Yet the interwoven and equally ubiquitous presence of antisemitic tropes in Irish religious and political discourse complicate any straightforward narrative of elective affinity.[5] Tackling this question, Marilyn Reizbaum has referred to a "double vision" of "contradictory images" that "corresponds to the historical split in perception of the Jews as at once a noble, ancient people, but unacceptable as individuals in

47

modern society."[6] Reizbaum's account speaks primarily to temporal and psychological configurations of Jewishness; the abstract "Hebrew race" can exist safely only as a proxy for an Irish "nightmare of history," whereas Jews in the "here and now" become "scapegoats in a country of scapegoats."[7] Yet perhaps ironically for a field so focused on James Joyce's minute re-creation of Edwardian Dublin, the role played by space in renderings of Irish Jewish cultural encounters is less evident.[8] The imprint of the "spatial turn" in Jewish studies has recently begun to tackle this lacuna, yet in the Irish context, the social and cultural production of space itself remains terra incognita.[9]

Sylvie Anne Goldberg has utilized the notion of an *espace-temps juif,* or "Jewish space-time," to denote both a "physical place where Jews are located" and a "time-related plan conveyed by tradition."[10] What we might term an "Irish Jewish space-time" saw the confluence of these elements around sites of representation and everyday life. As Con Leventhal later wrote in the *Bell,* the uniquely Irish gibe of "Jewman" was rooted in an obsession with origin; akin to "Frenchman" or "Corkman," "Jewman" denoted the need to simultaneously emplace and "other" Irish Jews.[11] Underlying this preoccupation was the familiar trope of the "wandering Jew" as "a sojourner in all lands, [but] a citizen of none," existing "where [there] are no happy homes of men."[12] New Jewish immigrants were thus caught in a pincer movement between at least two related narratives of temporal and spatial displacement: ancient biblical "exile" and imminent repatriation to a desirable "race-centre."[13] Both were suffused with philo- and antisemitic elements accentuated in distinct spatial settings, from enactments of the "stage Jew" in Dublin theaters to re-creations of an authentic "homeland" in Dublin's Christian-led Palestine Exhibitions of 1898 and 1908.[14] Even the farcical efforts of the British Israelite sect to excavate the Hill of Tara in search of the "Jewish Ark" between 1899 and 1902 spatialized claims to Irish heritage via the analogy itself.[15]

This chapter takes a new approach by investigating conflicts around the construction of Jewish space in Ireland within both the Jewish community and the wider Irish society. Here, antisemitic constructs of the diseased and degendered Jewish body were closely linked to notions of spatial disorder. Ultimately, I argue, Zionism provided a mechanism through which different sections of the community united to reinforce the physical, social, and sexual boundaries that came to constitute Jewish space and identity. It was in this sense, ironically, that the "familiar difference" of Irish Jews was made acceptable in an increasingly nationalist society. Completing the "arc" of Irish Jewish space-time made Irish Jews the quintessential "insider-outsiders," caught in perpetual motion between two dominant narratives of spatial legitimacy.

Transgressing Separate Spheres: "New Jerusalem"

What would later become known as Dublin's "Little Jerusalem" emerged from the 1880s onward, the city's Jewish population rising from 189 in 1871, largely situated in the city center, to 2,665 in 1911, mostly congregated in a new "Jewish quarter" south of the Liffey.[16] Yet during most of that period, the term was little used; instead, journalists and commentators referred to the area around Clanbrasil Street and the South Circular Road as a "New Jerusalem."[17] The difference is slight but instructive; the more recent nomenclature not only situates the neighborhood alongside ethnic enclaves in multicultural cities across the world but also serves to diminish the physical imprint of the Jewish presence itself.[18] "New Jerusalem" surely implied, by comparison, a wholly different set of constructive and re-creative connotations, not least the relative "newness" of the built environment itself that emerged in the 1870s and 1880s, partly thanks to the Dublin Artisan Dwelling Company.[19] Perched alongside the Grand Canal, the neighborhood was neither central nor suburban; as with Cork's "Jewtown," the physical fabric of "New Jerusalem" originated in a spirit of working-class reform and respectability, yet also lay proximate to an urban "underworld" of vice and prostitution beyond the remit of middle-class supervision.[20]

In a letter to the *Jewish Chronicle* in 1889, the lawyer Ernest W. Harris complained that "a very large number of families . . . have established in a district of this city a sort of *Ghetto*, which I think is greatly to be deplored," going on to describe the risk of "their children growing up with the ideas of their parents instead of having an education to suit them . . . in the land of their adoption." To the small preexisting community of "English" Jews of which Harris was a leading member, the emergence of a Jewish colony of "foreign" Yiddish-speaking European migrants radically destabilized the balance of visibility and "managed difference" that had hitherto prevailed.[21] While several scholars have argued that middle-class Jews "privatized their Jewishness" in order to acculturate without losing their identity, in Ireland there is also evidence of performances of "public Jewishness" that have tended to affirm and reproduce narratives of tolerance.[22] This point is particularly true of what Natalie Wynn has recently termed the "'no persecution' myth," a "mantra" repeated by nationalists, unionists, and community leaders alike that Jews never faced historical harassment in Ireland. Thus, in 1882 the nationalist *Irishman* lauded "Hebrew families residing in Dublin [who] bore grateful testimony to the enlightened fellowship of the Irish people by attending the centenary celebration of O'Connell's birthday."[23] Alongside funeral elegies, High Holiday sermons, and council chamber speeches delivered by communal leaders, the physical presence of St. Mary's Abbey Synagogue and most of Dublin's old Jewish establishment in the city center gave the community a legible "familiar difference."[24] By comparison, the "physically and psychologically . . . closed" world of New Jerusalem represented an identifiable but "impenetrable" mass on the physical margins of urban life.[25]

Antisemitic attacks and efforts to "reform" the new arrivals thus inevitably came to focus on the new spatial imprint of "foreign" Jewishness in Ireland. As putatively both "pauper immigrants" and "wandering Jews," migrants encountered a racialized discourse that rooted social and biological ills *within* Jewish space.[26] As elsewhere in Europe, "physical and cultural boundaries between public and private" were confounded by a "third boundary," that excluding "alien" Jews from the "social body" of the nation.[27] Thus, as "ghetto" space threatened to expose the acculturated "privatization" of Jewish life, the hidden domestic sphere of Jewishness itself became a threat to the nation's "public health." The *Evening Herald* of Dublin worried about the spread of cholera to Ireland in 1892: "When pauper aliens are landed by hundreds at a time in a country of which they know neither the language or the customs their helplessness and their misery often make them a positive danger to the public health."[28] Unsurprisingly, most of the antisemitic attacks on Jews in Dublin, Cork, and Limerick from the late 1880s referred to the "large number of the [Jewish] immigrants who settle in the blocks of small red brick houses," supposedly crammed into "one to two rooms."[29] In practice, distinctions between private lodgings and the "sweating dens" of "blackleg Jews" were often blurred: "If smallpox gets a footing in Cork," one writer argued in 1894, "the making of clothes in crowded [Jewish] tenements . . . [in] cases of contagious disease might remit very serious consequences."[30]

Just a few months earlier, members of the South Dublin Anglican Church Sanitary Association had met to hear a paper titled "Sanitation as Taught by the Mosaic Law" that lauded "a code of sanitary laws of Divine origin."[31] Indeed, praise for the "temperate and hygienic habits" of the Jews on such occasions as the opening of Tara Street Baths coexisted alongside narratives of filth, overcrowding, and disease.[32] The "dirty" world of the immigrant might consciously be distinguished from the civilizing efforts of "native" "white Jews," but it was the former who posed, as another hostile commentator argued in 1900, "a great source of danger to the public health and the morality of the city."[33] The confluence of physical and moral danger often referred to "scabs" or "usurers," yet from the 1890s on, the Dublin press reveled in exposing "domestic" crimes involving Jews, especially instances of suicide, bigamy, divorce, breach of promise, domestic abuse, or criminal insanity.[34] One columnist even drew on the work of Italian criminologist Cesare Lombroso in 1901 to show that levels of insanity among Jews were "four to six times greater," citing three known cases of insanity among the "alien Jews" of Dublin.[35] Major cases such as the suicide of Joseph Reuben and his wife in 1894 or the salacious Harris divorce trial of 1906 tended to cast Jewish men as greedy, heartless, and cruel to women. The same year as the latter case, the Church of Ireland Ladies' Union for Jewish Missions was told that Jewish women should be targeted for conversion, "because Jews have a low idea of the value of womankind."[36] And just as the same outfit recommended attempted conversion "when the Jewish men and women were softened by sickness," the typical Jewish housewife of the "old type" was depicted as "a small, sickly looking woman with black eyes and shrivelled skin."[37]

If the idea of the "dirty Jew" collapsed boundaries between public and private through connotations of filth and disease, it was depictions of the Jewish peddler and moneylender that cast the immigrant as an agent of the same corrosive process in non-Jewish life. In the context of the broader late-Victorian shift toward predominantly domestic work patterns among Irish women of the middle and lower middle classes, the Jewish peddler was seen as destructive of an incipient division of labor inherent to the separation of spheres.[38] From the beginning, the alleged "victim" of the "weekly man" was cast as the "artisan's wife," "silly women and giddy girls" left vulnerable in the absence of male protection.[39] Moreover, the "threat" posed by the money-lending peddler was more than narrowly financial; one antisemitic letter writer described in the *Daily Nation* during 1897 how "a foolish country girl, or a young married woman, may be tempted by the plausible arguments of the pedlar into buying articles or wearing apparel which she could very well do without and which really add nothing to her cleanliness or attractiveness . . . worthless and vulgar imitations of things worn by more opulent folk. . . . [H]owever, as the feminine mind judges, the style of dressing entered upon must be continued and seemingly new indebtedness must be insured, and fresh tribute paid to the pedlar."[40] Here, it was the opportunities for consumption offered to women that served to threaten the balance of power within the household economy and "put an end to thrift in their homes."[41]

Important too was the blurring of boundaries between urban and rural space, the latter increasingly regarded as the site of an unspoiled national culture under threat from "Anglicization."[42] Incredibly, given the relative poverty and predominantly urban character of Jewish immigrants to Ireland, antisemitic commentators linked Jewish peddlers to both "gombeen men on a large scale" and "alien" landlords in the aftermath of the Land War (1879–82).[43] An editorial in the liberal nationalist *Freeman's Journal* argued in 1885 that "the landlords are holding out against the tenants . . . because the Jews are holding out against the landlords." "If the Jews were at once run out of Ireland," another writer suggested in 1887, "there would be very little difficulty about getting proper reductions in the rents, easy sale to the tenants, or Home Rule itself." Later evidence given by the likes of Frederick Falkiner, the notoriously antisemitic recorder of Dublin, to the parliamentary select committee into money lending during 1898 stoked images of "villages and mountain hamlets" "infested" by peddlers. The following year, one writer went so far as to urge the unification of the Irish Party in order to tackle "the inroads of the ubiquitous Jewish vendors, who have already . . . mortgaged many farms of the peasants throughout Ireland." A decade later, an antisemitic placard of the Dublin Town Tenants Association asked provocatively, "Are the Jews going to monopolise Dublin?"[44]

Communal Space and 'Public Jewishness'

Cemeteries and synagogues—which ideally sought to create a "union of hearts" around religious festivals and rituals of birth, death, and marriage—proved vital battlegrounds for control over collective representation of Irish Jewry to the wider community.[45] Events such as funerals often involved elaborate public performances of hierarchy and order, providing a platform from which leading members of the community affirmed their authority to speak for all.[46] The funeral procession in 1880 for Alderman Herbert W. Harris, "godfather" of Dublin Jewry, saw a procession symbolically connect his private residence to the communal spaces of St. Mary's Abbey Synagogue and the Jewish burial ground at Ballybough, staging "ancient Jewish lamentations" for an "ornament to society." Standard references to the presence of a "large muster of Christian friends" further personified the mantra of "no-persecution."[47] The funeral of another communal leader, Marinus de Groot in 1901, similarly materialized the "familiar difference" of Jewishness by paying spectacular tribute to "the old stock of British Jews which know how to reconcile strict orthodoxy with the exigencies of modern life."[48]

From the 1880s, the presence of new arrivals necessarily complicated these rituals, as communal hierarchies themselves came to be
challenged. The opening of a new Jewish burial ground at Dolphin's
Barn in July 1898 saw one such conflict pit the respectable "English"
establishment against Robert Bradlaw, "the prince of the 'foreign'
community."[49] It was claimed that the latter "effected to control, rather
more than he was entitled to do, the management of the cemetery" to
enable "the extension of his sphere of influence" to "representing the
general body."[50] The new cemetery, intended for "the requirements
of the poor," also came under attack from non-Jews citing recurrent
tropes of "disease," "filth," and "pollution."[51] The cholera panic of the
1890s had prompted the *Evening Herald* to warn its readers of Jewish
migrants being "married on the grave of a person who had died of
cholera."[52] Echoing such fears, a local landowner complained in 1899
that interments first occurring "under cover of darkness" had lately
become "bold and confident" and risked rendering the water supply
around Dolphin's Barn "poisonous." An official sanitary inspection
ordered by local magistrates failed to close the cemetery, but critics
suspected the law was being "strained to meet the requirements of
aliens and Russian refugees."[53] Images of subterfuge, contagion, and
illicit influence racialized spatial threats to local property, as the cemetery was feared to be "detrimental to the inhabitants and persons having *vested interests therein.*"[54]

Similar struggles for communal representation were evident in
1902, when the new Limerick Holy Burial Society, or Chevra Kadisha, denounced "quarrelmongers . . . who intrigued against us at
every stage because they were not appointed by our community as
its leaders," and thus "defiled the name of the congregation of Israel
before the gentiles."[55] The society called on its members to "donate
money to buy a tract of land in our city for our deceased . . . so that
we shall not be the object of derision in the eyes of the gentiles in
whose midst we live, who say: it is not enough that the Hebrews be
wanderers throughout their lifetimes but also after their death . . . as
it befits every holy community to build a home for the living and a
home for the deceased."[56] Connections between the "wandering Jew"

and Gothic representations of the undead were also central to the "crypto-Jewish" figure of Dracula, made famous in 1897 by Bram Stoker, who grew up near both the "suicide plot" and the old Jewish cemetery at Ballybough.[57] Indeed, images of Irish Jews as "vampires" and "bloodsuckers" were part and parcel of a wider biological and racialized rendering of Jewish space; one antisemitic correspondent wrote during the Limerick Pogrom of 1904 that "Ireland's body is a body diseased . . . [and] if she is to survive as a nation she must rouse herself and shake off the Parasites, who, if they could, would bleed her blue veins white."[58]

In some cases, this rhetoric also found its way into conflicts over institutional control within the Jewish community; in 1897 the *Daily Nation* reported a distinction made by one Jewish witness to the select committee on money lending between "the upper and lower middle classes" and "money lending vampires," though the term was refuted in the *Jewish World*. Nonetheless, the *Jewish Chronicle* shortly afterward took the committee's evidence as an "opportune" moment to warn Dublin's Jews to "dissociate themselves . . . from the evil reputation" of moneylenders, quoting the chief rabbi's injunction that "the synagogue must leave no stone unturned to purify its courts from such contamination."[59] Following the refusal to admit moneylenders to free membership of St. Mary's Abbey Synagogue in 1881, Dublin saw six independent orthodox *hevrot*, or small synagogues, established between 1883 and 1893.[60] Despite partially successful efforts to unite the community around new synagogues on Adelaide Road (1892) and Greenville Hall (1924), splits recurred in Cork and Limerick during 1891, 1896, and 1902 based on a violent combination of liturgical conflicts, personal animosities, and social status.[61] Having divided, the separate spaces themselves became a focus of moral attack, as in 1891, when nonconformists were castigated for meeting in an "unsuitable dwelling" and "imbibing strong drink within their so-called synagogue," before "washing their dirty linen in court."[62] The same year, it was claimed that "uncleanliness exists in the synagogue," and "private house" meetings continued to be cast as unfit for marriage rites and other ceremonial functions.[63]

As elsewhere, new doctrines of "social hygiene" meant Jewish rites were increasingly "linked with every idea and practice that produces cleanliness . . . mirror[ing] *bourgeois* notions of normality and respectability."[64] Confronting prejudices that "alien Jews . . . contravened established hygienic standards"—including the characterization of tuberculosis as a "Jewish disease"—anthropologist Maurice Fishberg pointed to lectures delivered in Dublin by the Irish-born physician and eugenicist Edward Mapother illustrating Jewish "immunity" to cholera.[65] Fishberg's 1911 study, *The Jews: A Study in Race and Environment*, would later prove influential on James Joyce, and this and earlier work on Jewish ethnography received praise in Irish nationalist and intellectual circles.[66] The author's key augment that Jews were above all "a product of the *milieu* in which they found themselves" raised environment to the greatest of all socializing factors, with a concomitant emphasis on "social, sanitary, and hygienic conditions."[67]

Between *Heim* and Homeland

Natalie Wynn has written convincingly of the "formalisation of a communal narrative" around Irish Jewish "origin myths" that combine "inaccuracies, conflations, decontextualized titbits of fact, and outright fiction."[68] Such myths can obscure the subtle dynamics of regional difference and generational replacement; of the 2,877 Jewish residents in Dublin recorded during the 1911 census, just shy of half were Irish born, with those hailing from western Europe or Britain making up another 13 percent. Even the roughly 40 percent who classed themselves as Russian-born included references to Poland, Courland in northern Latvia, or specific towns in the Kovno district of Lithuania, such as Wexly and Telsch.[69] Indeed, in at least some cases, Wynn has argued that "notions of asylum-seeking" and what David Cesarani has termed myths of "accidental arrival" were constructed in the second generation to harmonize family experiences with collective narratives of tolerance and integration. The old *heim*, as in Hannah Berman's novel *Melutovna*, was somewhere to "strive to get the hell out of" a "place of shtetls and pogroms, in no sense a homeland."[70] Similarly, the notion that all Irish Jews descended from the single shtetl of Akmiyan, and that communities like Cork's Jewtown all but replicated that "self-contained Lithuanian village," homogenized an array of individual genealogies around a single collective place of origin.[71] Fixing two locations in space and time and establishing an irreversible vector between them powerfully resisted the placelessness of "wandering feet."[72]

Closely associated with questions of origin were issues of representation and identity, which would be profoundly impacted by the growth of Zionism. Rory Miller has argued that the speed with which Ireland's new Jewish migrants "swept away" the old elite was unprecedented among host societies and closely linked to its evolution into "the most Zionist community in western Europe."[73] Two years before a branch of the Chovevei Zion was founded in Cork, *Ha-Melitz* (the Advocate), the strongly Zionist first Hebrew-language newspaper in the Russian Empire, thanked "our brother Jews in the city of Cork" for welcoming recently arrived migrants, particularly "maintaining the Jewish women as they provided the food for the Sabbath." The *Warder* later noted of Ireland's new migrants, "Most of them march behind Zionist ensign and wear the Zionist badge."[74] Yet while Zionism helped to give public form to a renewed "pecking order," it also aided the "blurring" of internal communal boundaries by reinforcing "separate spheres" of activity under a single patriarchal leadership.[75] Irish Zionism went further than most in seeking to radically redefine the "boundaries and hierarchies" of social and sexual difference; the Dublin Daughters of Zion were perhaps the earliest women's Zionist organization to be formed in the English-speaking world, predating similar groups in Britain and America.[76] Yet the communal leaders Nick Harris later highlighted as *balabatim* [*sic, Baal-Ha-Batim*], or "masters of the House," were "keen" and "ardent" Zionists who played host to revisionist leaders and headed local organizations. As George Mosse has argued, Zionists resisted the gendered and spatial dysphoria of antisemitic characterization by asserting masculine sovereignty.[77] These ideological shifts unsurprisingly sharpened the spatial imprint of Jewish life in Edwardian Ireland.

Part of this rising conception of racial and cultural difference expressed itself in a renewed concern over the policing of boundaries, be they physical, ethnic, or sexual. As early as 1899, Dr. George Wigoder told a gathering in Dublin that Zionism was "a living thing now": "This new movement originated in Vienna, where Jews tried to find their deliverance in assimilation. But . . . they were given to understand that it is not exactly the talith and phylactery which make the Jew. It is in the blood."[78] Early dissonant voices worried that "Zionism will lay the foundation for future Anti-Semitism," and one commentator, most likely journalist and future convert Edward R. Lipsett, criticized the movement as a "sublimated form of Jingoism."[79] Yet within a decade, the Dublin Jewish Ladies Society was represented at the first Women's Zionist Conference, and the Jewish Literary Society regularly discussed "the claims which the Zionist movement had on the Jewish people" and "the glorious Jewish past which still lives in the Holy Land."[80] This emotional and psychological phenomenon was also physically emboldening. Chaim Herzog later recalled, "[As] the concept of a Jewish state emerged in our collective consciousness [it] added considerably to our sense of pride . . . [and] strengthened our entire community." Yet the Edwardian period also saw rising communal anxieties over the "lukewarm methods . . . being employed to ward off the evil of assimilation," and the movement continued to grow.[81] A debate at the Jewish Literary Club in 1909 on the "great evil" of intermarriage ended in a consensus that "each race should keep more to itself" and denounced "the waverers and the weaklings who left the nation."[82]

An important symbolic turning point came in 1909, when a faction of second-generation community leaders calling themselves the "Young Jews" confronted the regular presence of the Society for Promoting Christianity amongst the Jews on the boundaries of Jewish space. Two of the leaders of the Judæo-Irish Home Rule Association founded the previous year, Joseph Edelstein and Philip Wigoder, led a counterdemonstration and spoke at a "rival platform" to open-air Protestant street preachers at Portobello, adjacent to Little Jerusalem. The meeting ended in chaos when Edelstein was arrested by police for assaulting Isaac Luft, a Jewish convert who rose to speak.[83] Pamphlets circulated among the community asked, "How many homes they have ruined?," and an "oath" was later read to the crowds denouncing both missionaries and converts:[84] "We, the Jews of Dublin, here assembled . . . solemnly affirm that we shall not have conversations with missionaries; also that we shall rigorously boycott any Jewish pervert. That we shall take great care of the future of our children, and in every way to combat the endeavours of the society to rob the great Jewish people of their inheritance."[85] Similar concerns over the protection of children from the activities of missionaries fed into a nexus of women's and children's communitarian organizations; Jessie Spiro Bloom, who was heavily involved in the Dublin Hebrew Ladies Charitable Society during her youth, recalled how the Adelaide Girls Club was founded explicitly to prevent the conversion efforts by Christian missionaries. The Jewish Lads Brigade and Jewish Athletic Association similarly sought to "smooth out the ghetto stoop" and "fitted boys to be alert, strong, efficient men . . . morally, intellectually, and physically," who could "repel invaders from their homes." Nick Harris's memories of the "many street fights" of his youth occurred along the physical boundaries of Little Jerusalem around Grenville Terrace, where he confronted antisemitic gangs and worried "what would happen if they attacked a Jewish boy who could not defend himself."[86]

Conclusion

The emergence of Zionism utterly transformed the "familiar difference" of Irish Jewishness, resetting social, sexual, and ethnic boundaries between public and private and creating a new form of "public Jewishness" palatable to Irish society.[87] For different reasons, both cultural nationalists and Protestant evangelicals embraced Zionism without, in any sense, overwriting their fundamental antisemitism. Arthur Griffith moved away from his early alliance with the inveterate antisemite Frank Hugh O'Donnell, who saw Zionism as a global conspiracy, and toward revivalists such as Aodh de Blacam, who embraced Zionism as a "Jewish nationalism" worthy of imitation.[88] This model was replicated in various forms throughout the advanced nationalist movement, which blended classically antisemitic tropes with admiration of Jewish linguistic and cultural distinctiveness.[89] For missionaries, its appeal was the inverse; by creating a homeland and nationality,

Zionism served to divorce the racial and religious dimensions of Jewish identity and pave the way for conversion. The Reverend Charles S. Painter, secretary of the London Jews' Society, told a Dublin audience in 1906 that the Jewish Territorial Organization showed "the most hopeful symptoms that the promise would be fulfilled that the scattered Israelites would gather together again in their old land." At the Palestine Exhibition organized by Dublin missionaries two years later, a lecturer on Zionism told his audience that the movement meant that "if a Jew became a Christian he did not cease to be Jew."[90] For mainstream Catholic nationalists, Zionism was merely "a new name for a very old idea," concluding a process under way over the "nineteen centuries that have elapsed since the Diaspora."[91] The constructed dysphoria of Irish Jewish space was ultimately resolved by completing the loop of Irish Jewish space-time, psychologically emplacing "wandering Jews" in an imminent homeland. But the cultural hybridity and feelings of "unhomeliness" created in this "in-between" space in turn created their own psychological ripples through memory, space, and time.[92]

4

Irish Representations of
Jews and Jewish Responses/
Jewish Representations of Jews
and Irish Responses

NATALIE WYNN

Irish Jews, as a relatively unknown and exotic species, have traditionally attracted a great deal of popular interest both from within the
broader Jewish community and from beyond. The novelty value of
the "Irish Jew" has led to the production of a wide range of material, literary, historical, and fictional. Although the general fascination with Irish Jewry has increased since the 1990s, corresponding to
the decline of the community itself, the academic field of Irish Jewish
studies remains in its infancy. Many areas of Irish Jewish historiography—such as Irish-Jewish relations—remain mired in the nostalgia
and minority politics of a community past its prime, whose long-term
future hangs in the balance. Although much has been written about
the position of Jews in Irish society, rigorous, critical, and objective
analysis are notably absent from these assessments. The positive tone
of most existing appraisals has barely been queried, and potentially
controversial aspects of Irish-Jewish relations have been suppressed
within the recognized history of Irish Jewry. This chapter challenges received wisdom by demonstrating some ways in which negative stereotypes of Jews have shaped aspects of traditional Irish Jewish
"historiography." This historiography is revealed to be the product

of a circular process whereby Jewish sensitivity toward non-Jewish disapproval in the late nineteenth and early twentieth centuries has generated a narrative that has been readily accepted and repeated by historians of Irish Jewry, thus reinforcing its claims. The absence of any sound theoretical framework by which to measure and analyze anti-Jewish sentiment in the Irish context has contributed to the inability or reluctance (or both) of scholars to reflect sufficiently on the nature of their sources.

Defining *Antisemitism*

It should hardly be necessary to state that before any discussion of anti-Jewish prejudice can take place, it is vital to clarify what exactly is under discussion. However, even in the academic setting, the loaded nature of the term *antisemitism* and the strong emotional responses it evokes render clarification as vital as ever. While for the majority its meaning appears blatantly obvious, the definition of *antisemitism* in Jewish studies, in its purest sense, is very narrow. Jewish studies pins it down to a specific historical context (the demagogic politics of late-nineteenth-century Germany) and a clear set of (racial) criteria.[1] To contemplate antisemitism in any straightforward sense as a social phenomenon with a long, relatively unbroken history from antiquity via the Middle Ages to the present is anachronistic and overly generalized. Doing so subsumes the unique cultural and historical nuances of time and place into a sweeping, emotionally and politically loaded, and relativized view of history. The whole rich panorama of Jewish experience—good, bad, and indifferent, as it has been in different times and different places—is thus understood primarily in terms of recent, devastating, and far-reaching events.[2] The ongoing impact of the Shoah on the Jewish psyche should not be underestimated in terms of its influence on contemporary self-understanding and identity. To judge the Jewish past through the Shoah's lens has a distorting effect.

In Jewish studies a variety of terms are used to convey the nuances attached to different forms of anti-Jewish prejudice according to historical context, such as *anti-Judaism*, *Jew hatred*, and *Judeophobia*. Nevertheless, the shortcomings and inadequacies of any terminology are frequently emphasized by those individuals who study this phenomenon.[3] Significant too is the term favored by sociologist Zygmunt Bauman, *allosemitism*. This term refers to the notion that Jews are so different from the mainstream that in order to describe or understand them, a range of radically different concepts and categories is required. In Bauman's words, Jews represent "ambivalence incarnate," the "weeds" in modernity's "gardening" project of ordering society. Other scholars likewise observe that anti-Jewish prejudice is more about constructs of "Jews" as opposed to any observable reality, or experience, of "real" Jews.[4] Even though there undoubtedly is a connection (or connections) between the various manifestations of anti-Jewish prejudice and their related discourses over the centuries, the precise links are notoriously hard to nail down. Indeed, the nature of anti-Jewish sentiment tends to reveal more about the fears and anxieties of particular societies at a given time and place in history than about "Jews" or "Judaism" per se. David Nirenberg has recently examined this tendency of non-Jewish thinkers from antiquity to the modern era to reflect on the societies and issues of their time through the lens of "Jews" and "Judaism." The term chosen by Nirenberg to describe this intellectual pattern, *anti-Judaism*, is traditionally applied to theologically driven expressions of anti-Jewish prejudice. The range of cultural, religious, and intellectual constructs involved—and their nebulousness—should arouse suspicion toward any claims of a seamless continuum of "antisemitism" throughout Jewish history.[5]

In sum, scholars continue to grapple with many of the issues, not least how best to advance our understanding of the phenomenon (or phenomena) popularly known as antisemitism. Therefore, it is crucial for anyone purporting to discuss antisemitism to be clear as to how exactly they understand this term with reference to their own particular findings. In practice, the opposite is often the case, with many scholars who write about antisemitism remaining unaware of the intricacies and nuances involved. Their conclusions, though misrepresentative, can have considerable impact on our understanding of Jewish and non-Jewish relations in a given setting, with the Russian Empire a classic example.[6] Underresearched Jewries, such as the Irish case, are especially prone to such misleading scholarship, with few pausing to question received wisdom. The broad and imprecise interpretations of antisemitism that are characteristic of the Irish context have allowed scholars such as Dermot Keogh and Cormac Ó Gráda to sidestep conclusions that are potentially uncomfortable for the Irish, whether Jewish or non-Jewish. As their work has been widely lauded as "the final word" on Irish Jewry, it has been easy to dismiss or ignore alternative voices such as Gerald Moore or Ronit Lentin, whose findings are rather less palatable.

Considering Antisemitism in the Irish Setting

The mass emigration period triggered a reversal in the fortunes of the Irish Jewish community, which had been regarded by observers as being in a state of irreversible decline just a few years previously.[7] Although Ireland never became a major destination for East European Jewish immigrants, they arrived in significant-enough numbers to create in microcosm the types of social, cultural, and economic challenges that were experienced by established Jewish communities throughout western Europe and in the United States. Ultimately, Irish Jewry was completely regenerated as a result of accelerated immigration, seeing the creation of a rich communal infrastructure and experiencing something of a golden age in the 1940s and 1950s that is still fondly remembered. Even at the peak of its growth, the Jewish community never constituted more than a tiny minority among the Irish Catholic majority.

The comings and goings that have defined the Irish Jewish landscape for more than a century eventually began to take their toll. Irish Jews initially traveled onward in search of economic opportunities. As decline set in, the motivations changed: the search for bigger communities with better facilities and a more vibrant Jewish social and cultural life.[8] The issue of integration tends not to be openly acknowledged, as it dissonates with the image that the Irish Jewish communal establishment is keen to portray: one of a continuous Jewish presence since the Middle Ages; largely cordial relations between Irish Jews and non-Jewish ruling powers and neighbors; a community that has punched above its weight in terms of its contribution to Irish cultural, political, and economic life; and one that was sufficiently integrated into Irish society to take up the cause of Irish independence and militant Irish nationalism.[9] One enduring myth, popular since the nineteenth century, asserts that Ireland is the only country in the world where Jews have never been persecuted.[10] In this vein, the notorious Limerick Boycott of 1904 has been presented as "acharacteristic and atypical," "an aberration" in an otherwise unblemished Irish record.[11] The rose-tinted claims of the communal establishment are bolstered by the glowing reminiscences of expats.[12]

The sources suggest a different reality, pointing to a process of "indigenization" by the official community that presents Jews as a constant, steady, and integrated element of Irish society. This representation has entailed the writing of the community "in" to seminal and formative events of recent Irish history and the claim that Irish Jews have made a disproportionate contribution to Irish public life.[13] Although this assertion would appear to beg the question of why precisely such an exercise would be necessary for a comfortable, well-integrated, and accepted minority, it is a question that until relatively recently even scholars have shied away from asking. Instead, historians such as Keogh and Ó Gráda have allowed themselves be led by the "approved" version of Irish Jewish history, as received from the individuals and amateur historians whose views are in line with the claims of the communal establishment. Their work therefore reflects the largely unreflexive nostalgia of anecdotal sources, while serving to reify it as "objective" history.

Particularly problematic is the existing discourse on antisemitism in the Irish context. The majority of commentators have not only failed to interrogate the term, its meaning, and its significance but also never paused to consider its appropriateness to the Irish setting. It has been assumed that the reader understands exactly what is under discussion, even as the discussion wavers between a variety of forms of anti-Jewish prejudice, each with its own subtle nuances. This assumption of a set of definite, if unspecified, criteria by which to classify antisemitism has steered the debate toward a set of black-and-white conclusions, namely, whether negative sentiment toward Jews in Ireland should be taken seriously as antisemitism. The absence of any serious analytical framework has given rise to a polarized debate and a methodological cal vacuum. Here the emotiveness of the term *antisemitism* is particularly unhelpful, fostering a sense that if the level of prejudice is not comparable to Nazi Germany or czarist Russia, then it is "mild" or insignificant and therefore does not merit rigorous investigation in its own right.[14] Indeed, the majority of incidents are relatively minor— uncomfortable as opposed to physically threatening or violent—but these experiences do tend to indicate that Jews are perceived by some Irish people as somehow different from themselves and not quite Irish. This perception leads many Jewish people to feel—although they may be reluctant to admit it—that they will never fully be accepted or be Irish enough to be entirely at ease in Irish society.[15] Lentin has argued that this sense of unease has been a significant factor in persuading many younger Irish Jews to emigrate in recent decades.[16] While many have purported to be looking for bigger, more vibrant communities, this discomfort equally implies that they will feel more at home in places where it is less unusual to be Jewish or where it is easier to be anonymous.

Irish Jews, the Economic Stereotype, and the Historical Record

The impact that negative popular sentiment can have on collective Jewish memory and, by extension, on the more formal historical record is well illustrated through the ubiquitous stereotype of "the economic Jew." Derek Penslar, author of the most extensive analysis of Jewish economic stereotypes to date, argues that these clichés represent a constant and prominent strand of anti-Jewish discourse in Europe since the early modern period.[17] Penslar's study constitutes a significant advance in our understanding of the extent to which economic stereotypes have shaped both non-Jewish and Jewish thinking regarding "the Jew," while highlighting just how much work has yet to be done in this area. Economic stereotypes remain a difficult topic for scholarly investigation, having a power and longevity that render them sensitive and potentially contentious subjects for research. The awkward and inauspicious aspects of Jewish economic activity, in particular, require a great deal of reflection and honesty from historians. The topic is further complicated by the matrix of twentieth-century polemics: from the anti-immigrant discourse of the mass-emigration period to Nazi representations of Jews and Judaism. Economic discourses of the Jews are still, therefore, a relatively unexplored area, where research is tentative and ongoing.[18]

To an extent, the historical narratives of those Jewries that experienced the economic, social, and cultural challenges of mass emigration have been molded by Jewish responses to negative stereotyping, especially to economic discourses of "the Jews." In the first place, as Penslar emphasizes, the attitude of the Western Jewish communal leadership toward poverty and need was shaped by the bourgeois economic and cultural milieu that they shared with their non-Jewish counterparts, inclining them to feel a similar distaste for their less fortunate brethren.[19] The Jewish establishment, with an eye to the fickle tide of non-Jewish public opinion, was also deeply sensitive to unflattering popular perceptions of Jews. Communal authorities were keen publicly to distance the "official" community from the disreputable economic pursuits and practices that symbolized the essential "foreignness" of their East European counterparts in the popular mindset. While no immigrant community was immune to sharp practice by any means, including the Irish one,[20] the prejudice of Jewish elites has been noted by historians such as David Feldman, Mordechai Rozin, and Bill Williams (Britain) as well as Zosa Sjazkowski (Germany and the United States), and it is the elites whose voices tend to dominate the sources for much of the mass-emigration period. Thus, it is important to remember that the commentary of the nineteenth- and early-twentieth-century acculturated Jewish establishment on their immigrant brethren was molded by contemporary political conditions and exigencies and should not be taken at face value today.

In the Irish setting, the influence of economic stereotypes is visible in various pronouncements on immigrant Jewish mores. It has been remarked that the beginnings of integration brought about an increase in materialism among the newcomers. This negative quality has been linked to a growing religious laxity and a straying from traditional values, whereby the acquisition of and respect for Jewish scholarship were supplanted by a thirst for material gain and economic betterment.[21] However, our suspicions should be raised by the judgments implicit in these assessments. I contend that presuppositions regarding Irish Jewish materialism, economic practices, and involvement in money lending have been molded by an interplay of non-Jewish economic stereotypes and Jewish sensitivity toward these stereotypes. These questionable assumptions have influenced traditional understandings of certain periods and events in the Irish Jewish past. This point needs to be duly acknowledged, reflected upon, and interrogated, with implications for not just the historiography of Jews in Ireland but beyond its shores.

Myer Joel Wigoder's assertion that in Ireland "the predominant factor is money; learning and dignity are relegated to the background" is a prime example of how important primary sources have been subjected to the influence of economic stereotyping and the personal baggage of commentators. Wigoder, author of the only firsthand Irish immigrant memoir, describes how Jews whose traditional learning had ensured them a high social standing in their birthplaces found themselves excluded from Dublin synagogues through poverty. Poor scholars are contrasted with the brash parvenus whose wealth had earned them an unmerited prestige within Dublin's communal institutions. However, once Wigoder's remarks are read in context, they become much more nuanced than a straightforward critique of the local immigrant community. He notes that the unsystematic flow of immigration "has played havoc with the [former] social values" and concludes that "the process of developing a balanced community will take two or three generations," because "the community is virtually in a state of flux."[22] Wigoder recognizes that the unsettling processes of emigration, resettlement, and acculturation had taken their toll on traditional Jewish values within the community. Wigoder himself was a somewhat more complex character than is generally assumed. His memoir shows that he valued secular education as well as the traditional Jewish scholarship and observances to which he dedicated himself throughout his life. Wigoder was linked through marriage to Robert Bradlaw, a man whom he clearly respected, contrary to Mark Duffy's portrayal of Bradlaw as precisely the type of nouveau riche that Wigoder disparaged.[23] Rivlin's understanding of Wigoder's comments is influenced by her own favoring of "Observant" (with a capital *O*, as she spells it) forms of Judaism, to which a straightforward interpretation speaks volumes.[24] Although her bias is a lot more subtle than Duffy's, it is nevertheless distorting in terms of the general understanding of an important source such as Wigoder.

Duffy's assessment of Bradlaw draws on criticisms emanating from Dublin's Jewish establishment, which he fails to treat with due caution. These critiques attribute the split between established and immigrant factions of the community and the founding of the Dublin New Hebrew Congregation in 1883 to disputes over immigrant involvement in money lending. Representatives of the DNHC refuted these allegations, citing religious grounds for the schism.[25] Duffy's class-driven analysis is deeply influenced by Bill Williams's seminal work, *The Making of Manchester Jewry, 1740–1875*. However, Duffy uses Williams's work selectively, focusing on its social and economic aspects while missing its subtleties. He also fails to nuance it, on the one hand, to Dublin's distinct local context or, on the other hand, to the broader processes of Jewish mass migration. This oversight detracts from the potential value of Williams's findings as a model for understanding interactions between native and immigrant Jews in the Irish setting.[26] Although Duffy's study of Irish Jewry ended with his master's thesis, his findings have cast a long shadow through their influence on Cormac Ó Gráda's assessment of Jewish economic activity in Ireland; while Duffy's work has been ignored by the majority of chroniclers of Irish Jewry, Ó Gráda's most certainly has not.

Ó Gráda's detailed analysis of the Irish Jewish involvement in money lending is innovative in situating lending in general within the wider socioeconomic context of late-nineteenth-century Ireland. Ó Gráda argues that, despite the stigma attached to this profession, moneylenders performed an important function in a society where the vast majority were too poor to have access to any other form of credit. Yet his conclusions are contradictory. Ó Gráda's primary sources lead him to state that Jewish lenders tended to loan minor amounts to the poorest classes on little or no security. This money lending was an unofficial, small-scale, and risky sideline that came with a high possibility of default. Ó Gráda's assertions are corroborated by the census data for 1901 and 1911. The data provide little direct evidence of Jewish money lending, and even indirect evidence (euphemisms such as *collector* or *agent*) is slight.[27] Ó Gráda then effectively contradicts himself by concluding that the Jewish involvement in money lending was significant, citing Duffy's claim that a wealthy, influential class of lenders rapidly emerged from the ranks of Dublin's immigrant Jewish community as personified by Wigoder's purported nemesis, Bradlaw. Duffy's assertions are, in fact, unsubstantiated; there is little hard evidence to indicate the precise nature of distinctions of class, ethnicity, and culture within Dublin's immigrant community at this time.

Ó Gráda furthermore fails to recognize the polemical qualities of his contemporary Jewish sources. Even though he does acknowledge Jewish sensitivities toward money lending past and present, he accepts contemporary Jewish commentary as a straightforward critique of immigrant mores and occupational patterns. Ó Gráda thus interprets Anglo-Jewish exhortations to Irish immigrant Jews as contemporary analyses of local conditions rather than as an anecdotal source to be treated with due caution. He cites the exhortations of the chief rabbi of the British Empire, Hermann Adler, that Irish immigrant Jews comport themselves and conduct their business dealings in such a way as to earn the respect of their non-Jewish neighbors—that is, by becoming less visibly "Jewish" and by adopting what were deemed to be more respectable occupations and personal habits. Ó Gráda is unaware that similar speeches were delivered to immigrant communities the length and breadth of the British Isles. For example, in 1893 at the Great Synagogue in London, Adler urged an immigrant audience to behave in such a way as "to evoke the good-will, the esteem and favour of your fellow-citizens" as a prelude to addressing "the important subject of cleanliness in your persons, your dress, and your dwellings."

These comments bear striking similarity to the Reverend Lewis Mendelsohn's inaugural address to the Dublin Hebrew Congregation, cited uncritically by Ó Gráda as representative of local realities, "to act honourably, fairly and kindly towards their fellow-citizens of all creeds and classes, and thus assist in being the means of ennobling the Jewish race, and securing the respect of those amongst whom they are destined to live."[28] It is interesting to note that, although Mendelsohn appears to have been well received by all ranks of Dublin's Jews, such appeals did not always go down well even with the local Jewish establishment. An ironic piece from the *Jewish Chronicle* satirizing the relationship between the Anglo-Jewish authorities and their so-called provincial satellite communities places the following, presumably fictitious, remark in the mouth of one of the leading members of the Dublin Hebrew Congregation: "Well, Sir, when the Chief Rabbi pays us his next Pastoral visit let him not lecture us."[29] Adler's pastoral sermon to the congregation the previous year had again included recommendations regarding personal habits, business dealings, and relations with the host community.[30] Cumulatively, his comments reflect Anglo-Jewish elite assumptions that immigrant Jews were incapable of behaving appropriately on either a personal or a professional level.

In Limerick, sensitivities toward economic discourse encouraged the Jewish establishment in both London and Dublin to suspect the worst at the outset of the boycott. The Limerick community's internecine squabbles, including an acrimonious schism in the late 1890s or early 1900s, were freely aired in the local press as well as making their way into the *Jewish Chronicle*.[31] A distaste for money lending was cited by the breakaway faction as underpinning the split. Yet these claims could equally be understood as an appeal for legitimation and endorsement by the outside world over their more established rivals, especially given the emotiveness of the image of "the Jewish money-lender" for both Jews and non-Jews. Indeed, local King's Counsel R. Adams attributed the split more plausibly to petty ritual differences, while one member of the Limerick Jewish community, Sol Goldberg, remarked ironically that even the community itself did not know what the quarrel was actually about; Goldberg attributed the schism to arrogance and bad behavior.[32] The willingness of acculturated Jews to buy into negative economic discourse was exposed in the course of an investigation into local Jewish business practices by representatives of the Board of Deputies of British Jews. The president of the Dublin Hebrew Congregation, Ernest Harris, shared the investigators' initial assumption that the business practices of many Limerick Jews were disreputable and a cause of friction with their non-Jewish neighbors. Actually, the report exonerated the community and was noted by one deputy, J. J. Jaffe, as having refuted the suspicions of some of his colleagues that Limerick's Jews were retrograde and somehow responsible for the boycott.[33] Harris likewise had reached the conclusion that they were "respectable" traders who earned a precarious living and were often cheated by their customers. He described Limerick as "a small city where religious toleration has never been one of the characteristics of the majority of its population."[34]

One intriguing example of the impact of non-Jewish discourse on the self-image of the immigrant community itself is Joseph Edelstein's pulp novel *The Moneylender*, published in Dublin in 1908. Edelstein's stated purpose in writing the book appears to have been somewhat apologetic in seeking "rather to expose the causes of usury for eradication than the effects for vituperation."[35] As Edelstein saw it, the hatred that met Jews everywhere led them to take revenge by the only means open to them—usury—thus creating a vicious circle of resentment between themselves and non-Jews. However, the good intentions of the novel—such as they are—are easily outweighed by its melodramatic tone, exaggerated and unsympathetic Jewish characters, and a front cover that would not have looked out of place in Nazi Germany. A contemporary review by J. Emerson Scott, included in the 1908 edition of *The Moneylender*, finds the vulgarity and ostentation of the characters convincing. Scott describes them as a "mixture of childish simplicity and worldly cunning . . . drawn from the living model," an impression that speak volumes as to the potency of negative Jewish stereotypes. *The Moneylender* ran to five editions between 1908 and 1931, causing considerable embarrassment to the Jewish community and indicating the extent of local non-Jewish fascination with the novel's subject matter.

Given the tone of *The Moneylender*, its use by Ó Gráda as a historical source is somewhat perplexing. It may best be understood in terms of contemporary literary expressions of Jewish self-hatred, which often employed the crude popular stereotypes of the majority community. Edelstein's reliability is further compromised by his eccentricity, a point that appears to have escaped Ó Gráda altogether. Edelstein, who spent time in the infamous Grangegorman psychiatric hospital, is described by Asher Benson as "one of the lost souls of early 20th-century Irish Jewry" who occasionally "went off the rails."[36] Edelstein is best remembered nowadays as a cofounder of the controversial but short-lived Judæo-Irish Home Rule Association, which is discussed by Heather Miller Rubens elsewhere in this volume. The association was established in 1908—the same year *The Moneylender* was published—and is often regarded as an indication of Jewish nationalist sympathies.[37]

In sum, Ó Gráda's attempt at an objective analysis of Jewish economic activity is undermined by his failure to subject traditional economic discourses on Jews to the same degree of interrogation as negative stereotypes of money lending and lenders in general. Although he begins with some promising observations on the function of money lending in nineteenth- and twentieth-century Irish society, he allows his findings on Jewish economic activity to be shaped, and ultimately outweighed, by negative stereotypes, even to the detriment of his primary evidence. Ó Gráda's conclusions are sadly indicative of the potency and longevity of this imagery, even in countries such as Ireland, where the Jewish presence has always been marginal and no Jew has ever been prominent in Irish economic affairs.[38] Thus, his work represents little advance, from a historiographical perspective, on the findings of nonprofessional historians such as Duffy and Rivlin.

Conclusion

This chapter opened by showing that antisemitism and anti-Jewish prejudice are far from being the straightforward, somewhat "obvious" phenomena they are frequently assumed to be. Instead, anti-Jewish prejudice has been shown to be a complex and nuanced matter, requiring a careful choice of language and clear criteria before any worthwhile observations can be advanced. The virtual absence of any such clarifications in the Irish context has created a polarized debate. This discussion has focused on efforts to "prove" whether antisemitism exists in Ireland to any noteworthy extent rather than analyzing evidence of negative non-Jewish attitudes toward Jews in order to reach a set of objective conclusions as to the nature and extent of non-Jewish sentiment in Irish society.

The effect of negative non-Jewish sentiment on the Irish Jewish psyche has also been emphasized as an issue that has barely been touched on by commentators. Here the example of economic discourse is particularly informative, in its influence on analyses of Jewish history during the mass-emigration period by historians of all shades: professional, amateur, Jewish, and non-Jewish. Centuries-old assumptions of the nature of Jewish economic activity have been shown to have shaped historical narratives of Irish Jewry in a circular process. In the late nineteenth and early twentieth centuries, acculturated Jews allowed their sensitivity to non-Jewish critique to influence their perceptions of their immigrant brethren. This awareness reflected their own fears that their hard-won foothold in non-Jewish society was precarious and potentially threatened by accelerated East European immigration. The biases of the Western Jewish establishment, and their attempts publicly to distance themselves from the newcomers, were echoed in contemporary publications such as the *Jewish Chronicle*. Chroniclers of Irish Jewry, lacking expertise in Jewish history and historiography, have failed to recognize such sources as representing only one voice within the Jewish community. The commentaries of acculturated Jews have been taken at face value as authoritative contemporary accounts rather than being treated with due caution as anecdotal and potentially tainted. The adverse assessments of the most politically influential faction within British Jewry have been allowed to influence the interpretation of sources from within the Irish immigrant community itself, such as Wigoder and Edelstein, effectively distorting later historical analyses. Existing scholarship on Irish Jewry, both Jewish and non-Jewish, is notable for the absence of the kind of insights that are to be gleaned from Jewish studies. This point underlines the importance of Jewish studies perspectives to the critical analyses of contemporary, popular, and anecdotal sources on Jews anywhere. As things stand, the power and longevity of economic stereotypes are visible in the work of Jewish and non-Jewish chroniclers of Irish Jewry alike, and few of their readers have paused to question it.

Without an appropriate critical framework by which to assess the sources and to objectively assess Jewish and non-Jewish relations within the Irish context, existing historical narratives have been constructed by way of a circular process. The evidence would undoubtedly benefit from being reappraised in light of the negative stereotypes and anti-Jewish sentiment in general. It would allow us to construct a more rounded picture of the situation in Ireland and how it might relate to unfavorable discourses of Jews elsewhere. Equally important, such methodological advances might also encourage a greater degree of introspection and reflection among all chroniclers of Irish Jewry, Jewish and non-Jewish, scholarly and nonprofessional—as well as their audiences—as to why negative stereotypes of Irish Jewish economic activity are so readily and universally accepted.

PART TWO | **Realities**

5

From Richard Lalor Sheil to Leon Pinsker

*The Jewish Question, the Irish Question,
and a Genealogy of Hebrewphobia*

SANDER L. GILMAN

"What Is It You Fear? What Is the Origin of This Hebrewphobia?"

It was cold and wet in February 1848; indeed, it was one of the wettest Februarys across England and Wales that anyone could remember. The House sat the evening of February 7, 1848, and none of its members could escape the damp, the cold, and the noxious "Great Stink" of the Thames. The river had become "the common sewer of London": "the recipient of all the excrementitious matter from men and animals; of dead cats, dogs, rats, and a quantity of other vermin besides; of the filth and refuse of many hundred manufactories; of the rejected animal and vegetable substances, in a state of decomposition, from the market places; and, lastly, of the foul and gory liquid issuing from slaughter-houses, skinners of beasts, and preparers of tripe."[1] Charles Barry's semifinished new Palace of Westminster (Houses of Parliament) stood sadly next to it, often exposed to the weather and stench. And its members suffered each and every time they sat.

Two topics were to be debated—seemingly unrelated. The first was the ongoing catastrophe of the Irish Famine, which had begun in 1845 and was growing more desperate each day. It had begun with the continent-wide potato blight in the early 1840s but was exacerbated in Ireland because of a wide range of factors, from the overreliance of the Irish on this crop to British land politics and the notorious Corn Laws, that restricted the importation of grain to alleviate the Famine. The second topic was occasioned by the election in 1847 of the city banker Lionel de Rothschild to the City of London constituency. Rothschild, a practicing Jew, would not take the oath that required he state "I make this Declaration upon the true Faith of a Christian." Whig leader Lord John Russell introduced the Jews Relief Act, also called the Jewish Disabilities Bill, following the election to allow him to take the oath without this caveat.

The debate about the Irish Famine centered on the perceived inaction of the government to relieve the suffering that had grown so extreme as to become the defining factor for Irish political figures. John O'Connell, the member of Parliament for Limerick, not present on the floor, requested through a colleague that the government respond to the following question: "Whether, considering the enormous and every-day growing increase of destitution in many parts of Ireland; the nearly total want of means among her small farmers and agricultural labourers to purchase food and maintain their families; and the inability of the poor-law to support the overwhelming pauperism of the country—the Government have not some measure ready for the providing of relief by means of food or employment, and thus far preventing the wholesale wasting and destruction of human life among the poorer classes of Ireland."[2] Before dismissing the question as unanswerable, the home secretary, Sir George Gray, opined that "the Government was not prepared to submit to Parliament a proposition for the resumption of public works, or the system which superseded the public works; that was to say, the system of feeding all the destitute poor of Ireland by means of advances of public money." Private charities under the auspices of the poor laws were doing a more than adequate job, now feeding children in schools as well as providing assistance to the deserving poor. Their work "bear[s] testimony to the visible and daily improving condition of the poor unhappy children, to the cheering and beneficial reaction which this provision has had upon the parents." One of those individuals massively contributing to this futile private effort was Lionel de Rothschild, who had been among those lawmakers who helped set up the British Relief Association in 1847. The reality, of course, was very much different, and mass starvation had begun to kill what would eventually number a million inhabitants of Ireland and drive roughly an equal number abroad.[3] But Parliament was little interested in this crisis at the moment, and thus, in complex ways, modern Irish national identity dates itself from the Famine and the tepid British response, even when evoking Oliver Cromwell and the land seizures of the mid-seventeenth century as the wellspring of Irish political identity. The Famine came to define an Irish Catholic identity and thus Irish national politics, at least retrospectively, in opposition to Anglican Britain, as Claire Mitchell notes: "The construction of Catholic Irishness was strengthened by the disaster of famine from 1845 to 1849. . . . Religious affiliation became increasingly a surrogate for national identity as the effective agent for communal solidarity."[4] In Parliament that evening, such sectarianism seemed less central.

The Irish members, specifically the Roman Catholic members, were seated because the Catholic Relief Act passed in 1829 had allowed Catholics to take the oath of office in Parliament to join their Protestant colleagues. Quakers and other nonconformists had been allowed to "affirm" their oath rather than "swear it" after an act in 1833. Parliament had thus moved from a narrowly Anglican to a broader Christian body. Jews, however, still had to take a Christian oath. The future Conservative prime minister Benjamin Disraeli, while a Jew at birth, had become an Anglican at twelve when his father broke with the London congregation and converted. When he entered the House in 1837, he was able to swear the oath with no qualms of conscience. Lionel de Rothschild, a City banker, was, unlike Disraeli, a practicing Jew and refused to take the required oath as formulated.[5] Rothschild, whose wealth financed many imperial adventures under Victoria, was elected to the House along with the liberal Whig prime minister Lord John Russell from the City of London. To enable his compatriot to take his seat, Russell introduced the Jewish Disabilities Act to eliminate the problem with the oath. Russell, one historian claims, "was more concerned with the removal of obstacles to civil liberty than with the creation of a more reasonable and civilized society," and certainly this action was intended to have that effect.[6] The rest of the evening of February 7, 1848, was spent debating this bill, which did not deal, as was stated at the beginning of the debate, with religious freedom in Britain but considered the specific claim that members of Parliament had to subscribe to specific Christian beliefs.

After midnight the ninth speaker arose to debate the measure. He was Richard Lalor Sheil, Whig member for Tipperary (until 1841) and then for Dungarvan, who had sat in the Commons since 1831.[7] His maiden speech was on the second reading of the First Reform Act (1832) that year, which drastically overhauled the franchise to vote as well as the constitution of the Commons. Sheil came from a very wealthy Catholic family with continental connections and later married a very wealthy widow, so he was both cosmopolitan and independent in his outlook. Educated at Trinity College, Dublin, he was one of the Irish stalwarts who had accompanied Daniel O'Connell (the Emancipator) to London to protest the suppression of the Catholic Association, of which he was a founding member, and continued to support O'Connell until Catholic Emancipation was granted in 1829.[8] He was also one of the leading Anglo-Irish playwrights of his day, which can account to some degree for the power of his public utterances.[9]

Unprepossessing in appearance to his contemporaries, as he was only five feet tall, he was acknowledged to be one of the greatest Irish orators of his day, in spite, as a contemporary member of the House noted, of his "'detestable' Irish brogue, [that] meant that 'he was not pleasant to listen to.'" William Gladstone was somewhat more complimentary, comparing his voice to "a tin kettle battered about from place to place, knocking first against one side and then against another. There was a peculiar character, a sort of half-wildness in his aspect and delivery; his whole figure, and his delivery, and his voice and his matter, were all in such perfect keeping with one another that they formed a great Parliamentary picture." Yet, as Gladstone also further commented, Sheil "was a great orator, and an orator of much preparation, I believe, carried even to words, with a very vivid imagination and an enormous power of language, and of strong feeling." George W. E. Russell noted in his memoir, "Sheil was very small, and of mean presence; with a singularly fidgety manner, a shrill voice, and a delivery unintelligibly rapid. But in sheer beauty of elaborated diction not O'Connell nor any one else could surpass him."[10] What is striking about all of these comments are the euphemisms ("half-wildness," "shrill") that branded Sheil as essentially Irish, at least to the ears of his English listeners. And *Irish* in Sheil's case really did translate into *Catholic* at the moment in Irish history when these two identities came to be coterminous.

Sheil's speech that evening incorporated the very opposite of the advice that he had given Disraeli after his disastrous maiden speech in December 1837, when Disraeli was laughed off the floor as he spoke in opposition to O'Connell on the question of filling Irish seats: "As it is you have shown to the House that you have a fine voice, that you have unlimited command of the language, courage, temper and readiness. Now get rid of your genius for a session. . . . Be very quiet. Try to be dull, only argue and reason imperfectly, for if you speak with precision they will think you are trying to be witty."[11] Disraeli listened to him and was able to defuse what had become not only a personal but also a political disaster. Part of Disraeli's problem was both the tone of his address and the fact that he appeared before the House with very long curled hair and dressed in the bright-green coat of a fop. Sheil understood the power of appearances; he knew he could not change his brogue, which marked him as irredeemably Irish, but he believed that Disraeli could alter his clothing and his tone, as he (or at least his father) had his religion.

The confluence between these two men came to a head on that February night. Disraeli backed the bill for Jewish Emancipation even though his party, the Tories, sitting in opposition, was clearly arrayed against it. The speech Sheil gave on the evening of February 7, 1848, was extraordinary in its precision and wit and powerful as much because of his brogue as in spite it. His contribution to the debate became one of the milestones of parliamentary oratory.[12]

Sheil began by distinguishing between religious affiliation and national identity, a central tenet of the Enlightenment discussion about the nature of the Jews and, one can repeat, part of the evolving changes in the very definition of the "Irish" at that moment because of the Famine. As Oliver Rafferty has also observed, "There was a tendency to read the Famine in religious as well as political and economic terms. In a certain sense the emergence of Irish Catholic identity in the modern era is perhaps uniquely a result of the historical experience of Ireland in the nineteenth century."[13] Sheil's speech was one of the last gasps on the part of a generation of Irish intellectuals to separate national and religious identity, in this case of British Jewry.

The Jews, according to Sheil, were not uniquely a "nation among nations" (as the post-Kantian idealist philosopher J. G. Fichte had claimed about them at the beginning of the century) but merely the adherents of a religion subscribed to by some British citizens. (Sheil uses the contemporary term *English*, referring to a collective British identity, even though the Acts of Union had been in force since 1707. *English men* came to be the collective for citizens of Great Britain incorporated in John Arbuthnot's 1712 figure of John Bull.) For Sheil,

> A Jew born in England cannot transfer his allegiance from his Sovereign and his country; if he were to enter the service of a foreign Power engaged in hostilities with England, and were taken in arms, he would be accounted a traitor. Is a Jew an Englishman for no other purposes than those of condemnation? I am not aware of a single obligation to which other English men are liable, from which a Jew is exempt; and if his religion confers on him no sort of immunity, it ought not to affect him with any kind of disqualification.[14]

Sheil states that this argument was precisely the one that he had advocated in the 1820s in the struggle for *Catholic* Emancipation. It was one of the central battles that came to define Catholic Irishness during and after the Famine. For Sheil, religion was the central line of demarcation, as it was religion, not nationalism or ethnicity, that had disenfranchised the Irish. The political reaction against the Catholics from Elizabeth to Queen Anne defined their marginality. (What that attitude meant in practice is complicated, as Sheil, in loud opposition to O'Connell, had advocated in 1821 Parliament's ability to veto the appointment of Catholic bishops, as it could Anglican ones, as a sign of Catholic loyalty.) For Sheil that Friday evening, Daniel O'Connell was an earlier embodiment of Lionel de Rothschild, the struggle for an Irish Catholic Emancipation identical to the religious freedom now requested for the Jews:

> I can speak as a witness as well as an advocate. I belong to that great and powerful community which was a few years ago subject to the same disqualification that affects the Jew; and I felt that disqualification to be most degrading. Of myself I will not speak, because I can speak of the most illustrious person by whom that community was adorned. I have sat under the gallery of the House of Commons, by the side of Mr. O'Connell, during a great discussion on which the destiny of Ireland was dependent. . . . How have I seen him [O'Connell] chafe the chain which bound him down, but which, with an effort of gigantic prowess, he burst at last to pieces! He was at the head of millions of an organised and indissoluble people. The Jew comes here with no other arguments than those which reason and truth supply; but reason and truth are of counsel with him; and in this assembly, which I believe to represent, not only the high intelligence, but the high-mindedness of England, reason will not long be baffled, and truth, in fulfilment of its great aphorism, will at last prevail.

But what was the rationale for those individuals opposing the emancipation of the Jew? Was it that the Jew was inherently different from, perhaps, the Catholic, as the latter was, at least, a Christian? No, his argument runs that some of his listeners believed in the inalterability of the Jew, of a specific Jewish nature. Sheil argues that the Jew, like the Irish Catholic, was not inherently different from all other human beings and could, indeed had, become British. Unlike Fichte's view, for Sheil national identity always trumped religious identity. "I know that there are those who think that there is no such thing as an English, or a French, or a Spanish Jew; a Jew is nothing but a Jew; his nationality, it is said, is engrossed by the land of recollection and of hope, and the house of Jacob must remain for ever in a state of isolation among the strange people by whom it is encompassed." Sheil's answer mirrors his understanding of the resilience of Irish identity under English subjugation and persecution:

> British feeling has already taken root in the heart of the Jew, and for its perfect development nothing but perfect justice is required. To the fallacies of fanaticism, give no heed. Emancipate the Jew—from the Statute book of England be the last remnant of intolerance erased for ever—abolish all civil discriminations between the Christian and the Jew—fill his whole heart with the consciousness of country: do this, and we dare be sworn that he will think, and feel, and fear, and hope, as you do: his sorrow and his exultation will be the same: at the tidings of English glory his heart will beat with a kindred palpitation; and when ever there shall be need, in the defence of his Sovereign and of his country, his best blood, at your bidding, will be poured out with the same heroic prodigality as your own.

Here one can imagine Sheil's high-pitched voice rising to a crescendo, his brogue-laced English attesting to the fact that he too felt "the tidings of English glory [as] his heart . . . beat with a kindred palpitation." And at this point in his speech, Sheil makes the most extraordinary claim concerning such beliefs in Jewish difference:

> If a Jew can choose, wherefore should he not be chosen? If a Jew can vote for a Christian, why should not a Christian vote for a Jew? . . . What is it you fear? What is the origin of this Hebrewphobia? Do you tremble for the Church? The Church has something perhaps to fear from eight millions of Catholics, and from three millions of Methodists, and more than a million of Scotch seceders. The Church may have some thing to fear from the assault of sectaries from without, and still more to fear from a sort of spurious Popery and the machinations of mitred mutiny from within; but from the Synagogue—the neutral, impartial, apathetic, and unproselytising Synagogue—the Church has nothing to apprehend. But it is said that the House will be unchristianised. The Christianity of the Parliament depends on the Christianity of the country; and

the Christianity of the country is fixed in the faith, and inseparably intertwined with the affections of the people.

"What is it you fear? What is the origin of this Hebrewphobia?" asks Sheil. It cannot be the difference of the Jew, because he has become British; it cannot be the faith of the Jew, because it is not like Catholicism or the nonconformists, which proselytize their faiths. Indeed, he claims, they are unlike those Highland Scottish Protestants who fought alongside their Catholic compatriots against the Crown following the Catholic pretender Bonnie Prince Charlie. "Hebrewphobia" is indeed the problem. It is the unsubstantiated fear of a "nation" (the imagined "Hebrews," as in 2 Corinthians 11:22), unanswered by the reality of a loyal British Jewry.

Does Sheil also imply by the term *phobia* that such opposition is a form of mental illness, a mass delusion? Is it a phobia to be treated like other such obsessions through medical intervention? And if so, what is its cause? Is it a disease of the Christian? Is hatred of the Jew a problem for the Christian, as "the Jew was selected as an object of special and peculiar infliction. The history of that most unhappy people is for century after century a trail of chains, and a track of blood." Yet there were Catholic "men of mercy [who] occasionally arose to interpose in their behalf," such as Saint Bernard. Sheil notes that "the Reformation did nothing for the Jew. The infallibility of Geneva was sterner than the infallibility of Rome." It was Christianity that carried the burden of Jew hatred, for "all of us—Catholics, Protestants, Calvinists—all of us who have torn the seamless garment into pieces—have sinned most fearfully in this terrible regard." But Enlightenment reforms of Christianity seemed to give "some consolation to a Roman Catholic to know that in Roman Catholic countries expiation of this guilt has commenced. In France and in Belgium all civil distinction between the Christian and the Jew is at an end." Catholics had abandoned Jew hatred, but what about the legacy of the Reformation, Sheil asks, "to this Protestant country a great example will not have been vainly given"? Great Britain could join the league of those countries expressing toleration, not prejudice, through the action proposed that evening.

For Sheil, Christian Hebrewphobia was simply a form of irrational prejudice that could be overcome through the power of the Enlightenment, already accomplished, as he states, in Catholic countries. Britain, too, had seen this shift away from unenlightened prejudice, through, he implies, the opening of Parliament to Catholics and thus to the Irish. "There did exist in England a vast mass of prejudice upon this question, which is, however, rapidly giving way. London, the point of imperial centralisation, has made a noble manifestation of its will. London has advisedly, deliberately, and with benevolence afore-thought, selected the most prominent member of the Jewish community as its representative, and united him with the First Minister of the Crown. Is the Parliament prepared to fling back the Jew upon the people, in order that the people should fling back the Jew upon the Parliament?"

The City of London had elected Lionel de Rothschild as well as the prime minister to represent their seats, and, he implies, it was the City that was on the cutting edge of reform. The opponents of Jewish Emancipation suffered not from a mental aberration but rather from an unsubstantiated prejudice, a violation of the terms of the Enlightenment political notion of the presumed equality of all men (with clear and present exceptions, including all women and, given this debate, the Jews). Hebrewphobia was merely the old fear writ new, both on the evening of February 7 as well as in the debates about prejudice in the Enlightenment. The debate continued, and the House supported the bill to alter the manner of taking the oath. As positive as this outcome sounds, we might add here that although the Commons passed the bill, it was turned down twice in the House of Lords; this result was repeated with a new bill in 1851. It was only in 1858, after Rothschild had been twice reelected to his seat, that a third bill was approved to allow the House to have its own rules for membership.[15]

Now Sheil was quite aware that *prejudice* is not a neutral term. All of these concepts have long and complicated histories. French philosopher Baron d'Holbach dismissed prejudice in the Enlightenment as harmful and incompatible with virtue. Immanuel Kant too saw prejudice as violating the rule of judging without reflection, and he simply dismissed it, as it was opposed to true principles rather than true statements. However, the concept was partially recuperated in the work of Georg Friedrich Meier in Germany, who argued that although prejudice was always an error, it may be faulty only from the standpoint of its form and true in regard to its content. No one thinks of it as having a psychological component, but it was already debated in the eighteenth century as to what social function it served.[16] Sheil follows the older Kantian notion of prejudice and introduces the term *Hebrewphobia* to summarize it.

Why does Sheil evoke the phobic in his talk if he does not believe that prejudiced individuals are suffering a form of mental aberration? In Sheil's day, the very notion of phobia had reached beyond the merely medical. Indeed, the most often cited phobia in the medical literature of his day was hydrophobia, rabies, which even in the mid-nineteenth century before the work of Louis Pasteur was no longer to be associated with the run-of-the-mill various forms of mental illness, from acrophobia to photophobia, which are much less often cited.[17] Phobias were popularly understood at the time "to be a fear of an imaginary evil, or an undue fear of a real one."[18] While the metaphoric use of phobias proliferated in the early nineteenth century, it was only in the mid-nineteenth century that the French conceit of labeling dislike of nationalities as phobias (as in *Anglophobia*) had appeared in English. Indeed, Sheil's use may be counted among its earliest appearances, as it was not until 1851 that the *Times* used *Anglophobe* for the first time.[19] Sheil uses it only to signify a chronic aversion to the Jews, and certainly framing his defense of the Jews against Hebrewphobia was a sense that "Irishphobia" was as endemic a disease in Great Britain.[20]

The Jews were thus ironically seen as a collective, even though Sheil's argument, taken from the debates about Catholic Emancipation, was that as a religious community they could also be simultaneously a loyal member of a nation-state. The argument was thus not that prejudice made those individuals who attacked the Jews (or the Catholics) mad; rather, they took a specific and incomplete understanding of both religious liberty in a parliamentary monarchy and the very notion of the Jews within Christianity. Ignorance rather than madness was the problem of anyone opposed to the inclusion of the Jews.[21]

That was 1848 and in Great Britain. Sheil's background as a law-yer (and, one can add, as a playwright exposed to Continental debates about prejudice) who had fought the successful battle for Irish Cath-olic Emancipation shaped his argument. For him, the continuity of Irish Catholic Emancipation was the final emancipation of the Jews. His rhetoric was of his time, but it is also quite clear that it was shaped by the linguistic fashions of his time, not by any evocation of a medical model for prejudice. Fast-forward four decades, and we can see a radi-cal shift in the readings of prejudice against the Jews very much within a medical model that had become the fashion of its day.

Judeophobia Is a Psychic Disorder

In 1882 the proto-Zionist physician Leon Pinsker (1821–91) published *Mahnruf an seine Stammgenossen* (*Auto-Emancipation*). Pinsker was born in Polish Russia and educated at the University of Odessa, where he trained to be a physician. His medical training was modern, which in the nineteenth century meant German and biologically oriented. Horrified by the series of pogroms against the Jews beginning in 1871 in Odessa, Pinsker, writing in German, pleaded for a Jewish state on the basis of the inherent nature of Jew hatred (*Judenhass*) in Europe. As a physician, he used the category of mental illness to explain this hatred, calling it an obsession of the European Christian regarding Jews as "for the living . . . a dead man, for the natives an alien and a vagrant, for property-holders a beggar, for the poor an exploiter and a millionaire, for patriots a man without a country, for all classes a hated rival."[22] He undertook the first systematic attempt at analyzing Judeophobia as a disease of late-nineteenth-century Europe that could never be cured:

> Along with a number of other unconscious and superstitious ideas, instincts, and idiosyncrasies, Judeophobia also has become fully naturalized among all the peoples of the earth with whom the Jews have had intercourse. Judeophobia is a form of demonopathy, with the distinction that the Jewish ghost has become known to the whole

race of mankind, not merely to certain races, and that it is not incorporeal, like other ghosts, but is a being of flesh and blood, and suffers the most excruciating pain from the wounds inflicted upon it by the timorous multitude who imagine themselves threatened by it. Judeophobia is a psychic disorder. As a psychic disorder it is hereditary, and as a disease transmitted for two thousand years it is incurable.[23]

For Pinsker, it is in racism as an "inherited predisposition" that madness lies.[24] Pinsker was the first to provide a clinical definition of the term as well as a forensic label to answer the widely popular term *antisemitism*, which had become the marker for the political attack on Jewish Emancipation after the 1880s. While *antisemitism* may have looked to Pinsker's contemporaries like a "scientific" term, it was clear that it had primarily a political purpose. Indeed, the term seems first to have appeared in 1860 in the Austrian Jewish scholar Moritz Steinschneider's use of the phrase "antisemitic prejudices" (*antisemitische Vorurteile*) in categorizing French philosopher Ernest Renan's contrast between the "Semitic" and the "Aryan" soul.[25] The term, however, was popularized only in the 1880s by the journalist Wilhelm Marr in his widely read 1880 pamphlet attacking the Jews, *Der Weg zum Siege des Germanenthums über das Judenthum* (*The Way to Victory of the Germanic Spirit over the Jewish Spirit*), in which the word first appeared to mean "Jew hatred."[26] That year Marr founded the League of Anti-Semites to combat Jewish influence in Europe. The term had a clearly political meaning thereafter, not as a pejorative label for a prejudice but as a call to arms.

Pinsker also isolated the etiology of the madness of the Jews from the inherent racism of "Judeophobes." For him, it was the Enlightenment demand that the Jews become "like everyone else" in a national society—become Germans, French, English, while repressing their own Jewish national identity—that was the cause of their madness. This belief is, of course, exactly the antithesis of Sheil's argument that Jews in Great Britain could become "Englishmen" once the limitations on their legal status were eliminated. Pinsker agreed with the common notion of the day that the Jews were predisposed to mental illness, but he saw the endless torment from the pressure to acculturate, not from religious persecution, as the cause. The statelessness of the Jew in the age of nationalism condemned him to be an outlier, as "the stigma attached to this people, which forces an unenviable isolation among the nations upon it, cannot be removed by any sort of legal emancipation, as long as this people produces in accordance with its nature vagrant nomads, as long as it cannot give a satisfactory account of whence it comes and whither it goes, as long as the Jews themselves prefer not to speak in Aryan society of their Semitic descent, and prefer not to be reminded of it, as long as they are persecuted, tolerated, protected, emancipated. . . . Intelligent and rich in experience . . . we have never asked whether this mad race . . . will ever come to an end."[27] For Pinsker, it was self-abnegation through acculturation and assimilation, both seen as equivalent, that was the source of Jewish madness.

Pinsker's ideas seem to be a radical break from the claim of nineteenth-century biological psychiatry that madness lies in the predisposition of racial cohorts to madness. His attribution of Jewish madness to the loss of nation, and with it independence, and the resulting fall "into a decay which is not compatible with existence as a whole vital organism" responds to such constructions. As a result of this decay, according to Pinsker, Jews began to seem to others like ghosts—which is the root of Judeophobia, as "the fear of ghosts is something inborn." It is interesting how the metaphor of ghostliness is concrete enough for Pinsker to incorporate it, as though literal, into a medicalizing statement. Pinsker's claim that the madness of the Jews was the result of faulty acculturation was well known in the critical literature about European Jewry at the time. Intellectuals of the late nineteenth century agreed that the Jews were mad, but some thought that their madness was a reflex of antisemitism internalized as self-hatred. Friedrich Nietzsche's poetic reading of Spinoza makes this point quite clear. Christianity's claim of universal love was the Jew's vengeance for his treatment by Christianity:

Unheimlich glimmernder Rachebrand:
—am Judengott fraß Judenhaß!—
—Einsiedler, hab ich dich erkannt?

An eerily shimmering fire of vengeance:
—The Jewish God devoured by Jewish hatred—
Hermit, have I recognized you?[28]

Ultimately, Pinsker's argument relies on the notion that "the misfortunes of the Jews are due, above all, to their lack of desire for national independence" (2). Nationalism would cure self-hatred, but nothing could cure the obsessive racism of the world in which the Jew was exiled. But was it the Christian alone who was racist? Was it this category that alone perpetuated Jew hatred, or was it also the fault of the Jew, who had lost any sense of national identity? And if so, what about other forms of racial hatred that were not tied to the experience of Jews in the West? Sheil's nuanced argument about the complexity of Christian responses to the Jews as citizens of a national state, which had claims on the loyalty of all religious groups, is dismissed by Pinsker, seeing the world not from the Houses of Parliament but from the bloody streets of Odessa.

The argument rests on the image of psychopathology. Pinsker writes, "In a sick person the absence of desire for food and drink is a very serious symptom" (2), and "We would hear nothing of taking our malady at the root, in order to effect a complete cure" (11). His essay uses pathological language for both Jews and antisemites and acknowledges fault on the part of the oppressors, while placing the onus for change on the oppressed. Pinsker writes, "If the basis of our reasoning is sound, if the prejudice of the human race against us rests upon anthropological and social principles, innate and ineradicable, we must look no more to the slow progress of humanity" (9). Yet Pinsker also makes a biological and therefore racial argument, quite counter to Sheil's Enlightenment claims about humanity. Mired in the scientific discourse of his time, he saw the struggle for Jewish mental health as analogous to, but different from, the other great struggle of the day, the emancipation of the African slave, only recently freed in the United States and six years away from emancipation in Brazil. Pinsker, however, assuming black inferiority through the lens of contemporary racial science, writes that the Jews must be emancipated:

"Like the negroes, like women, and unlike all free peoples, they must be *emancipated*. It is all the worse for them if, unlike the negroes, they belong to an advanced race, and if, unlike women, they can show not only women of distinction, but also men, even great men." He saw a specific national state as the catalyst of the moral, mental, and physical regeneration of the surplus Jews (a version of the Victorian notion of the deserving poor) who were saved by the actions: "Our greatest and best forces—men of finance, of science, and of affairs, statesmen and publicists—must join hands with one accord in steering toward the common destination. This would succeed chiefly and especially in creating a secure and inviolable home for the *surplus* of those Jews who live as proletarians in the different countries and are a burden to the native citizens."[29] This claim was rooted in a science that had different valences in the claims of the European Jew and the black slave. Pinsker's views on race, difference, and disease became part of the ideology and the vocabulary of Zionism and indeed of the debates about the source and nature of prejudice in general.

Such views came to be projected onto other groups seen as mentally ill. Theodor Herzl, for example, attacked his Jewish opponents in October 1897 as *Mauschel*, an unhealthy ghetto Jew without the mental capacity to understand the need for an independent Jewish national identity. Such an understanding was defined by him and his supporters, including Max Nordau, as demonstrating a healthy, rather than pathological, psyche.[30] Herzl labeled those Jews who were opposed to Zionism as corrupt and saw the proof in their attitude toward Zionism: "*Mauschel* was quick to put forward an insidious catchword against the Zionists: namely, that they are Jewish anti-Semites. We? We, who acknowledge before all the world, without consideration for our acquired positions and our advancement, that we are Semites; we who cherish the cultivation of our national heritage, who stand by our unfortunate brethren? But *Mauschel* figured out with lightning speed what we are: we are anti-*Mauschel*."[31] Being anti-assimilationist, Herzl argues, was seen in the eyes of acculturated European Jews as a form of self-hatred. The early Zionists also made the counterargument.

Max Nordau, a neurologist and one of Herzl's earliest supporters, had argued in his famed pre-Zionist text *Degeneration* (1892) that "all the particular 'manias' and 'phobias' which at present swarm in the literature of mental therapeutics" were simply signs of the "great emotionalism of the degenerate." Nordau's "degenerate" is the embodiment of modernity, of the speed of modern life, of self-absorption. His prime examples were Wagner, Nietzsche, and Dostoyevsky. By 1896 his focus was on the psychopathological response of the Jews to antisemitism: "It is the greatest triumph of anti-Semitism that it has brought the Jews to view themselves with anti-Semitic eyes."[32] For the early Zionists, identification with the aggressor defined not only anti-Zionists but also acculturated Jews.

Prejudice against the Jews, however defined, came to be seen as a form of mental aberration in an age when medical discourse had high esteem. The late-nineteenth-century age of Pinsker and Nordau was exactly such a moment. The cure was a new nationalism that would immunize its citizens from the infection of hatred.[33] The world of mid-nineteenth-century parliamentary debate, the world of Sheil and Rothschild, did not need to characterize such views as pathological—just prejudiced. Thus, the analogy between Irish Catholics and British Jews worked well as a means of equating groups who were the target of such prejudice. No pathology present; no cure necessary. Just political will and the call of justice. The difference may well have lain in the robustness of the British system, which was able to alter such views over time. Pinsker, coming from imperial Russia, saw no such option. Time and place distinguished one from the other.

6

Rebellious Jews on the Edge of Empire

The Judæo-Irish Home Rule Association

HEATHER MILLER RUBENS

In 1908 members of Dublin's Jewish community formed the "Judæo-Irish Home Rule Association" and formally announced Irish Jewish support for Irish national aspirations. Members of the British Jewish community, in both Dublin and London, strenuously objected to the formation of this group and called for these Irish Jews to not involve their Jewishness in politics.

In this chapter I trace the newsprint narrative in the British Jewish and Irish press surrounding the short-lived Judæo-Irish Home Rule Association. In examining this public exchange, I explore three sets of interrelated questions. First, how was a public Jewish identity in the British Isles understood and expressed at the beginning of the twentieth century? Were Jews solely a religious community? Were Jews a national or ethnic group? How should Jews, whether religious, ethnic, or national, participate in politics—collectively or individually? Second, how does one understand the Irish Home Rule movement? Was Home Rule at heart a national struggle, a religious struggle, or both? Does the religious nature of this political conflict allow Jews to opt out of the struggle, or must Jews choose to align? If Jews must choose, what should guide their choice of alliance? Third, what exactly is the nature of the relationship between the Irish Jewish and British Jewish communities? Are these two Jewish diasporas of equal footing, or are Irish Jews somehow beholden to British Jews owing to the structures of empire?

Jewish Identity

On Thursday, September 10, 1908, the Judæo-Irish Home Rule Association held its inaugural meeting at the Mansion House in Dublin. At this meeting, the newly formed association passed the following resolution as its first act: "That this great meeting of Jews . . . resolve[s] to support such measures that will tend to secure for the people of Ireland a full grant of self-government, such as accepted by the Irish Parliamentary Party, to foster Irish industries and in general to promote the welfare and prosperity of Ireland." Jacob Elyan, the association's first chair and a longtime fixture in the Dublin Jewish communal leadership, expanded on this mission, saying that the Judæo-Irish Home Rule Association sought both to put Irish Jews into closer relations with their fellow Irishmen and to correct false conceptions about Irish Jewish insularity, which manifested as popular ideas that Irish Jews were indifferent toward Irish politics and the general welfare of their Irish neighbors. In his view, this association meant to "dispel the delusion and darkness" that surrounded the Irish Jewish community and would do so by lending moral and material support to the cause of Irish Home Rule.[1]

Two additional Judæo-Irish Home Rule executive members further explained the unique perspectives that Irish Jews brought to the Home Rule cause. Citing the 1905 Russian Revolution as an example, Joseph Edelstein, the association's secretary, explained that Jews had extensive experience in the pursuit of liberty and economic equality throughout the world that they would bring to the Irish cause. Arthur Newman, another founding board member and prominent Irish Jewish leader, also reflected broadly on the role of Jews in the history of liberation politics. Newman asserted that Jews had long experienced intolerance and persecution and thus were in natural sympathy with those peoples, like the Irish, who had been persecuted. Newman went further, asserting that Jews were ready once again to be politically proactive in human history and that Irish Jews in particular were ready to take up the Irish cause. Newman imagined the average Irishman wondering how Jews could "account for sleeping away their political time over the past 2,000 years? Was it conceivable to the Irishman that Jews could be satisfied to go on wandering from country to country, living on sufferance everywhere, whilst the smallest of nations had managed to extract themselves from oppressive situations and emerge as states?"[2] Indeed, according to leaders of the Judæo-Irish Home Rule Association, the time for Dublin's Jews to act was now, and the political cause to support was Irish Home Rule.

As expressed in the resolution, and further explained by the executive committee, the Judæo-Irish Home Rule Association did not directly address Jewishness as a religious identification. Rather, the important takeaway lesson was that Jews were a collective, a people who could and should act politically as a defined group in local politics. Taking this view, Jews were not individual citizens of the Jewish religious persuasion who confined Jewish action to the religious sphere. Rather, Jews, as a collective, were encouraged to join their Irish neighbors in the work of political liberation and economic betterment for their local communities. In this view, the connection between the Irish and Jewish communities was twofold: First, the Jews and the Irish shared a common home that they wanted to run locally and improve through local means. Second, both communities were peoples who shared a history of oppression and a common desire for political liberty. For the Judæo-Irish Home Rule Association, the Irish and Jewish communities had a common homeland, a similar history of oppression, and a shared desire for local governance. Religious identification would not necessarily cement these bonds but perhaps provide a stumbling block to the association's aims. The category of religion did not play into the shared identification of Ireland as a homeland and was absent from this association's discussion of a shared history of oppression.

However, not all of Dublin's Jews understood themselves in these terms, nor did they contend that the Irish Jewish community should involve itself in the struggle for Home Rule. Philip Wigoder, a Dublin physician active in Jewish affairs, attempted to interrupt the meeting and offer a counterresolution opposing the very notion of a Jewish Home Rulers club. He was denied the floor. The chairman told him that if he opposed the formation of the Judæo-Irish Home Rule Association, he should not have come to the founding meeting. Rather, it was suggested that he form his own club. However, Dr. Wigoder did not need to start his own organization to find others opposed to the very idea of a Judæo-Irish Home Rule Association. All he needed to do was to turn to the existing organs of the British Jewish establishment and engage a working model of Jewish community that was religiously circumscribed.

Dr. Wigoder publicly voiced his negative opinion of the Judæo-Irish Home Rule Association in both the *Jewish World* and the *Jewish Chronicle*, London's main Jewish periodicals. Within the week his letters to the editor were published in both newspapers, accompanied by editorial commentary supporting his opposition to the Judæo-Irish Home Rule Association. Dr. Wigoder's letters asserted the following points: First, this organization did not represent the dominant Irish Jewish opinion. He supported this claim by saying women and non-Jews mostly populated the crowd at the meeting and that the members of the association board were organizing only to further their personal careers with Irish Party politics. Second, Dr. Wigoder argued that Jewish political associations were generally dangerous endeavors. While Dr. Wigoder asserted a general opposition to all types of Jewish political organization, he was particularly concerned with the development of the current association in the Irish context. He writes, "As you are aware, Irish politics are largely a matter of religion, and the danger of religion in politics is only too well-known. Hence, the advisability of steering clear, as a religious body, of all local political questions." Instead, Wigoder advises Jews to join a local organization such as the Home Rule Gaelic League or Sinn Féin as individual citizens but not to do so as a Jewish group.[3]

Both editors at the London-based newspapers the *Jewish World* and the *Jewish Chronicle* affirmed and expanded on Dr. Wigoder's sentiments. The *Jewish World* at the time was generally proimperial and firmly wanted to assert that the Irish matter was part of domestic British politics. The *Jewish World* allowed for the fact that the welfare of the Jews in Ireland was undoubtedly tied up with the future of Ireland.

But, the editor asks, "Why, then, form a *Jewish Home* Rule Association? We cannot insist too often or too urgently on the fact that, except in matters where the principles of their religion are at stake, Jews have no right to interfere with British politics in any other guise than as British citizens. . . . [W]e are deeply concerned to see Jews banding themselves together into a political association to deal with matters which, as Jews, do not affect them in the slightest degree." The *Jewish Chronicle* offered a similar opinion, but with slightly more friendly, pro-Irish language: "Now, no objection of course could be raised to a Jew in Ireland voting as an Irish citizen for the policy referred to. But to his voting in that sense *qua* Jew, there is a strong objection indeed. . . . A collective Jewish vote, except in the rare cases where Jewish interests are seriously assailed or can be materially advanced can have only the effect of dragging the Jewish race or faith into political and religious controversy, and history warns us wither that leads."[4]

The *Jewish Chronicle* went even further to assert that if Jews sided with Irish Home Rule, they would be seen by the Unionist Party as disloyal and perhaps even as treasonous. For Dr. Wigoder and the British Jewish press, Jews were publicly a religious community and should function as individuals in political matters. The only reason that the Jewish religious community should engage in politics, particularly engage in the political process as a collective group, was when the Jewish religion was under threat or disability.

This position, typical of western European Jews, held significant historical weight in particular for British Jewry living in the metropole. The struggle for Jewish emancipation in the British Isles over the course of the nineteenth century played out in religious terms. And part of the understood structure of the emancipatory pact involved confining Jewishness to religious terms, while making one's political, indeed one's national, self allied with one's home country. This attempted division of religion and politics spoke to the larger history of minority emancipation within England's shores. Since the Reformation, Roman Catholics had served as the enemy within, the other par excellence in the British imaginary. Thus, the push for emancipation of minorities was to a large extent the story of the removal of religious disabilities, focused on the Catholic minority. When full Catholic emancipation was finally realized in 1829, the fight for Jewish emancipation began in earnest. Thus, from 1830 to 1858, London's Jews vigorously asserted that they were British citizens of the Jewish religion with a right to the removal of religious disabilities to political participation. With these disabilities removed, Jews could enter the political arena as individuals, while their group identity was confined behind the synagogue doors.

In sum, the British Jewish position as represented by Dr. Wigoder and the London Jewish press called on Jews to limit collective action to Jewish religious issues. Jews should not operate as a group in forming a Jewish political organization. For British Jews who had accepted the emancipatory model of Jewish identity, Jews were citizens of the Jewish religious persuasion and thus only publicly Jewish when religious issues were at stake. Thus, religious identity necessarily came into play in the British Jewish discussion of the Judæo-Irish Home Rule Association, as such an association was completely contrary to this model. Religion, then, was introduced by British Jews as a category of exclusion that would limit Jewish collective participation in the political process and discredit the premise of the association. In contrast, the Irish Jews lending Jewish collective support to the cause of Home Rule refrained from mentioning religion, or any other boundary marker to Jewish identity, perhaps in part because they knew the category of religion limited them politically. Instead, their claim was that Jews could act as a political group and could, and should, engage a variety of issues as a group. Religion played no part in this contention.

Irish Home Rule

How does religion factor into the characterization of Irish Home Rule? The disagreement between the British and Irish Jews under consideration here went beyond a difference in understanding the particularities of a public Jewish identity to also include a different characterization of Irish Home Rule. Was this conflict religious or national?

The British Jews mentioned here who understood Jewishness in exclusively religious terms also characterized Irish Home Rule as a religious struggle. That is to say, they emphasized the religious and not the national nature of the Irish Home Rule movement and did so, once again, in an effort to exclude Jewish participation. Dr. Wigoder highlighted the particular turbulent history between Catholics and Protestants that the Irish Question could be understood to foreground. The proffered conclusion was that a Catholic-Protestant struggle was not a Jewish problem per se. Or perhaps more accurately, the fight between Catholic and Protestant factions in Ireland was something Jews, as a religious group, could successfully abstain from and were advised to do so by maintaining their particular religious identity. The broad underlying assertion is that mixing religion and politics is messy business that is best to be avoided. In asserting Jewishness as a religious identity, and Irish Home Rule as a religious conflict, the British Jewish community sought to collectively opt out. The category of religion served as a refuge from political participation.

In contrast, the Judæo-Irish Home Rule Association did not bring religion into their discussion of Irish Home Rule but rather understood the conflict in national terms. As mentioned previously, the Home Rule cause was understood as the liberation of oppressed peoples living in an oppressed land. As the association's founding resolution foregrounds, the Home Rule struggle for them was one of political independence and economic autonomy. Hence, local Jewish involvement in such a struggle was a natural, even preferred, method for political engagement, as Ireland was their home and they considered themselves to be part of the Irish people. There is no mention of religion in this discussion.

Competing Diasporas

We now turn to the relationship between the Jewish communities of Dublin and London, as the distinct history of these two communities directly factors into the pronounced differences in the expression of a public Jewish self and a characterization of Home Rule. To a certain extent, the divide between British Jews and Irish Jews was a recent development in 1908. Most Irish Jews did not share the nineteenth-century history of British Jewish emancipation, and they were not

"British" by communal tradition or by birth. Indeed, the Irish Jewish community was a relatively recent expansion of the Jewish diaspora. As of the 1870s, there were only a few hundred Jews living in Dublin. It was not until the Litvak Jews immigrated at the end of the nineteenth century that a sizable Jewish community became apparent in Ireland. By 1900 the Dublin community of a few hundred had blossomed to more than two thousand Jews, and by 1914 Dublin's Jewish community hovered at three thousand, with the vast majority being recent immigrants from eastern Europe. This demographic shift brought with it a major difficulty for these different Jewish diasporas living within the British Empire. What exactly was to be the relationship between the expanding Dublin Jewish community and the London Jewish establishment? Or, in broader strokes, what was the relationship between the Jewish communities living on the peripheries of the British Empire to Jews living in the metropole?

Over the course of the nineteenth century, British Jewry had established two offices, sanctioned by the British government, to represent Jewish communities in the United Kingdom: the Office of Chief Rabbi of the United Hebrew Congregations of the British Empire and the Board of Deputies of British Jews. By the time the Judæo-Irish Home Rule Association had its inaugural meeting in September 1908, troubles between these London-based authorities and Dublin's Irish Jews were already brewing. In the previous year, the Board of Deputies had sent a delegation to investigate the activities of the Irish Jewish community, and the Office of the Chief Rabbi continued to try, with little success, to exert authority over the various Jewish congregations operating in Dublin.

Indeed, a year prior to the founding of the Judæo-Irish Home Rule Association, the *Jewish World* did an exposé for London Jews that highlighted the fractured and unruly nature of Dublin Jewry. "It may be said, and with a double significance, that in communal affairs the vast majority of the Dublin Jews of the Irish capital steadfastly refuse to be governed by London—i.e., from the Chief Rabbi's office—the conclusion is that they must be in the full enjoyment of the sweets of Home Rule." In an editorial in the same issue, there was a call for the respectable element of Irish Jews, that is to say the British Jewish element, to "conciliate the foreign Jewish element, and bring Irish Jewry into line with Anglo-Jewry."[5]

Knowing the intercommunal power struggles between Irish Jews and British Jews in the previous few years, the Irish Jewish call to support Home Rule took on an interesting double significance. On one level, the Irish Jewish community wanted to integrate more fully into their local diaspora home, work for local government, and work for the local economic prosperity of Ireland, as stated in the association's resolution. For Dublin Jews, it meant committing to the political cause of Irish Home Rule and Irish prosperity in a concrete way and as an identifiably Jewish group. On another level, embracing the Home Rule cause affirmed that this Dublin Jewish community was distinct from the British Jewish community of London and autonomous from the British Jewish offices that attempted to exert authority over their communal affairs. Thus, in a very real sense, Irish Jews were also shouting their own war cry for communal Home Rule to the British Jewish establishment. From the British Jewish perspective, the vast majority of Jews living in Dublin were not Irish but recent immigrants benefiting from the policies of the British Empire. As such, London's Jewish authorities preferred that the Dublin community understand themselves as British Jews who benefited from British immigration laws rather than identify as Irish Jews committed to the project of Irish independence.

Thus, a peculiar dynamic developed between the two diaspora communities, which was exacerbated by a British Jewish imperial sentiment. The British government endowed the Office of the Chief Rabbi and the Board of Deputies with real authority over the Jewish communities throughout the empire. London's Jewish periodicals regularly reported on the happenings of Jewish communities from all over the empire not simply as a matter of interest but because these communities were understood as an extension of British Jewry. Each of these three London-based organs (the Office of the Chief Rabbi, the Board of Deputies, and the Anglo-Jewish press) worked to ensure that the various Jewish communities throughout the empire behaved in a manner complementary to British rule. In this capacity, then, these British Jews worked to support continued English dominance and took on an imperial posture in relation to their coreligionists elsewhere in the empire. Thus, there was great displeasure that some of Dublin's Jews had privileged an Irish Jewish identity over and against a British Jewish one.

Conclusion

The founders and defenders of the Judæo-Irish Home Rule Association never described Dublin's Jewish community in religious terms, nor did they discuss the Home Rule struggle as a religious conflict. Rather, Home Rule was couched in terms of political and economic liberation, a liberation movement that Irish Jews could and should participate in as a collective group. Indeed, the experience of the Jewish community as an oppressed people seeking liberation was underscored as an asset to Irish self-determination. In contrast to understanding Jewish identity primarily in terms of collective peoplehood, British Jews defined Jewish identity in individual and religious terms. Opponents of the Judæo-Irish Home Rule Association understood the Home Rule movement as a struggle between Catholic and Protestant factions. Understanding Jews as religious individuals and Irish Home Rule as a religious conflict was a strategy of exclusion adopted by the British Jewish community that demanded that Dublin's Jews opt out of supporting Home Rule. Religious identification was deployed to circumscribe political action in the context of Irish Home Rule and support the structures of empire. Indeed, the difference here between Jewish supporters and Jewish opponents of Home Rule highlights an important observation—in 1908, how one answered the Jewish Question dictated how one answered the Irish Question.

While the Judæo-Irish Home Rule Association existed for only a short time and did not succeed in playing a significant role in the future struggles of either the Irish or the Jewish communities involved, its creation in 1908 is an instructive flash point that helps focus scholarly questions on the different ways Irish and Jewish identities were understood and articulated at the beginning of the twentieth century.

The birth of this association provides a snapshot of competing claims regarding the boundaries of religious, ethnic, and political categories and competing modes of answering both the Jewish Question and the Irish Question. Exploring this particular newsprint exchange allows us to see the diversity of ways early-twentieth-century Jews understood themselves in Ireland and England. In particular, this instance highlights how giving primacy to a Jewish religious identity affirmed the structures of empire and a hierarchy of diasporas, while laying claim to a primarily Jewish political identity contested imperial norms and challenged the primacy of Jews in the metropole.

7

Rethinking Irish Protectionism

*Jewish Refugee Factories and the Pursuit
of an Irish Ireland for Industry*

TRISHA OAKLEY KESSLER

Economic nationalism advanced in the 1930s in response to rising unemployment, concerns about national identity, and a downturn in the economy.[1] Ireland, like many other countries, initiated protectionist policies that began to shape the economic and cultural life of the nation. Eamon de Valera, the leader of Fianna Fáil, Ireland's new governing party in 1932, offered a national solution to Ireland's economic problems. In his promise of a self-sufficient industrial Ireland, de Valera adopted a heightened nationalist discourse and called for a wall of protection to allow foreign up-to-date technology and ideas to enter Ireland but not the stranger, who, for too long, had taken employment from the Irish people.[2] Issues of inclusion and exclusion came to the fore and shaped Ireland's pursuit of industry. Rather than viewing protectionism solely as a doomed policy that failed to stimulate long-term industrial growth, this chapter uses the prism of Jewish refugee industries to explore how protectionism raised questions of national identity and change, which played out in complex ways in 1930s Ireland.[3]

As Jewish communities in Europe were "othered" and expunged from the economic life of their native countries, a broad range of Irish voices pressured the government to bar Jews entering the economic life of Ireland. Oppositional voices raised fears that Fianna

Fáil's industrial drive was bringing Jews into the Irish economy, which was harmful to the nation. A developing anti-Jewish economic discourse was used to portray Fianna Fáil's economic policies as nonnational and fraudulent. Although Ireland offered very little refuge to Jewish refugees, some refugee workers and industrialists did settle in Ireland.[4] They were given employment permits because their manufacturing skills were of use to the nation.[5] A carefully constructed narrative presented these foreign workers as serving the development of an Irish industrial modernity. Obscuring their voices within an Irish industrial narrative, these factories and their products underwent a process of "becoming Irish," and as a consequence this moment when provincial Ireland encountered the Holocaust has been lost in the margins of Irish history.[6]

Jewish Refugee Workers Arrive in Provincial Ireland

In November 1938, Thea Dziwietnik, a Jewish refugee worker at a newly opened hat factory in Galway, wrote to her former Austrian employer now living in Brussels,[7] "I am doing well in business and my performance is satisfactory . . . but the sorrow is making me gloomy and on top of this I feel like a traitor to my family. I am sitting here home and dry and my people are overloaded with grief."[8] She had much about which to be worried. After Kristallnacht, earlier that month, her brother had been taken into German Preventive Custody, and it was unclear whether he was in a prison or a concentration camp.[9] Her correspondent, Victor Böhm, knew well the difficulties she faced, for he too was exiled from his Austrian home and concerned about his extended family and colleagues. As a director of a large and successful hat-manufacturing business in Austria and Czechoslovakia, Victor, his brothers, and his immediate family were now residing in Brussels after Nazi processes of expropriation and Aryanization forced the sale of their factory in Vienna and the confiscation of their larger industrial premises in Neutitschein, Czechoslovakia.[10] Victor's letter to Thea forms part of a larger correspondence with Jewish refugee hatters who were scattered across the globe, having found settlement through the trade networks of the Böhm brothers.

Thea was one of twenty-five expert technicians, many of them refugees and previous Böhm employees, who arrived in Galway in 1938.[11] Established by two Jewish businessmen from Paris, Henri Orbach and Marcel Goldberg, Les Modes Modernes was the flagship factory of a new Irish hat industry supported by protectionist measures.[12] Its managing director, Orbach, had embraced the opportunity to invest in Ireland and had borrowed money from colleagues and family to provide a capital investment of £40,000 matched by Irish investors.[13] Although Orbach and Goldberg were both French citizens, as Jews they were forced into hiding after 1940 and their principal factory in Paris was taken from them and assigned to the Commissariat Général aux Questions Juives in 1941.[14] Trapped in France and desperate to return to Ireland, Orbach and his sister, Sophie Philipson, the wife of Serge Philipson, manager of the factory in Galway, were deported to Auschwitz in February 1944.[15]

Two further factories funded by Jewish refugee businessmen, one manufacturing hoods from raw materials and the second producing ribbons and accessories, were located to Castlebar and Longford. Western Hats, Castlebar, was established through a partnership between Franz Schmolka, a successful hat manufacturer from Czechoslovakia, and Senator Edward Claessens, a prominent industrialist in Verviers, Belgium, as well as an active politician for the Catholic Social Party. As Jewish industrialists began to look for settlement in other countries, Belgium as an important center for textiles became a place of refuge. Following a similar process as the Bruder Böhm brothers, Franz Schmolka used his trade networks to find safe passage for his family and friends, many from his hometown, Komotau, a predominantly German town in the Sudetenland that was declared "judenrein" on September 23, 1938.[16]

Finally, Emil Hirsch, an industrialist from Vienna, arrived in Ireland in December 1938 with family and workers to establish a ribbon factory in Longford. Hirsch had, like many Jewish businessmen, delayed leaving Vienna until after the Anschluss, perhaps struggling to find settlement or hoping that the situation would calm. However, as the work of Herbert Strauss shows, Kristallnacht proved to be the decisive moment for large Jewish industries that had continued to operate against mounting difficulties. They were now forced to liquidate. With very little capital, Hirsch was helped by a colleague within the Austrian hat industry to facilitate business renewal in Ireland and provide safe passage for family and friends.[17]

Protectionism: A Special Path for Ireland

The destruction of Jewish industries across Europe and the search for settlement by Jewish refugees came at a moment when Ireland was pursuing a native industrial drive to create a self-sufficient Irish economy. Like other political leaders, Eamon de Valera had promised a national solution to Ireland's economic problems, which steered Fianna Fáil to electoral victories in 1932 and 1933. De Valera's commitment to produce native manufactured commodities, supported by protectionist measures, advanced an existing nationalist economic narrative that had deep roots within Ireland's formative struggle for independence.[18] De Valera reshaped this ideological vision within a discourse of contemporary economic needs and formulated an economic approach to deliver Ireland from rising unemployment and emigration.[19]

In his pursuit of a special path for Ireland, de Valera crafted an industrial vision to create employment through the production of all the food and necessities required to maintain its population.[20] A sizable number of jobs were to be allocated to the expanding clothing and footwear industries, both of which received increasing protectionist measures to establish factories in Ireland.[21] Protectionism, a policy to steer economic nationalism, was in the eyes of Fianna Fáil a means of import substitution, particularly products imported from Great Britain.[22] Trade statistics for 1932 reveal the rising numbers of imports for apparel, textiles, and footwear, and an internal Department of Industry memo on the Irish hat industry disclosed the import numbers for ladies' hats, which in 1935 amounted to almost two million.[23]

The development of a substantial hat industry, particularly ladies' hats, was a response to both Ireland's dependence on the British hat industry and the need to expand new industries to generate employment. By 1935–36 it was evident that Fianna Fáil's industrial drive was slowing down, and the challenge of a saturated marketplace, in which a limited number of Irish produced goods had market viability, became a concern for the government.[24] Business leaders questioned Fianna Fáil's ability to absorb Ireland's employment numbers through its industrial drive and argued a policy of import substitution could not fully industrialize a nation that lacked essential resources and raw materials.[25] Political discourse focused on the demise of Fianna Fáil's much-promised employment creation scheme, and communities across Ireland still waiting for their factory expressed anger and frustration at the lost opportunities a new factory could have brought with employment and spending power.[26]

Protectionism: A Lifeline for Jewish Refugees?

The need to explore new manufacturing possibilities influenced the decision of the Department of Industry and Commerce to reply to a memorandum received from the Council for German Jewry (CGJ) in June 1936. Following the 1935 Nuremberg Laws, greater numbers of Jews in Germany, many newly classified by this legislation, sought refuge abroad. As Herbert Strauss argues, patterns of emigration reflected the increased levels of persecution that Jews faced.[27] In response, a campaign was launched in Britain by the CGJ to focus on the contribution Jewish refugees could offer the nation in terms of their skills. The CGJ turned their attention to the British Dominion States, and the Department of Industry received a memorandum regarding the possibility of Jewish refugee industries contributing to the Irish economy. It displayed a good understanding of Fianna Fáil's economic policy, noting, "Many German manufacturers were now looking to find new means of livelihood and could find the required capital to produce new products, which would help improve Ireland's trade balance through the diminution of imports."[28] Citing the success of a number of new enterprises established by experienced German Jewish refugees in England, the council suggested that the Irish Free State might be willing to accept a limited number of German Jewish manufacturers. Its arguments were compelling. Rather than looking for employment, refugees on this scheme would create employment.[29]

Already the manufacture of new lines in Britain had initiated between six and seven thousand jobs within industries producing electrical equipment, chemical and pharmaceutical products, leather and rubber goods, furniture factories, and the making of apparel.

The memorandum spoke to the growing acceptance by the British government that Jewish industrialists could be of use to the country in terms of job creation and developing important exports. The newly passed Special Areas Act (1934) designated four areas in need of economic rejuvenation to which Jewish industrialists could be steered in negotiations regarding settlement.[30] Although the term *refugee* was not used in an open invitation to "foreign nationals" or "aliens" to settle in Britain, it was clear that this offer spoke to Jewish refugee industrialists.[31] British consulates used their diplomatic services to inform Jewish communities that residence permits would be issued to industrialists willing to move to certain areas. Furthermore, incentives in the form of newly built factories at reduced rents on specially constructed trading estates in each depressed region reflected the British government's acknowledgment of the refugee status of these industrialists, who by 1936 struggled to move any substantial assets out of Germany.[32]

During a period when Fianna Fáil's policy toward Jewish refugees was deeply restrictive, the response to the CGJ by John Leydon, the secretary of the Department of Industry, was encouraging. The department would be prepared to recommend to the Department of Justice the granting of alien permits for a certain period of employment if an enterprise offered *"value to the country."*[33] The possibility that some Jewish refugees could enter Ireland marked a modest shift in Ireland's response to Jewish refugees that had been lamentable after 1933. As early as April 1933, Leo McCauley, secretary of the Berlin Legation, had warned the Department of External Affairs that the legation had received an increasing number of inquiries and applications for visas from Jews of Polish and other nationalities desiring to leave Germany. The legation, he reassured the department, "had discouraged such persons from going to Ireland, as they are really only refugees; and it assumed that this line of action would be in accordance with the Department's policy."[34] New restrictions requiring return visas to countries of origin for all applicants wishing to enter Ireland provided foreign legations with authority to decline refugee applications.[35]

Mirroring other nations, Ireland refused to process refugees as a separate entity, and the Aliens Act 1935 subjected all nonnationals to the same clauses without favoring refugees over others.[36] In reality, Jewish applicants for Irish visas were subjected to extra scrutiny. As the work of Goldstone argues, being Jewish mattered, and bureaucratic responses to applications from Jewish refugees were governed by anti-Jewish mentalities.[37] Questions regarding Jews and integration surfaced, and issues of inclusion and exclusion were determined by the larger project of nation building and a narrowing of a national identity that negotiated "Irishness" in terms of being Gaelic in culture and Roman Catholic in belief.[38]

As the Department of Industry began to scope the possibilities of Jewish industrialists aiding Irish industry, decisions were governed by Fianna Fáil's industrial policy of import substitution. A lifeline was offered to those enterprises that could manufacture new commodities, as in the case of the new hat industry. Protectionism as a means to drive an industrial Ireland became a blunt instrument to determine who would or would not be offered settlement. For those Jewish businessmen who approached the Irish legations in Berlin and Paris with their credentials, letters of reference, and business proposals for the production of commodities already overproduced in a saturated Irish market, it was clear that the Department of Industry would reject their applications.[39] Rising numbers of applications reached the department in 1938, reflecting the perilous position Jewish communities faced. It also spoke to a new focus on Ireland, as Jewish communal networks highlighted Ireland's industrial needs. De Valera's call, as president of the League of Nations Assembly, for nations to rescue "suffering refugees" was reported in the *Jewish Chronicle*, the leading Anglo-Jewish newspaper. Furthermore, as J. J. Lee observes, an explicit recognition of "the Jewish congregations" in the 1937 constitution was "a gesture not without dignity in the Europe of 1937."[40]

To aid the Department of Industry in finding potential industrialists, an unusual partnership formed between a nonnational Jewish businessman in Dublin, Marcus Witztum, and Fianna Fáil senator Sean McEllin. Witztum, having lived and worked in numerous countries, had developed extensive trade networks in the European textile industry that were of use to the department. Senator McEllin, a key player in Fianna Fáil's industrial program, had experience, through his work in developing the Irish sugar-beet industry, in bringing outside technical skills to Ireland. Although Ireland could not compete with the inducements offered by Great Britain, it could offer forms of protection through tariffs and quotas. This framework made Ireland an attractive place for partnerships between Jewish and non-Jewish investors to place some capital alongside the manufacturing skills of their Jewish colleagues desperately looking for settlement. Traveling back and forth to Europe, McEllin and Witztum guided industrialists to potential sites in the West of Ireland, where McEllin had a family and political base.[41]

Witztum, in particular, devoted much of his time advising Jewish refugees how to obtain work visas for Ireland.[42] He was carefully monitored, with Liam Archer at the Department of Defense noting:

> Marcus Witztum, a Jew, now Irish, formerly Argentinian, and prior to that a Polish National, is recorded as a director of three companies in Ireland since 1932, and seemingly believes he can influence policy in these matters. . . . There are frequent statements in the correspondence of the Jewish Community that Marcus would obtain visas from the Government. The opinion formed from the Witztum correspondence is that he is no more than an adroit company promoter, he is evidently much used by alien Jews to secure entry permits to this country and in the Jewish Community here is regarded as having considerable influence in this connection.[43]

However, archives testify to a number of potential negotiations between the Department of Industry and Jewish industrialists who, with the help of Witztum, had found Irish partners willing to form companies.[44] Unfortunately, many of these opportunities foundered; the requirements demanded by the department were time intensive, and many industrialists failed to secure them as persecution intensified:

"Any persons desirous of engaging in industry in this country should therefore submit in full particulars of the proposed scheme, including information as to the financing, the type of goods to be made, the processes to be undertaken, the raw materials to be used, the technical skills available, the employment to be given, the proposed output, the prices at which the goods would be sold as compared to the existing prices, and reference as to standing in business and previous trading."[45] With tenacity, Witztum and McEllin located a number of Jewish refugee industries to Ireland, of which a new hat industry was perhaps the most successful. Although the hat industry created employment for more than six hundred workers, not all other prospective industries were welcomed. In the case of a large shoddy cloth factory that was to move to Ballina, with investment from a Czech industrialist, Dr. Kroner, promising employment for between eight hundred to one thousand workers, oppositional voices used the factory as an example of Fianna Fáil's failure to support the Irish woolen industry.[46] Although moneys were raised within the town to contribute to the factory and Dr. Kroner, then resident in Dublin, had deposited an amount of £20,000 in an Irish bank, the factory failed to materialize.[47]

The exact numbers of refugees who arrived with new factories is not clear, but a conservative number would be seventy in total.[48] The Departments of Justice and External Affairs reminded the Department of Industry that issuing visas for foreign nationals, that is, Jewish workers, would necessitate their staying in Ireland.[49] Their use to the nation had to be carefully weighed. At times correspondence between each department was tense, as Sean Lemass, the minister for industry, requested greater numbers of permits to be given to expert technicians. In the case of five foreign workers, a letter from John Leydon to Joseph Walshe, the secretary of the Department of External Affairs, noted the following: "That employment permits under Article 5 (2) (b) of Aliens Order 1935 have been granted to six workers for Les Modes Modernes—September 1938—five of the aliens, described as Austrian nationals, the minister feels justified in granting these permits notwithstanding the difficulties that may arise regarding the repatriation of these aliens once their permits expire."[50] Sean

Lemass's determination to drive forward his vision of an industrial Ireland demanded all sorts of compromises, and as a consequence Fianna Fáil's protectionist policies were layered with complexities. The arrival of Jewish refugees was not a humanitarian response to the plight of Jews in Europe. Decisions were determined by their use to the nation. The ones who did arrive struggled to help family members gain visas for Ireland unless they offered particular skills.[51] An application by Thea Dziwietnik's brother, Adolph, who had been released from prison, to travel to Ireland was refused, as were other applications by workers for family members to settle in Ireland.[52] Those refugees who were given employment permits arrived in a country in which a large section of its citizens were deeply suspicious of the presence of alien Jews in Irish industry.

Protectionism: A Contested Policy "Othered" into a Negative Jewish Space

Ireland in its pursuit of a protected economy, like other nations during this period, raised questions of national identity and notions of who was included and excluded in the economic life of the country. A multitude of voices from within the business community, the Irish diaspora, veterans (including female republican movements such as Cumann na mBan), and individuals pressured the government to close the doors on further numbers of Jews establishing themselves in Ireland.[53] Joseph Walshe, the secretary of the Department of External Affairs, noted as much in his response to the high commissioner regarding the memorandum from the CGJ: "Numerous protests have been made to the Government in recent years regarding the number of alien Jews who have established themselves in this country and the Minister would not look with favour on any policy which might tend to increase that number."[54] A fear that large numbers of alien Jews had settled in Ireland had been fomented by a complex and mutable body of oppositional voices that had used the presence of Jews in Irish industry as a tool to attack Fianna Fáil's industrial policy. Arguing that Eamon de Valera's protectionist policies favored Jews, these voices used the Irish Parliament, Dáil Éireann, and Blueshirt rallies to voice dissent to

Fianna Fáil's economic policies. The Blueshirts, a protofascist move-ment originating out of the Army Comrades Association, flourished with growing membership from farmers, aggrieved by the economic war with Great Britain from 1932 to 1938.[55] De Valera's decision to refuse payment of land annuities owed the British government saw retaliatory British protectionist policies raise duties on agricultural products and initiate cattle quotas, which diminished export markets and severely impacted farmers' welfare.[56] Farmers were doubly disad-vantaged by protectionist policies that diminished their income and increased the cost of living as a consequence of wage inflation.[57]

Agricultural communities felt marginalized by Fianna Fáil's new industrial focus, which was seen as benefiting urban workers with increased wages and employment benefits such as paid holidays and set working hours governed by international labor laws.[58] Furthermore, some argued that the beneficiaries of this new industrial Ireland were women workers, who, with money in their pockets, could potentially destabilize Irish family life.[59] The formation of a new political party in September 1933, Fine Gael, merged the political voices of Cumann na nGaedhael, the Blueshirts, and a farmers' party, the National Centre Party. A weighty political voice emerged to address concerns about political and social change, the impact of the economic war, and the hegemony of Fianna Fáil with its economic policies that favored urban working-class communities.[60] As newly established factories created footprints of Fianna Fáil power across the country, oppositional voices seized an opportunity to "other" Fianna Fáil's industrial policy into a negative Jewish space.

The notion that Jews were a destabilizing force in society gained currency in the 1930s, as nation-states struggled with questions of national identity in response to worldwide depression.[61] Ireland was no exception. Between 1933 and 1934, a dangerous discourse developed that accused Fianna Fáil of allowing increasing numbers of alien Jews into the Irish economy. As Lemass faced political pressure to provide data about new factories, which he resisted, the opposition party filled an empty statistical space with foreign names, mostly Jewish. For example, after the launch of a new Viennese sausage factory in Naas,

Cumann na nGaedhael representative Patrick McGilligan argued the following in the Dáil:

> I intend to do nothing more than to mention the names of the directors and to indicate, as it should be indicated, to this House that if people are buying sausage products it can hardly be said that the money recovered from the customer goes to the nationals of this country. It is part of the programme of the Minister for Industry and Commerce that in the case of factories that are established except under license capital should be controlled, in the main, by Irish nationals. Here you have names as examples of Irish nationals: Franz Vogel, Caplal, and Witstun [*sic*].[62]

An extended list of names followed in November, and this tactic appeared no fewer than eleven times in Dáil debates between July 1933 and May 1934.[63] A focus on naming as a validation of "Irishness" within industry contributed to a dangerous narrowing of a national identity. For Jews working in business, whether Irish born, naturalized, or recently settled in Ireland, such a discourse "othered" them.[64]

Questions of national identity and national characteristics were also highlighted in a discourse of non-native-run factories as sites of danger and alien practices. A negative focus on Jews and industry became a tool used by politicians to position newly protected factories as potentially unsafe places. Fine Gael legislator Richard Mulcahy associated such factories with the sullying of an Irish industrial tradition of fair practice and good working conditions.[65] In a lengthy Dáil debate on factory conditions, Mulcahy distinguished between those patriotic men trying to establish new businesses from their homes and so-called alien workshops operating in the back lanes of Dublin with the smell of Whitechapel about them.[66] Tapping into notions about the dangers of factory work, Mulcahy and others identified Jewish factories as sites of employment for women and juveniles in appalling conditions.[67] In doing so, Fine Gael politicians attempted to place Fianna Fáil's industrial policy within a discourse of sweatshops and profiteering. Attributing negative economic characteristics to Jews spoke to a long history in anti-Jewish Christian thinking about Jews and economics. As Jerry Muller argues, the long shadow of usury colored the way Christian societies thought about Jews in the economic space.[68] Attempts to make Jews visible in the Irish economy through a prism of exploitative practices echoed previous moments in Irish history when Jews in Ireland were othered as harmful to Irish society.[69]

"Becoming Irish": Protectionism and an Irish Ireland for Industry

Negotiating the presence of Jewish businessmen and workers in provincial Ireland demanded a carefully constructed narrative from Fianna Fáil. Les Modes Modernes, Galway, soon faced accusations from Fine Gael politicians that its female employees earned "slave wages," while its directors earned vast fortunes.[70] Encouraged by leading Fine Gael politician James Dillon, Les Modes Modernes hats were boycotted by consumers and wholesalers, which placed the owners in a precarious financial position and challenged Fianna Fáil's investment in the factory as a flagship of its industrial policies.[71] To assure the public that this new hat industry was working in the best interests of the nation, Sean Lemass presented the factories as Irish in the making. To control the way Irish society encountered these factories, Lemass promoted a process of Irishization, which used legislation, brand development, as well as a developing narrative of an Irish modernity that served an Irish Ireland to promote the hat industry as serving an Irish industrial landscape.

To ensure that ownership was in Irish hands, these factories were subjected to the Control of Manufactures Acts of 1932 and 1934. This legislation determined that the majority of shareholders of new industries were Irish citizens, and, in addition, the majority of the board, excluding the managing director, had to hold Irish citizenship.[72] This legislation was a cornerstone of Fianna Fáil's pursuit of economic nationalism. By individualizing who was Irish in the industrial life of Ireland, the concept of "foreigner" was narrowed from an overseas corporation to a single person. Every individual on a board of directors was now accountable: Was he Irish or not? As McGilligan had shown, naming as a construction of an Irish national identity exerted a powerful influence in Irish society. Knowing who was Irish was particularly important in a period of change, and it was no surprise that new legislation to monitor name changing was introduced in 1936.[73]

These acts also ensured that greater preference shares were given to Irish directors who had invested relatively small financial assets in these companies. Mary Daly has argued that many foreign investors manipulated the share issues to circumvent the acts with help from prominent lawyers. For these Jewish industrialists, however, who were dependent on the government for employment permits, adherence to the acts was important. The prospect of safe settlement in Ireland involved an exchange in which these once successful industrialists in their native countries accepted a reduced role in new business partnerships. They had reduced voting rights regarding decisions within the business, and the Irish directors became the public faces representing the factories in any official capacity, whether summoned to meet a bishop or welcoming Eamon de Valera to the factory.[74]

To assuage residual fears about rising numbers of Jews entering Ireland, these businessmen were presented as European industrialists with considerable manufacturing and design skills. Ireland's industrial drive would be served by Austrian expertise in production methods and Parisian designs of dernier cri hats to fashion Irish heads.[75] While a passing mention was made of the "political troubles" that compelled these industrialists to leave their native lands, the larger narrative emphasized their industrial experience.[76] Presented as brokers of an industrial modernity, each industrialist offered expertise that was key to the larger project of nation building. Lemass recognized the value of an industrial modernity in terms of its use to the nation and formulated an industrial narrative that was modern in function but substantially Irish in its substance. Hugh Campbell describes this twin imperative of Irish modernity in terms of "essentialism" and "epochalism." Ireland desired to be a formative modern nation as well as representative of a "national spirit."[77]

New factories with foreign investment became fully Irish through the skills of Irish workers and the siting of these factories within the rural idyll of green pastures. A modern Irish industrial landscape was introduced to the Irish public through a language of design and progress. In the case of Les Modes Modernes, Galway, Irish workers would benefit:

> The building, which was erected by Messrs J Stewart and Sons, Lower Salthill, Galway, at a cost of £11,000 is of the latest modern factory design, comprised of fourteen compartments, and with a total inside measurement of 140 feet by 80 feet. The roof is of the northlight truss type, ensuring perfect daylight lighting. The offices are to the front of the building and have a total measurement of 80 feet by 25 feet. There is also a large display room to the front. The heating of the factory and offices is on the modern unit system. These units can be reversed in summer and utilised as coolers.[78]

State-of-the-art factories, like Les Modes Modernes', served Irish workers engaged in a national endeavor to deliver a self-sufficient industrial nation. Western Hats, Castlebar, was acclaimed as the "most modern hat factory in the world" in its use of new construction techniques of reinforced concrete rather than steel girders, which allowed for broader internal spaces for production lines and a greater proportion of exterior walls to be devoted to exterior windows.[79] However, as the *Irish Press* reminded its readers, it was equally important that these "well-lit healthy offices" enabled "members of staff to look out on the busy scene of earth being upturned . . . to produce food for the nation."[80] Ireland's rural landscape tamed the functional purpose of an industrial Ireland and protected its workers from the potential evils of an industrial modernity.[81] As Lemass remarked at the opening of a new factory in Nenagh, workers looking out on green fields avoided "the evils of slumdom, and the evil of the drab and uneventful lives that characterized industrial countries."[82]

An industrial language also introduced the public to new industrial processes. Press reporters walked their readers through each hat factory, explaining hat manufacturing and how newly skilled Irish workers were more than capable of mastering processes to produce Irish products of a very high quality.[83] Yet within this encounter, these Jewish businessmen and workers became obscured in an Irish industrial discourse that focused on their presence as performing a functional role. Press photographs always positioned them standing by machinery or holding the latest manufactured product. Just as they facilitated the construction of modern factories, these foreigners were present to transfer manufacturing skills and expertise to Irish workers.[84] Irish workers, guided by foreign experts, were capable of handling the most advanced machinery and technological processes, and in doing so the workers became the manufacturers of these hats.

As these products entered the Irish marketplace, it was essential that Irish women bought them. Brand development was used to persuade consumers that Les Modes Modernes hats, made by Irish hands yet guided by Parisian experts, would keep women abreast of world style trends.[85] Parisian chic now infused Irish-made products. Foreign experts, brought over by Lemass, served Irish women as brokers of fashion and modernity, and in return Irish women were expected to serve the nation through their purchase of these hats. A form of citizen consumerism permeated the narrative of Irish protectionism, and wearing Irish-made hats became a national duty to keep Irish citizens employed.[86] Consumer pressure and a heightened discourse about employment also framed Irish society's perception of these factories.

Conclusion

The arrival of a new hat industry to Ireland with Jewish refugee workers offers a prism through which to explore how Fianna Fáil's pursuit of economic nationalism shaped Irish society in unexpected and contested ways. As the rise of nationalism(s) and ideologies across Europe embraced forms of othering and scapegoating to make sense of a politically and economically unstable world, so too did Irish voices during the 1930s. Fianna Fáil's policy of protectionism was layered with complexities, and Jews became a fault line in a contested discourse of national identity and change. For Jewish refugees in search of settlement, employment permits were issued to those individuals who could offer some manufacturing skills that were of use to the nation. Protectionist policies as a means of import substitution determined their fate.

An urgency to present these factories and their products as Irish suppressed any engagement with the lives of these workers as refugees whose families were scattered across the globe or still trying to leave an increasingly dangerous Europe. It was almost impossible to help family members gain visas for Ireland unless they offered particular skills that were useful. The government showed little benevolence toward these workers or industrialists who invested considerable capital investment in the Irish economy. Yet the presence of these factories with Jewish refugee workers helped skill a new generation of workers in hat and ribbon making and created employment opportunities for more than six hundred Irish workers in provincial Ireland.

PART THREE | Migrations

8

Irish, Jewish, or Both

Hybrid Identities of David Marcus,
Stanley Price, and Myself

GEORGE BORNSTEIN

An early episode satirizing antisemitism in James Joyce's monumental novel *Ulysses* pops up at the end of episode 2 (Nestor), when Stephen Dedalus collects his pay from the ironically money-counting West Briton headmaster Mr. Deasy. Deasy calls Stephen back to hear a short anti-Jewish joke. "'Ireland, they say, has the honour of being the only country which never persecuted the jews. Do you know that? No. And do you know why?'" he asks. "'Because she never let them in,' Mr. Deasy said solemnly," as he coughs up a phlegm ball.[1] Both the joke itself and its unattractive delivery by a coin-obsessed foreigner testify to Joyce's (and perhaps Stephen's) disapproval. But Ireland had let them in, of course. The earliest mention comes from the *Annals of Inisfallen*, dated 1079, which records, "Five Jews came over the sea with gifts for Tairdelbach, King of Munster, and they were sent back again."[2] There was a Jewish mayor of Youghal in the sixteenth century, and after Cromwell allowed the Jews back into the British Isles in 1650 a few, mostly Sephardic, found Ireland as well. The population continued to grow in the eighteenth century, and one, Baron Lionel Rothschild, finally took his place in Parliament in the nineteenth. Persecution of the Jews in the Russian Empire swelled the ranks of emigrant Jews considerably, with fifty-three hundred living in northern and southern Ireland by World War II. Still, the concept of an Irish

Jew sounds odd to most ears, and author and editor David Marcus, himself one, could label his 1990 collection of short stories *Who Ever Heard of an Irish Jew?*[3]

Along the way and into the present, Jewish Irish numbers gyrated up and down, depending among other things on the ability to find a Jewish marriage partner among so few choices and a resultant number of mixed or hybrid matchings. *Hybridity* seems the obvious term for such intermingling, as Leopold Bloom's biography illustrates: he identifies as Jewish but is technically not one by lacking a Jewish mother, does not keep kosher, and so on. Culture works that way, too. "From the very beginning we must call into question any notions of pure traditions or pristine heritages, or any civilization or culture having a monopoly on virtue or insight," writes African American cultural theorist Cornel West in a formulation that applies to the vexed past of Ireland as well as of America. "Ambiguous legacies, hybrid cultures. By hybrid, of course, we mean cross-cultural fertilizations. Every culture that we know of is a result of the weaving of antecedent cultures." Or as jazz trumpeter Louis Armstrong more pithily put it in dismissing race consciousness in jazz musicians: "These people who make the restrictions, they don't know nothing about music. It's no crime for cats of any color to get together and blow. Race-conscious jazz musicians? Nobody could be who really knew their horns and loved the music."[4]

Issues of hybridity and mixing play out in two Irish Jewish autobiographies, David Marcus's punningly titled *Oughtobiography* (2001) and Stanley Price's *Somewhere to Hang My Hat* (2002).[5] Both grew up in Ireland, but whereas Marcus lived abroad in England for thirteen years before returning to Ireland to follow up on his influential editing of *Irish Writing*, Price in contrast left the country for good for England and then America. Price confesses that "though I was never to live there again, my Irish background was to run through my life like a thin green line" (142). The subtitles of both autobiographies stress their hybridities: Marcus calls his *Leaves from the Diary of a Hyphenated Jew*, while Price settles on simply *An Irish-Jewish Journey*. Both suggest what the Anglo-Irish sometimes called "the agony of the hyphen," an identity split between two contrasting cultures. Stanley Price is a distant cousin of mine, sharing the last name of my mother (Celia Price) and her birth family, and we share a common ancestor in the improbably named Charles Beresford Price, his grandfather and my great uncle, who is said to have become so seasick on the journey from the Baltic that when the boat stopped to refuel in Cork Harbor, he got off and decided to immigrate then and there, a story in itself. Partly for that reason, I conclude with my own observations drawn from visiting Ireland for more than forty years of great change.

Marcus's subtitle indicates his main drift by tagging himself as a "hyphenated Jew." As he explains on the last page of the prologue, "That inner me was formed by two things—music, and the ongoing trauma of having to juggle a hyphenated heritage of being both Irish and Jewish" (xiv). On the one side lay the duties of Orthodox Judaism, with its 613 mitzvoth, or commandments, and on the other the multiple obligations of an Irish citizen in a militantly Catholic state. There was minimal overt antisemitism, though on one occasion at his Presentation Brothers school Marcus found himself cast as Shylock in *The Merchant of Venice*. His delivery of Shylock's famous speech "I am a Jew. . . . If you prick us do we not bleed?" met with a round of applause from the boys, but he was transferred to a different role the next day lest the casting be criticized as antisemitic. Then there was not the compulsory Hebrew of Orthodox Judaism but the compulsory Irish of the Republic in those years. As journalist Medb Ruane wrote later in the *Irish Times*, "My generation was administered Irish the way we were administered cod liver oil" (quoted in Marcus, 6–10, 30).

Marcus made his mark as an editor, of course, first of *Irish Writing* and then, after the English sojourn, of *New Irish Writing*. With the help of coeditor Terence Smith and mentor Sean O'Faolain, *Irish Writing* devoted itself largely to Irish short stories. Starting at a young age, Marcus recruited both famous and emerging authors. He gives an especially hilarious account of his visit to Drishane House to recruit the aging Edith Somerville for the cause. Unused to such lofty surroundings, Marcus moves from intimidation to near panic. As an Orthodox Jew, he had never eaten nonkosher meat, yet sapped by the ordeal of keeping up a literary conversation with Somerville's nephew, the distinguished medievalist Sir Neville Coghill, Marcus decided "to swallow the meat along with one of the fundamental taboos of my upbringing" (53). His home had also been nonalcoholic, yet he accepts a tumbler of Paddy whiskey that almost knocks him out. The hulking Coghill (Marcus calls him Karloffian) was, of course, the distinguished and witty translator of Chaucer's medieval text into modern English, including his version of the end of "The Miller's Tale": "And Nicholas is branded on the bum; / And God bring all of us to Kingdom Come."[6] Fortunately for Marcus, Somerville did agree to contribute to the fledgling journal. The comic aspect of hovering between two cultures, Jewish and Irish, takes on a more sinister side after the comedy at Drishane House. On the return train, an unknown woman suddenly sits down in his carriage and breaks into a lament for the Irish Republican Army (IRA) prisoners interned in the Curragh before launching an antisemitic rant. "It was the Jews, them Satan divils. They're behind everything in the country," she exclaims. "Horrible, ugly creatures with black, oily hair and hooky noses and cruel, devilish eyes. That's how you'd recognize them. Oh I'd know a Jew anywhere! . . . They can't fool me." "Well, here's one who *has* fooled you," exclaims Marcus. "You see, I'm a Jew" (76–77). Ruminating further on the IRA members behind bars, he reveals that his mother had been driven out of Limerick by the pogrom of 1904 and later become a member of Cumann na mBan, the women's wing of the IRA.

Between the original *Irish Writing* and its successor, Marcus became one of the most influential Irish editors of his time, known particularly for introducing new writers. The former *Irish Writing* boasted Patrick Kavanagh, Conor Cruise O'Brien, Edith Somerville, and Padraic Colum among its essayists, with Benedict Kiely, Frank O'Connor, Sean O'Faolain, and Liam O'Flaherty among native writers and especially Jean-Paul Sartre and William Saroyan among distinguished foreigners. The latter offered work by Hugh Leonard, Con Houlihan, Samuel Beckett, and novelist Ita Daly, whom Marcus later married. The long-term marriage to Daly matched the hybridity featured in Leopold Bloom's marriage to the Gentile Molly in that Daly herself was not Jewish. At the same time, Marcus made his first and perhaps least successful effort at a novel, *To Next Year in Jerusalem*, a phrase from the Passover Haggadah recited by Jews every year. As he wrote of his own Irish Jewish story just accepted by *New American Writing* for what seemed the then prodigious sum of $315 (then over £100), "I was flabbered and I was gasted" (108). Despite the jump in confidence that prompted him to submit the novel in the first place, he continued to have doubts even after publication. Set in the West of Ireland, the novel told the story of a doomed romance between an Irish Jew and a young Catholic woman. Nervous about comparison with the then hard-to-come-by *Ulysses* in Ireland, Marcus defended himself by arguing that "mine was the first Irish-Jewish novel by a real Irish-Jewish writer, with a real Irish-Jewish main character which Bloom, being born of a non-Jewish mother, was strictly not" (107).

As Marcus comes to realize during his thirteen years in London, "The comparative rarity of an Irish-Jewish heritage was the quiddity on which my identity was founded" (139). Chronicling adventures like that one with the Dickensian-named Jewish Sabbath Day Observance Employment Bureau, where his Jewish identity was doubted, and the Guildhall Insurance Company, where his boss reveals himself as a closet Jew, he encounters Ingrid, a German-born woman astonished that as a Jew, he accepts her (154–59). After his return to Ireland, Marcus began work on his historical novel *A Land Not Theirs*, which explores the Jewish community in Cork during the War of Independence, torn between the struggles for freedom in Palestine and in Ireland.[7] Surprised by the offer of £15,000 for it, he noted that readers were mostly complimentary, though ironically the reviews in British Jewish organs were the most critical. He saw it as the chronicle of "people—the British, the Irish, and the Jews, a unique *ménage à trois* on a site which the Irish owned, the British held, and where the Jews . . . found sanctuary" (219). The remark unknowingly (or perhaps knowingly) echoed a once widespread American adage on New York and Chicago: "The Negroes built it, the Jews own it, and the Irish run it," among other variants.

Toward the end of his memoir, Marcus mentions his meeting with William Saroyan, whom he calls "the first hyphenated American I had ever met" (240). Saroyan was an Armenian American whose first short story collection, *The Daring Young Man on the Flying Trapeze* (1934), led off with his story "Seventy Thousand Assyrians." Once a great people, the Assyrians then numbered only seventy thousand, with the Armenians after the genocide numbering fewer than a million themselves. "'You understand it,' Saroyan said. 'You felt it, as the Assyrians felt it, as I felt it, and as you, a Jew, would have felt it'" (238). That remark pointed Marcus toward awareness of interethnic hybridity, for which he invokes the old joke about the Irish priest traveling in America who in a small town comes across a store with a sign reading "Cohen and O'Toole." He enters and encounters an old man with a beard and wearing a yarmulke. "'I've just come in to tell you,' said the priest, 'how wonderful it is that your people and mine have become such good friends—even partners. That's a surprise.' The old man sighs, 'I've got a bigger surprise for you. I'm O'Toole'" (242).

The autobiography of novelist and screenwriter Stanley Price also revolves around hybridity. Like Marcus, Price's grandparents hailed from Lithuania. As he writes of his father, "As an Irishman and a Jew, he had lived in a double diaspora" (8), as had his father's father, the comically named Charles Beresford Price, Beresford being the name of an English family of large landowners who settled in Ireland and that served as an incongruous middle moniker for the Lithuanian refugee. Again, his grandson identifies a double heritage, "comic Irish, tragic Jewish" (19). The grandson observes that both the Irish and the Jews had each suffered a large diaspora and that a letter in the *Cork Examiner* from 1884 observed further of the new refugees that "these haggard, emaciated, tattered-clothed, Jewish immigrants look not unlike our own impoverished people after the Famine" (31). On the other hand, a somewhat later piece from Dublin in the London *Jewish Chronicle* contended, "The Jews understand the Irish little; the Irish understand the Jews less. Each seems a peculiar race in the eyes of the other; and in a word, the position of Jews in Ireland is peculiarly peculiar. . . . Nowhere else is the term 'Jewman' known, here we hear nothing else" (34). One place where that term could be heard was in

John Synge's masterpiece, *Playboy of the Western World*, in whose third act Pegeen Mike fantasizes about "a Jew-man, with ten kegs of gold."[8]

As mentioned, Price was the name of my mother's family, and Stanley is my distant cousin. In the book he tells a story of Charles Beresford Price's immigration to Ireland that also prevailed in my own family, even though the two sides of the ocean had never had contact with each other. The only difference was that my family ascribed the exchange to a customs official, while *Somewhere to Hang My Hat* ascribed it to a gunman during the Troubles. Here is that version: "At one point, when stopped at a barricade and challenged, 'Are you a Protestant or a Catholic?' 'A Jew,' he had replied. 'Are you a Protestant Jew or a Catholic Jew?' his questioners persisted. When he again replied, 'A Jew,' one sentry is said to have shouted to the other: 'Let him pass—no religion!'" (67). But Charles Beresford Price did have a religion, and his records persist in Dublin's Irish Jewish Museum, dedicated in 1985 by Chaim Herzog, then president of Israel. Differing views of that religion were prevalent at the time and later in Ireland, as in the debate between two prominent leaders, Michael Davitt and Arthur Griffith, both of whom Price quotes. Davitt, leader of the Land League, vented passionately in Leopold Bloom's newspaper, the *Freeman's Journal*: "There is not an atom of truth in the horrible allegations of ritual murder against this persecuted race. . . . I protest, as an Irishman and a Christian, against this spirit of barbarous malignity being introduced into Ireland. . . . Like our own race, the Jews have endured persecutions" (59). In contrast, Griffith, who sided against Dreyfus, among others, concluded a vitriolic passage by blaming Jews with the sarcastic image of "Jewish auctioneers to sell us up in the end for the benefit of all our other Jewish benefactors" (60).

Price found similar bifurcation in English culture when he moved to England at the age of twelve. "As a devout Jew, my parents wished me to become an English gentleman, or at least an Anglo-Irish-Jewish gentleman," he recalled (135). But in London, as in America at the time, day schools maintained firm quotas against Jews, usually around 10 percent. That created an immediate sense of difference among Jewish boys, sometimes approaching alienation and a sense of never being able to fit in properly. It often led to alienation from parents as well. Price explains, "In wanting the best of both worlds for their children, British and Jewish, it never occurred to them that there might be any conflict involved for their children" (132). As the horrors of the concentrations camps became known, a sense of separation only increased. Price found himself "trying to cope with the change from Ireland to England, from being an Irish Jew to being an English Jew," the more so as, "despite the Holocaust, anti-Semitism was still alive in Britain" (146).

In opposition to the tensions, counterexamples of harmony did beckon. One was embodied in Robbie Briscoe, a hero of the Irish Revolution who became the first (of only two) Jewish lord mayor of Dublin and an international example of goodwill toward Jews. Vladimir (Ze'ev) Jabotinksy, militant Zionist and founder of the Haganah's more activist cousin, the Irgun organization, wrote to Eamon de Valera for instruction on how the Irish had fought a successful guerrilla war against the English in Ireland, a success that he hoped to replicate in British-controlled Palestine. De Valera turned him over to Briscoe, the highest-ranking Hebrew in the IRA, and the two became fast friends. Jabotinsky stayed in Ireland for a month and later wrote in his autobiography that he returned home to "form a physical force movement in Palestine on exactly the same lines as Fianna Eireann and the I.R.A."[9] Briscoe remained popular abroad, not always so militantly. When he arrived in Boston, with its hordes of Irish émigrés, Mayor John Hynes introduced him to a vast crowd with words that began like a standard joke before turning back on itself: "Once there was an Irishman and a Jew—and here he is, Robert Briscoe!" (192). Yet despite such inspiration, Price ended up with "the divided self that haunts all expatriates and exiles." He did finally win a place to hang his hat after all, even if it meant having two passports (237).

Many aspects of Marcus's and Price's autobiographies turned up in my own life in America. Immediately after transfer to a new private day school came awareness of difference and etiolation of links to parents. Until the age of eleven, I had grown up in a neighborhood of St. Louis that was heavily Jewish, as were most of my schoolmates. But that situation changed in the year before I finished elementary school. The principal called in me and my parents to say that I should take the entrance exam for what was then the best school in the city and sub- urbs, St. Louis Country Day. I was about to learn the lesson that the writer Calvin Trillin did when growing up across the state in Kansas City. "The real Jews were in New York," he thought. "New York was also where the real baseball players were—the Kansas City Blues were a farm club of the New York Yankees. . . . We were farm-club Jews."[10]

Country Day changed my world, including my relation to Juda- ism and to my family. At the age of twelve I encountered scions of the St. Louis elite and indeed of the whole country. My schoolmates now included heirs of the May Company department stores, Budweiser brewery, and McDonell aircraft, among others. Most of the parents, too, had attended elite colleges, though mine had no college and, indeed, had not even graduated from high school, during the Depres- sion having gone to work instead. The antisemitism was mostly under the table and of a social nature, showing itself in the exclusion of Jew- ish boys from some social events and the occasional flare-up, as when in the role of bus monitor my junior year I stopped a rambunctious large boy from harassing a smaller one. "I'm not going to have a Jew meddling in my business," snarled the offender. Unable to think of another course of action, I slugged him. We were both brought to the headmaster's office, and to his credit Headmaster Harper excused me back to class but kept the offender to read him the riot act. I remem- bered the incident the next day when we were singing the Doxology hymn in morning chapel:

> Thank God from whom all blessings flow,
> Thank him all creatures here below
> Thank Him above ye heavenly Host
> Praise Father, Son, and Holy Ghost.

The Jewish boys, as usual, kept silent or hummed instead of singing those words.

The school was small in those days, with only forty-three students— all boys—in my senior class. Despite unmentioned social restrictions, there were no academic ones, and Jewish boys were among the top students. Three of us were among the six who went to Harvard, one of them a lifelong friend, and a similar number went to Yale and Princeton. By then, such colleges had become mostly meritocracies, with social restrictions receding (except for the "final clubs" at Harvard and "eating clubs" at Princeton). Yet as the number of otherwise-qualified Jewish students rose after the turn of the twentieth century, so did limits on their numbers. It was true of Harvard as well as the others, and while there I lived in Lowell House, named for former president A. Lawrence Lowell, who led the fight for restrictions on admission to both college and country, serving as vice president of the Immigration Restriction League as well as president of Harvard.

The only tenured Jew in literature that we knew about at Harvard was Harry Levin, the eminent scholar of Shakespeare and others, and the pickings were even skimpier at Princeton, where, following Chaucer's admonition in *The Merchant's Tale* that "sundry scoles maken sotile clerkis," I moved for graduate school.[11] There the only tenured Jew in English was the Anglophile eighteenth-century scholar Louis Landa, from Tyler, Texas, whose ethnic background was revealed to us by a graduate student from the same town. Within the then Anglocentric curriculum I gravitated toward a thesis on Ireland's greatest poet, W. B. Yeats, partly because of the beauty of his poetry but also because as an Irishman, he was the closest thing to a fellow outsider available to me as a choice. My uncertain status revealed itself in an end-of-the-year mandatory conference with a graduate adviser, who asked whether I was in the right field and elaborated that "English literature is basically a Christian literature, and as a Jewish boy you will never understand it fully." So much for the educational value of literature; after fifty years, I still remember his bigotry. I ended up writing a dissertation on Yeats and Shelley, outcasts from the canon in different ways, Yeats for being Irish and Shelley for being a romantic when romantics were out of fashion in the academy.

I learned more about Yeats and Ireland during frequent trips starting in the late 1970s. Ireland then was a poor, almost Third World country, with the Celtic Tiger still nearly two decades in the future.

Outside of Dublin, roads were narrow and winding (though still charming), thatched-roofed cottages were frequent, and the food disappointed but the singing did not. Nor did the friendliness toward Americans; with forty million people of Irish descent in America, nearly everyone in the home country had relatives or friends living there. Widespread ambivalence and even disapproval of Yeats surprised us, though. Many Irish then saw him as more Anglo than Irish and distrusted his English affinities and sometimes snobbery; a taxi driver delivered a diatribe even as he brought us to the Abbey Theatre, which he regarded as its opponents in Sean O'Casey's autobiography had fifty years before.[12]

Fortunately, none of it affected the Yeats children, Anne and Michael, themselves Anglo-Irish. They each went on to distinguished careers, Michael as a barrister and politician, Anne as an artist and stage designer for the Abbey. They both inherited, too, manuscripts and artworks of their father and their uncle Jack Yeats. Of these works, they served as exemplary guardians, regarding their inheritance as material belonging to the nation and in their temporary custody. Before their impressive donations to the National Library of Ireland, the archives were housed mostly in their homes in the Dublin suburb of Dalkey, the literary ones mostly but not exclusively with Michael and the artistic ones mostly but again not solely with Anne. Unlike consulting the materials now in the National Library and its wonderful manuscript reading room with layers of security, studying them in the houses of Anne and Michael created an aura of intimacy and a sense of connection to the past. I remember one occasion when Michael perhaps mischievously asked if I would like to see the piece of carved lapis lazuli that inspired his father's famous poem. Falsely imagining it to be a small medallion-size object, I was startled when he placed the foot-high, heavy object in my hands. I almost dropped it as headlines like "American Oaf Shatters Precious Yeats Heirloom" ran through my head. Fortunately, I didn't. With Anne, I remember my wife watching the royal wedding of Charles and Diana on television in her house while I toiled on her father's manuscripts. By the end, they were good friends, and Anne exclaimed that despite her mockery of the occasion, "I do like a bit of pomp." Both Anne and Michael embraced their hybrid heritage.

So, too, did Yeats's designated biographer, eminent historian F. S. L. Lyons, who died in the midst of his work, passing the project on to his student R. F. Foster, a now celebrated professor of history at Oxford. Along the way, Lyons produced a superb little book, *Culture and Anarchy in Ireland, 1890–1939*, that traced the clash of four cultures in Ireland—native Irish, English, Anglo-Irish, and Scots Protestant in Ulster. Unusually for the time (1979) but not surprisingly given the author, W. B. Yeats plays a central role. But one thing that the astute Lyons did not perceive was the future rise of the Celtic Tiger, which, in transforming the economy with the help of low taxes, native talent, and European Union funding, changed everything, including improved roads, a booming economy (for a while at least), vastly improved food, more mobility, and of all things an influx of foreign workers. Ireland for a time became a net importer of jobs, much of it from eastern Europe as well as Africa and even Asia.[13]

Something else that neither Lyons nor others foresaw was the collapse of authority of the Roman Catholic Church in national life. Enshrined in the constitution, the church played an outsize role in de Valera's Ireland and after. When my wife and I began coming to Ireland, the influence and power of the church were everywhere and especially noticeable to me as a Jewish American visitor. That atmosphere changed suddenly under the combined impact of the sexual abuse scandals, in which young women were forcibly incarcerated on often dubious moral grounds and made to work in church-sponsored laundries without pay and pension, often for lifelong terms. The last one closed only in 1996. The church sexual abuse scandal completed the rout, with prosecutions intensifying in the 1990s amid revelations that hundreds of priests had abused thousands of boys and young men and some girls and women over the years. On a visit to Ireland in 2014, my wife and I noticed the absence of clergy in habits on the streets compared to their near-ubiquitous presence thirty years before.

Through those upheavals, the few-thousand-strong Irish Jewish community soldiered on, gradually declining as members moved to

England or the United States and then rising again under opportunities of the Celtic Tiger boom and later bust. Attitudes toward Irish Jewish connections on both sides of the Atlantic changed, too. When I began to mine the connection, there was little interest except for studies of Irish emigration to America. Even the study of Yeats blossomed first in the United States. When I asked a group of distinguished American historians about the connection of Jews and Irish, they told me that there was none. They knew nothing of the Jewish Robbie Briscoe's role in the Irish independence movement or his influence on Ze'ev Jabotinsky's thinking, of de Valera's planting a tree in an Israeli forest, or of the chief rabbi of Ireland emigrating to the Promised Land. All of it changed around the turn of the century. Dermot Keogh's groundbreaking *Jews in Twentieth-Century Ireland* (1998) was followed by titles such as Stephen Watt's new *"Something Dreadful and Grand": American Literature and the Irish-Jewish Unconscious* (2015), my own *Colors of Zion: Blacks, Jews, and Irish, 1840–1940* (2011), and Abby Bender's *Israelites in Erin: Exodus, Revolution, and the Irish Revival* (2015). All looked hard at connections of different kinds. National and international conferences began to feature connections, too, as with panels at the 2016 American Conference on Irish Studies meeting at Notre Dame. This book itself testifies to the growing trend and seeks to extend it.

9

The Irish Victory Fund
and the United Jewish Appeal
as Nation-Building Projects

DAN LAINER-VOS

In 1919, during the high time of the Irish struggle for independence, the popular weekly *Gaelic American* implored its readers to donate money to the Irish Victory Fund: "[The Easter Rising martyrs] . . . gave their lives for Ireland's freedom. . . . Will we raise the amount [$40,000] for democracy, for human happiness, for unfettered knowledge, for lofty civilization, for the life of Ireland?"[1] Thirty years later, the United Jewish Appeal (UJA) used a somewhat similar tone to appeal to its donors: "On the day that the State of Israel introduced its full-scale austerity program so that its citizens could absorb more immigration, the United Jewish Appeal was $24,652,000 behind in its cash collections. . . . The Jews in Israel are giving a model of self-denial. . . . At the very least, it would remove any vestige of belief on the part of American Jews that too much is being asked of them."[2] Sacrifice and self-denial in the homeland justify demands for giving from fellow Irish Americans and Jewish Americans, respectively. An exchange of blood and money connects multitudes of people that face radically different life circumstances in bonds of obligation and solidarity.

These statements in the *Gaelic American* and UJA literature are anything but unusual. Yet despite the centrality of gift giving and reciprocity to the national rhetoric and the self-understanding of members, scholars have generally refrained from linking gift giving and nation building. Instead, scholars typically treat acts of giving and sacrifice as a testimony for the existence of the nation and an illustration of its potency. That subjects are willing to selflessly give seems to attest to the existence of a surpassing entity, that is, the nation. It is not necessarily wrong to treat giving to the nation as a sign of preexisting sentiments. It is only sensible to assume that people give to things they care about. Nevertheless, such treatment is misleading in that it treats the nation as an established fact or a thing.[3] Such misplaced concreteness prevents us from appreciating the role of gift giving in the process of nation building.

In order to understand how gift giving is implicated in the process of nation building, this chapter comparatively examines the formation of transatlantic gift-giving networks that connected Irish Americans and Jewish Americans to the national struggles across the ocean in the 1910s and 1940s, respectively. Instead of assuming that Irish Americans and Jewish Americans bear natural affinity to the Irish and Jews across the ocean, I explore the organizational practices that fundraising organizations developed in order to secure the flow of financial resources to these respective national movements and look on how these practices informed the kind of membership that diaspora subjects experience.

I argue the fund-raising mechanisms that connected Irish and Jewish Americans to their counterparts in Ireland and Palestine, respectively, were not merely instrumental tools for maximizing resources but a mechanism that produced a sense of national belonging among these groups. Furthermore, close examination of these practices suggests that the type of belonging these fund-raising drives carved for Irish Americans and Jewish Americans was distinctly unequal. Benedict Anderson famously argued that the nation is imagined as a horizontal community.[4] Examination of the practices used to summon members of diaspora communities, however, suggests a radically different imagination of the nation. Instead of a homogeneous social space (even only in one's idealized imagination), the nation is conceived from the get-go as a stratified entity with some groups, who allegedly sacrifice more, in the core of the nation and other groups in the periphery. A moral economy of sacrifice and giving stratifies and gives meanings to membership in the nation.

Comparing the Irish and Zionist homeland-diaspora encounters is particularly interesting, not owing to their similarity. Indeed, the Irish and Jewish homeland-diaspora relations differ in many respects. Many Irish Americans were born and raised in Ireland.[5] Most Jewish Americans, in contrast, had no personal links to Palestine. The settlement experiences of the two communities were different, too. Both communities suffered from negative stereotyping and discrimination on arrival, but in comparison with the Irish, Jewish migrants climbed the socioeconomic ladder faster and by the period examined here (1940s) most occupied middle- or upper-class positions.[6] The religious difference between the communities is obvious. Perhaps more important, the level of institutionalization of the communities was very different. While the Friends of Irish Freedom, the largest Irish American organization of the period, had permanent staff, outside of New York it relied exclusively on haphazardly recruited volunteers. By contrast, the UJA relied on its own field-workers and on professionally staffed Jewish Federations all around the country. Finally, during and after World War I, activists who engaged in diaspora activities in the United States, especially activities directed against Britain, risked being accused of divided loyalties. In contrast, during and after World War II, the attitude toward diasporic activities, especially by Jews, was more permissive.

While these differences were without doubt consequential, the Irish and Jewish national movements faced a similar predicament in their relationships with their compatriots. In both cases, the diaspora organizations had to reach large, diverse, dispersed, and largely unorganized potential donors and persuade them to give their hard-earned money in support of a faraway struggle, with no expectations of return. This similarity provides a basis for an exploration aimed at identifying the sociotechnical mechanisms that are involved in funding the nation in specific diasporic contexts.[7]

Gifting the Nation

Gift giving creates and reinforces social ties and obligations.[8] In Marcel Mauss's famous formulation, the practice of gift giving in "archaic" societies consisted of three obligations: the obligation to give, the obligation to receive, and the obligation to reciprocate a gift. The routine exchange of gifts and countergifts generates solidarity. Gift giving in archaic societies was also strongly associated with identity and social standing. Failure to give, receive, or reciprocate at the appropriate time and place and in the appropriate manner dishonors a person. Successful accomplishment of the gift-giving ritual, in contrast, bestows honor. Marshall Sahlins further shows how this dynamic of giving sometimes creates distinct inequalities and political domination, wherein one party gains unequal political status by outdoing all others in generosity.[9]

Like gift giving, nation building is a process that generates enduring solidarities between members who were previously only loosely associated. Nevertheless, scholars have generally refrained from studying gift giving as a mechanism of nation building. This avoidance, I suspect, is related to the modernity and scale of nation building. Unlike the tribal societies that Mauss studied, modern nations assemble vast numbers of individuals. The normative regulation that animates Mauss's model cannot work in the same way within the nation. Indeed, many scholars of gift giving argue that in modern societies, gift giving becomes largely an interpersonal matter and loses its larger societal role.[10]

Nevertheless, examining the connection between gift giving and nation building may be fruitful. The key reason lies in the way members of the nation themselves make sense of this membership category. Unlike gender or race, which are typically understood (if wrongly) as an ascribed category, members often understand their relations to the nation in active terms, as membership enacted and earned through active participation. This participation is very often conceived in terms of giving. Julie Peteet and Nira Yuval-Davis show how women, and the general public, sometimes see childbearing and mothering as a gift for the nation. Military service is also often conceived of as a gift to the nation that commands gratitude from a multitude of others. In a diaspora context, giving to the nation often takes a monetary form. Nina Bandelj, for instance, shows how actors interpret the decision to invest or not to invest in particular firms as giving to the nation.[11] The rights and obligations associated with membership in the nation are often understood as relationships of giving and receiving. These themes play a central role in the national rhetoric but are also important in the self-understanding of members.

Given the centrality of gift giving to national rhetoric and the self-understanding of members, it may be useful to treat Mauss's model not as a predictive hypothesis but as a sensitizing tool and to examine how nation builders tinker with gift giving in order to mobilize various groups for the national struggle. The focus of such an investigation should not be on just the motivations of actors but on the organizational challenge of giving to the nation.[12] The problems identified earlier—the absence of reciprocity, the lack of normative regulation, and the limited scope of modern gift giving—should not steer research away from these practices but rather orient us toward the challenges that nation builders confront when they use gift-giving practices.

Iddo Tavory's concept of "summoning" provides a useful concept for understanding the relationship between gift giving and nation building. Tavory examines the production of Orthodox Jewish identification in Los Angeles. Instead of assuming that the Orthodox Jewish community has clear boundaries, Tavory notes that the boundaries of this community are extraordinarily porous and examines the practices that draw subjects into membership in the community. The term *summoning* corresponds with Louis Althusser's concept of interpellation.[13] *Interpellation* describes the process through which ideology constitutes the subject by asking it to actively engage with certain prescriptions. Interpellation clarifies that rather than being imposed from the outside, subjects actively participate in their ideological shaping by responding to ideological demands. In the same vein, *summoning* comes to describe the interaction between the actors' self-projects and the situations they find themselves in and in which they are expected to act in certain ways. In the following pages, we will see how national ideological demands for selfless giving are taken up, first by nation builders who organize fund-raising events and then by donors who by responding to the request for monetary donations insert themselves into a nationally coded social interaction and come to understand themselves as members of the nation.

Fund-Raising and the Making of the Irish and Jewish Diasporas

This chapter explores the Irish and Zionist movements' attempts to secure funds in the United States for their respective national struggles. To study how practices of gift giving are implicated in nation building, this chapter takes on a processual organizational approach.[14] Rather than assuming that subjects are always already members of the nation, I focus on the difficulties associated with giving to the nation and analyze the practical solutions nation builders develop in order to streamline the relationships of giving to the nation.

The diasporic setting provides a strategic research site for such an investigation.[15] Unlike giving within nation-states, which is often conflated with the legal demands of a given nation-state, giving to the nation in diasporic settings is entirely voluntary. The ambivalent stance of communities—the fact that regardless of proclaimed affiliation, members of diaspora communities choose to live away from the homeland—accentuates this challenge. Studying how nation builders wrestle with these challenges thus provides an outstanding opportunity to understand giving to the nation, under extreme circumstances.

The chronological starting points of this investigation are the Easter Rising of 1916, in the Irish case, and 1939 and the beginning of the Holocaust, in the Jewish case. These two events mark the beginning of a period of intense mobilization, which provides an excellent opportunity to examine the innovations developed to enroll diaspora communities in the national struggle. I focus specifically on the activities of the Friends of Irish Freedom (FOIF) and its fund-raising arm, the Irish Victory Fund (IVF) and the United Jewish Appeal, the most significant Irish and Jewish fund-raising organizations of the period.

The Irish Victory Fund

The Irish struggle for independence gathered steam during the 1910s, beginning with the fight against conscription to the British army during World War I and on with the Easter Rising and the Sinn Féin victory in the 1918 election. In the United States, the Clan na Gael nationalist fraternity and its public front, the FOIF, also emerged as a dominant force.[16] Between 1917 and early 1919, membership in the FOIF rose from fewer than a thousand to more than thirty thousand members and 204 active branches. The number of Irish Americans affiliated with the FOIF through other Irish societies was much larger.[17]

The FOIF leaders launched the IVF during a large convention in March 1919, hoping to raise $2 million for the Irish struggle. During the convention, delegates from various cities pledged to raise more than $1.5 million. In the following months, Diarmuid Lynch, a veteran of the Easter Rising who fled to the United States and became the secretary of the FOIF, labored to turn these pledges into cash.

To set the tone for the campaign, the FOIF printed millions of leaflets and essays, highlighting the symbiotic nature of Irish and American patriotism and the duty to support Ireland's independence. A special poster featured a drawing of the Sixty-Ninth Regiment, a predominantly Irish American unit that fought fiercely during World War I. The poster listed dates of key battles in American history in which Irish Americans took part. These dates served as a reminder for the poster's key message: "America! Remember what you owe to Ireland."

Another key theme in the IVF campaign was the link between past and present sacrifices. A special leaflet distributed in Philadelphia, for instance, asserted: "[The Easter Rising] martyrs have passed upward to take their place beside that of dauntless champions of freedom—immortal on earth as they are in heaven. They gave their lives for Ireland's freedom. . . . Will we [Philadelphia Irish] raise this amount [$40,000] for democracy, for human happiness . . . for the life of Ireland?"[18] The leaflet summoned readers into a chain of giving,

beginning with the martyrs' ultimate sacrifice, still awaiting a countergift from the readers.

Given the federated structure of the FOIF, the IVF campaign
followed different trajectories, depending on local circumstances. In
Philadelphia and Buffalo, IVF committees worked in close cooperation
with clergy, which allowed activists to easily reach otherwise unaffili-
ated donors. Furthermore, the clergy provided each of the campaign
activists with an identification card that bore the signature of the local
campaign chairman and a priest. Certifying the collectors helped
recruit volunteers and increased public confidence.[19] In New York
City, the campaign advanced through close cooperation with various
Irish Patriotic and Benevolent Associations (P&B Associations).[20] In
addition to soliciting donations from members, the Mayo Men's P&B
Association committed the proceeds of its annual Sunday Picnic to the
IVF.[21] In other instances, fund-raising took a carnivalesque and even
coercive tone, as when Irish firemen in Boston blocked a bridge and
collected "donations" from passerby during a St. Patrick's Day parade.

Collecting the money was half the challenge. Lynch and his associates in the FOIF also had to make sure that the funds collected in
various locales were actually remitted to the FOIF headquarters in
New York. Part of the problem had to do with dishonest organizers
who might keep some or all of the money for themselves. In other
instances, however, the problem was too much enthusiasm on the part
of local activists. Lynch complained, "Devoted workers in the cause,
seeing the pressing need for Irish propaganda—are eager to apply a
portion of the Fund to good work in their communities. But no army
can win by letting the various regiments fight the enemy immediately
in front of them without regard to the situation on the battle-front
as a whole. . . . So it is essential that all collections be made with the
sole purpose of increasing the resources in the hands of the National
Council of the Friends of Irish Freedom."[22] To fight fraud and prevent
leakage of funds, the IVF instructed local activists to create special
finance committees manned by prominent community members.[23]
Lynch also urged IVF committees to print special pledge cards, issue
receipts to contributors, and identify collectors with special badges.[24]

During late 1919, Lynch and his colleagues' efforts began to bear fruit, and the FOIF headquarters received a steady flow of money from Irish communities around the country. By August Lynch reported that the IVF collected more than $1 million. The IVF's success allowed the FOIF to expand its activities. Early in 1919, the FOIF took over the Irish National Bureau in Washington and used it to press the Irish cause on Capitol Hill. Later, it also sent a committee of Irish American dignitaries called the American Commission on Irish Independence to Paris, with the hope of taking part in the post–World War I Peace Conference. The FOIF also sent money to Ireland to help finance an Irish delegation to the Paris Peace Conference. While only modest in size and loosely organized, the IVF collection thus helped catapult the Irish struggle beyond its immediate locale.

The United Jewish Appeal

American Jews have been raising funds on behalf of overseas Jews for decades. Prior to World War II, however, these efforts were typically split between organizations with different ideological leanings and concerns. The American Jewish Joint Distribution Committee (JDC), created during World War I, provided aid to Jewish refugees primarily in Europe but also in the Middle East and North Africa. The United Palestine Appeal (UPA) was controlled by the World Zionist Organization and funneled money to Palestine. The National Refugee Service, on the other hand, focused on helping Jewish refugees in the United States rebuild their lives. In late 1938, hoping to surpass past collections, the three organizations joined forces and launched the United Jewish Appeal.[25]

In order to approach donors in different locales, the UJA recruited a team of field-workers, but the bulk of the effort was entrusted with hundreds of Jewish Federations and Welfare Funds around the country.[26] Well established within their communities, the federations kept part of the collection to fund local needs and sent the rest to the UJA, which distributed the funds among its constituent organizations.[27] Struggles between local federations and the UJA, and between the JDC and the UPA, over the appropriate distribution of the collections were integral to the operation of the UJA.[28] In the early 1940s, given the catastrophe that unfolded in Europe, the JDC appropriated most of the money. After the war, the UPA became the major recipient.[29]

One of the UJA's key challenges was persuading federation leaders to accept challenging campaign quotas. Local activists used the previous year's campaign to calculate how much they would raise in the coming year, but Henry Montor, the executive director of the UJA, wanted to collect more contributions. This difficulty is related to the unreciprocated nature of donations. In gift *exchange*, actors use the previous gift as a guide for determining the size of the countergift, but donors to the UJA campaign received no prior gifts. In order to set a challenging standard of giving, Montor commissioned detailed studies of the needs of Jewish communities worldwide.[30] Perhaps more important, the UJA created a database of Jewish Americans that contained detailed information regarding the size of different Jewish communities and their socioeconomic composition. This community-level information allowed field representatives to compare one community with other similarly composed, but better-performing, communities around the country. By sparking community-level generosity competition, Montor and his associates persuaded local leaders to commit to yearly quotas that were previously considered unrealistic.[31]

To motivate individual donors, the UJA organized stratified generosity competitions at the individual level. Rather than addressing the community as a whole, the UJA created special events for different groups. Big donors were invited to special gala events where the key method was "card calling." At the right moment, after dinner and a few speeches, the campaign chairman would take the podium and call out names from specially prepared cards along with their donations in the previous year. Upon hearing their names, donors would stand up and announce their donations for the coming year. To encourage large donations, the organizers contacted a few donors ahead of time and secured their donations for the coming year. The startling generosity of the first givers forced others to follow suit.[32] By carefully engineering the pitch, the UJA increased the visibility of giving and ignited intense generosity competition among donors.

In large communities, intermediate donors were approached through small parlor meetings that were assembled along professional lines. The UJA's 1950 campaign in Boston, for instance, included more than one hundred luncheons and dinners, including special dinners for donors in the poultry industry, men's wear, women's underwear, and more.[33] These divisions created socially meaningful groups, where generosity competitions among peers were especially intense.

To approach small donors, the vast majority of the population, the UJA organized door-to-door canvassing campaigns. Montor noted that the sums collected in these campaigns were almost offset by the costs of collection, but it helped set the tone for the entire community and created a sense of shared responsibility.[34]

In the early 1940s, the calamity in Europe dominated the UJA's campaign. Trying to avoid despair, the UJA designed an emotionally charged message that addressed donors as potential lifesavers. A typical ad highlighted the effectiveness of giving and the responsibilities of American Jews:

> It costs six cents a day to feed a Jewish child in Poland. If six cents means the preservation of a life, that is surely little enough, but it's six cents for one meal, for one day, for one child. The days of want go on and the ranks of the hungry multiply. . . . Think of it, your contribution can keep scores, and, perhaps hundreds of children alive until this nightmare of cruelty is brought to an end. We have the responsibility; we have the power of life and death over these tragedy-ridden human beings.[35]

Toward the end of the 1940s, the campaigns focused on Palestine. These campaigns continued to emphasize the responsibility of American Jews, but they did so by comparing the sacrifices demanded from different Jews. A leaflet of the 1948 campaign of Greater New York, for example, asked readers: "How much does he give?" The inside of the leaflet explained:

> "He" is an Israeli, any Israeli. Chances are he earns between $100 and $125 a month for himself and his family to live on.

† He pays the highest taxes in the world, twice as much as we do.

† He gives his savings, wedding rings, prize possessions to raise extra funds for defense and housing. . . .

† He risks his life daily, working in the fields under enemy gun-sights or guarding a lonely settlement at night.

† He can't give much, but he gives big![36]

Instead of arguing "We are one," the UJA campaign in fact highlighted the differences between the life conditions of American Jews and the experiences of an abstract "Israeli," highlighting the exceptional sacrifices that Israeli Jews embrace.

Translating pledges into cash presented another challenge. To increase generosity, the UJA agreed to accept donations in installments, but doing so complicated collections. For this purpose, local committees were instructed to create pledge-collection committees that would remind donors, first in a letter and then, if necessary, by a personal visit. Furthermore, in the 1942 season, Montor insisted that donors who failed to pay their previous year's donation in full would not be allowed to make a new pledge. The implementation of this strategy and its success varied, but in some instances the combination of prompt reminders and a threat of exclusion from future events reduced the shrinkage rate—that is, the difference between the pledged amount and the actual sum collected—to merely 1.5 percent.[37]

As in the Irish case, making sure that donations actually were sent to the UJA headquarters was a particularly delicate challenge. Every year Montor and his colleagues had to negotiate with multiple local federations and haggle over the precise sums that would be kept for local needs. Montor insisted that the money was donated, by and large, to support Jews across the ocean. Local leaders were also concerned with the needs of their local communities. In some cases, local communities insisted on keeping reserve funds for unanticipated needs or to compensate for unredeemed pledges or unanticipated campaign expenses. To struggle against this division, Montor instructed field-workers to carefully inspect the campaign books and to stay in the community until the campaign funds were deposited in the UJA coffers.[38]

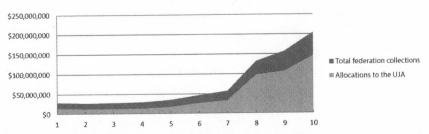

Total federation collections and allocations to the United Jewish Appeal, 1939–48.

The UJA's strenuous efforts bore fruit. During the 1940s, Jewish philanthropy grew from a modest and largely decentralized project into a central preoccupation of American Jewry. Alongside an increase in the number of Jewish households that donated, the UJA saw a tenfold increase in its collections (see diagram). In 1939 the UJA collections totaled a little more than $14.5 million. In 1948 the UJA collections exceeded $146 million. This dramatic increase allowed the UJA to provide substantial assistance to hundreds of thousands of Jewish refugees in Europe and later to take a leading role in the absorption of immigrants from all over the world in Israel.

Irish and Jewish Diaspora Fund-Raising

Placing the Irish and Jewish fund-raising campaigns side by side provides a striking illustration of the differences between the two projects but also highlights important similarities. In important respects, the two projects were of entirely different scale. The Irish American community, while displaying enthusiastic commitment, relied on loosely coordinated societies that operated almost entirely on a voluntary basis. As a result, the IVF was to a large extent a campaign created ad hoc in different localities. The problem was not that the Irish American community lacked an organizational basis. Irish Catholic parishes and the Irish Patriotic and Benevolent Associations served as the backbones of the community. However, many of these organizations did not support Irish nationalism and remained only partially involved with the IVF. In contrast, Jewish communities around the country, even prior to the establishment of the UJA, created a highly professionalized system of Jewish Federations and Welfare Funds. These federations, and the UJA, were not necessarily Zionist, but they were primarily concerned with general Jewish humanitarian issues. Nevertheless, the existence of this communal bureaucratic infrastructure provided the UJA with a convenient base for summoning local communities into engagement with Jewish supralocal projects.

The difference between the Irish and Jewish organizational infrastructure was particularly important owing to the nonreciprocal nature of diaspora gift giving. In gift exchange, of the Maussian model or the modern interpersonal variant, the size of gifts is linked to the previous gift, as practitioners try to maintain a balance and match the previous gift when they reciprocate. In the absence of reciprocity, however, the Irish and Jewish organizers had to find a way to set the standards for appropriate giving. Knowledge of the pool of potential givers is crucially important for this task. It allows organizers to not only pick challenging pacemakers but also stratify givers so that the pacemakers will be considered relevant. The differences between the cases here are dramatic. Lynch and his associates in the FOIF regularly claimed to be speaking on behalf of "Irish America," but in practice they had only a general understanding of where Irish Americans lived, their attitudes, how much they earned, and how much money they could potentially spare for Ireland. The UJA, in contrast, was able to use existing information and its field-workers to create a database that contained detailed demographic portraits of different communities and, perhaps even more important, lists of important donors and their past donations. This information allowed the UJA to tailor its campaigns to different subgroups in the community and to provide each subgroup with a challenging gift-giving standard.

Mauss describes how gift giving is related to social status. In this framework, the giving of a gift creates a debt. Failing to reciprocate dishonors the original recipient. Proper reciprocation, in contrast, honors givers. Sahlins shows how this dynamic sometimes generates generosity competitions. In the cases of the IVF and the UJA, however, gifts were unidirectional almost by definition. Thus, in order to create an obligation to give without the promise of reciprocity, the IVF and the UJA sought to ignite status competition *among givers*. Instead of trying to secure a countergift from recipients or humiliate recipients into submission, the leaders of the IVF and the UJA used the immediate context of fund-raising to encourage giving. Lynch, for instance, regularly listed in the *Gaelic American* the names of big donors, activists, and successful organizers. The trick was to try to dramatically increase the visibility of giving so as to encourage giving. Montor and his colleagues also publicized big gifts so as to honor givers, but by stratifying fund-raising events by gift size, the UJA was able to intensify competition by ensuring that donors competed against similarly endowed donors and that the honors associated with giving resonated with the relevant social circles.

The differences between the Irish and Jewish fund-raising campaigns manifested themselves in the amounts raised. In 1919 the IVF raised a total of $1,005,080. In comparison, in 1946 alone the UJA raised more than $100 million. Even controlling for class differences and inflation, these differences are dramatic. Focusing on monetary value alone, however, is a mistake. Aside from being an instrumental venue for transferring resources, the IVF and the UJA served as a key way through which Irish Americans and Jewish Americans related to their compatriots across the ocean.[39] It is therefore important to understand how the IVF and UJA shaped Irish American and Jewish American belonging, respectively. In other words, it is important to understand how these fund-raising projects summoned Irish Americans and Jewish Americans into their respective nations.

Both the IVF and the UJA campaigns took place in the context of dramatic historical events. It is tempting, therefore, to suggest that these projects were simply responses to events across the ocean—the anti-British rebellion in Ireland and the Holocaust and later the establishment of the State of Israel. This presumption is undoubtedly true. However, such a perspective radically overlooks the roles of the IVF and the UJA in shaping the meaning of these events and in offering a model response to them. The Irish rebellion and the Holocaust were conveyed to Irish Americans and Jewish Americans through newspaper reports and other media, but it was largely the IVF and the UJA that turned these events into a call for specific kind of action.

The Easter Rising could have been interpreted as a folly, a quixotic fantasy, or a dangerous expression of separatism in the midst of a decisive war. Indeed, the Easter Rising was presented this way in most mainstream newspapers in the United States. It was the FOIF and the IVF, to no little extent, that construed it as a gallant national rebellion that was in line with American ideals. Furthermore, Irish Americans in general supported the Irish Republicans, but even then many organizations believed that the proper Irish American response was trying to influence American public opinion and advocacy in Washington, not necessarily funding the fight in Ireland. Similarly, the initial Jewish American response to the terrifying news from Europe was despair. It was largely the UJA efforts that turned the news into a call for *monetary* action, which was the dominant Jewish American response (other than enlisting to the US Army, of course).[40] More than merely responding to historical events, the IVF and to an even greater extent the UJA shaped the meaning of the Irish rebellion and the Holocaust to their respective audiences and curated their responses to these events.

More to the point, the IVF and the UJA provided crucial institutional scaffolding that allowed Irish Americans and Jewish Americans to engage in meaningful action and to visualize their belonging in supralocal terms. Irish Americans were surely familiar with the term, but during the first decades of the twentieth century much of their everyday life was organized around different membership categories. At work and during much of their leisure time, they were something else altogether—workers, parents, parishioners, and so on. Even their seemingly "Irish" engagements were often organized on a subnational basis. P&B Associations and the playing of Gaelic games were organized on the basis of county of origin, and the animosities between different counties were sometime pronounced.[41] Similarly, Jewish American everyday life was largely unmarked in terms of nationality, and even their religious and communal everyday life was decidedly local, organized around local synagogues or other local organizations.

Through the IVF and UJA events, the nation as a relevant social category—one that commands affiliation and sacrifice—came to life. In
and through fund-raising events, the Irish or Jewish nation became
something for and in which Irish Americans and Jewish Americans
took responsibility and pride. In other words, the IVF and the UJA
summoned members of these respective diaspora communities into
meaningful membership in the nation.

A closer look at how the IVF and UJA addressed their donors
makes my argument about summoning clearer. "What will you give
to the work of Easter week? Will the Hibernians of Philadelphia contribute $40,000 to make the dream of Easter week come true?" the
Gaelic American challenged.[42] Similarly, the UJA's publicity manual of
1940 explicitly coached speakers to present the campaign as a "test"
for the community. To the extent that these challenges were meaningful, giving to the IVF and the UJA served as proof—to oneself and for
others—of membership in the nation. Rogers Brubaker suggests that
we think of ethnicity and nationalism not as a thing but as a mode of
cognition—as ways of interpreting events and making sense of one's
position in the world.[43] Viewed from this perspective, the IVF and
the UJA brought Irish Americans and Jewish Americans into tangible
engagement with the nation—one that they and others could see—
and thus provided the framework for making sense of their position
in the nation.

It is also vitally important that we examine the specific kind of
membership that the IVF's and UJA's summonings produced. First,
the IVF and the UJA summoned Irish Americans and Jewish Americans as members of diaspora communities. To spark generous giving,
the UJA and IVF (to a lesser extent) organized generosity competitions *among givers*. While the IVF and the UJA referred to Irish and
Jews across the ocean, the relationships with these compatriots were
almost entirely "imagined," in the sense that participation in fund-
raising events required no actual encounter with those compatriots.
One only needed to conjure their sufferings in one's imagination.[44] At
the same time, the structure and dynamics of fund-raising made the
immediate American diaspora community superpresent and relevant.

It was other Irish Americans and other Jewish Americans who participated in intercommunal and individual generosity competitions. Paradoxically, therefore, the absence of reciprocity left the recipients of these drives out of the picture. In this sense, the IVF and UJA drives served as mechanisms of "diaspora building" perhaps even more than nation building.[45]

In another important respect, however, the recipients of the IVF and UJA drives were never out of the picture. Both campaigns repeatedly compared the sacrifices demanded from Irish and Jewish Americans with the sufferings willingly embraced by or imposed on their compatriots across the ocean. The IVF, for instance, wrote, "In Easter Week (1916) a handful of heroes threw their precious lives onto the scale of Irish freedom. . . . Then the heart of the race beat high, the ancient spirit was seen to be unbroken, the blood of the people still a blood of warriors. . . . [W]hat would you give to the work of Easter week?"[46] The use of *scale* in this ad is telling, because the IVF literally urged readers to measure their sacrifice against the losses of the Easter Rising martyrs. The UJA used similar comparisons to motivate giving:

> [In the United States] . . . nobody shoots at us. There is no barbed wire coiled and glinting in our streets. We sleep without the abrupt staccato of a Sten gun shattering the night's stillness. Our busses are not armored, and we can travel from Newark to Philly or from Frisco to L.A. without death lurking behind every tree. Five, six thousand miles away from the bullets in Jerusalem . . . from the lonely boy with his rifle under the pale moon. . . . Yes, but we are together. . . . The whole building, fighting, frontline Yishuv is counting on us. Sure, we carry newspapers to work instead of grenades. Sure we never feel the sickening thud of a bullet. But we've got a frontline, and we cannot desert it or go AWOL for a minute for it's the one and the only way we can fight and build side by side with them.[47]

While the life circumstances of the two exemplary Jews in this ad are radically different, a thread of giving links them tenuously together.

To an extent, stressing the difference in the sacrifices demanded from compatriots across the ocean was just a clever means to extract additional funds. However, the gap between these two ways of giving can never be closed. Money can be accumulated and then given away without radically affecting the giver. Life, in contrast, is radically inalienable. No matter how much money one gives, this type of sacrifice will forever pale in comparison to the contribution of the national martyr or even the potential martyr (that lonely boy with the rifle). Thus, the IVF and the UJA summoned Irish Americans and Jewish Americans into a complex relationship with their respective compatriots. While the IVF and UJA summoned Irish and Jewish Americans to the nation and helped render membership in the nation relevant and meaningful, the membership positions they carved were unequal and attenuated.

Discussions on nation building, in diasporic contexts and elsewhere, typically highlight the unifying credo of national ideologies. Benedict Anderson famously argued that "regardless of the actual inequality and exploitation that may prevail in each, the nation is always conceived as a deep, *horizontal comradeship*. Ultimately it is this fraternity that makes it possible, over the past two centuries, for so many millions of people, not so much to kill, as willingly to die for such limited imaginings."[48] But the IVF and UJA campaign did not ask potential donors to imagine their membership as a horizontal comradeship of equals and did not blur the differences between various members of the nation. Rather, summoning Irish Americans and Jewish Americans into the nation rested on a concomitant drawing and blurring of boundaries within the nation.

In the ads above, the IVF and the UJA drew sharp distinctions between members in the nation in the homeland, who sacrificed or showed willingness to sacrifice blood, and members in the diaspora, who were merely required to part with their money, and in the very same paragraph folded those differences and emphasized shared obligations.

The imbalance between the two ways of giving for the nation creates a moral debt that, on the one hand, aids the instrumental task of fund-raising and, on the other, generates two unequal memberships in the nation. Whereas Anderson and many others acknowledge the existence of objective inequalities, they were fascinated by the alleged absence of such inequalities in the realm of idealized imagination of the member. In the quote above, Anderson further argues that the egalitarian nature of the national imagination is the inspiration for the incredible sacrifices that the nation successfully commands. But the cases examined here suggest that the nation in the first place is not really imagined as an egalitarian space, not even in the ideal sense. Rather, it is imagined as an onion-like entity, where different groups are positioned closer or further from an imaginary core on the basis of the sacrifices they endure or are willing to endure. A delicate balance between being alike and being different and less of a member was essential for the operation of the IVF and the UJA and for the nation-building processes they ushered.

The double movement I describe above, of concomitantly marking and blurring the differences between different groups, is not reserved for diasporic settings. At roughly the same time that the IVF and UJA campaigns unfolded in the United States, the Irish and Zionist national movements launched ambitious fund-raising campaigns in Ireland and Palestine. Uri Ben-Eliezer, for instance, describes how the Israeli Jewish public was induced to donate money for the purchase of arms in the early 1950s. To promote generosity, the organizers of Keren Hamagen (literally "Defender Fund") published the military's shopping list in the newspapers, complete with the price of each item. Lydia Benlulu, a mother of ten, decided to give back the gift of the hundred pounds she received earlier as a childbearing prize (1995). In Ireland, in 1919, the republican provisional government sold bonds in order to fund the struggle for independence. To inspire giving, the Irish republicans produced a short silent film in which national dignitaries, mostly mothers and widows of Easter Rising martyrs, lined up to purchase the bonds. As a desk, Michael Collins, then the minister of defense of the Dáil Éireann, employed the wooden block used to behead Robert Emmet, another republican martyr. The renowned bishop of Killaloe Michael Fogarty in a letter urged viewers to "give proof of the faith that is in us, we must not . . . fall behind our great American friends, it will be a shame to do so."[49]

While the contexts of these two national campaigns are radically different from the circumstances in the United States during the IVF and UJA drives, the rhetoric and underlying mechanism of summation are strikingly similar. In both cases, the great past or future sacrifice of a certain group (martyrs or potential martyrs) serves to prompt others to do their share. A stratified economy of gift and sacrifice, not identical but similar to the one ushered by the IVF and the UJA across the ocean, plays a role in the emerging national struggle.

IO

The Discourses of Irish Jewish Studies

Bernard Shaw, Max Nordau,
and Evocations of the Cosmopolitan

STEPHEN WATT

In the spring of 1895, George Bernard Shaw was enjoying a holiday at Beachy Head, near Eastbourne, gazing at the water from what are advertised as Britain's "highest chalk cliffs" and attempting to ride a bicycle for the first time in his life (or so he claimed). These leisurely pursuits were interrupted by a letter from Benjamin Tucker, editor of the American magazine *Liberty*, asking that he review Dr. Max Nordau's book *Degeneration* (1892), which by that time had been translated from the German and garnered a large readership in both Britain and the United States. Tucker sweetened his request by asking the novice cyclist to undertake a minor investigative chore: "I invite you, Shaw, to ascertain the highest price that has ever been paid to any man, even to Gladstone, for a magazine article; and I will pay you that price for a review of *Degeneration*."[1] Declaring this proof of "really great editing" on Tucker's part—and providing evidence for Declan Kiberd's assertion that Shaw "wrote mainly for money and earned lots"[2]—Shaw agreed, eventually damning the book as "manifest nonsense" in his letter-review "A Degenerate's View of Nordau," published in *Liberty* later that July. As a result, Shaw proclaimed, the *Degeneration* "boom" was now totally "exhausted," and Nordau would "never be heard from again," save for the fact that Shaw's review was reprinted in a later pamphlet series, requiring revision, a new title, and a preface (*MCE*

286). At least in this regard, Nordau and his screed against fin de siècle culture *were* "heard from again" in "The Sanity of Art," as Shaw's essay was retitled in 1908, and again in 1930 for the collected edition of his writing that included the lacerating subtitle "An Exposure of the Current Nonsense about Artists Being Degenerate."

Shaw's prediction of Nordau's imminent obscurity was hardly accurate, as over the next two decades he continued to write and speak publicly, especially on Zionism, famously advocating for a "Muscular Judaism" at the Second Zionist Congress in 1898 in part to counteract antisemitic denigrations of Jewish men as physically inferior.[3] Yet there are issues larger than Shavian hyperbole and masculinity to consider in both Nordau's attack on fin de siècle culture and Shaw's evisceration of it. Some, in fact, surface in the preface to "The Sanity of Art" and pertain directly to one project central to Irish Jewish studies, namely, the study of cultural constructions within which ethnic identity is formed and, in some cases, the terms by which identities might be juxtaposed or serve as substitutions for or as twins of the other to perform specific cultural work. In particular, I want to scrutinize Shaw's use of the term *cosmopolitan* both in introducing "The Sanity of Art" and in developing its critique of *Degeneration*, for both *cosmopolitan* and a larger sense of *cosmopolitanism*, terms that have gained theoretical traction recently in Irish studies and advanced discussions of Irish modernism in particular, look considerably different from the vantage point afforded by Irish Jewish studies.

Such a critical unsettling is hardly a unique project but is central to the evolution of most critical and interpretive discourses, and such is the case with the multidisciplinary thrust of the emergent discursive category called Irish Jewish studies. As Paul Bové reminds us when briefly looking back at the interpretive primacy of the so-called American New Criticism of the 1940s–1960s, "discourse" then functioned to "organize an entire field of knowledge," eventually becoming widely institutionalized and then naturalized to the point that, for a time, its effects were "not noticed" and its operations so removed from critical view that they remained unchallenged.[4] A certain irony inheres in this trajectory, as discourse as construed by poststructuralist thought is a material practice that aims to examine and trace critically the histories that interpretive monoliths like the New Criticism tend to obscure once their dominance in the academy has been firmly established. The various interests of contributors to this volume confirm the multidisciplinary bristle of a nascent Irish Jewish studies as exegeses of representations of Jews and Jewishness in nineteenth-century Irish literature are anthologized alongside essays that examine refugee factories in the protectionist Ireland of the 1930s, antisemitic representations of Jews in the Irish press and elsewhere, Jewish Dublin and the rise of Zionism, and myriad other historical, literary, and economic topics. Irish Jewish studies, if such a project can be said to exist at all, does so through the cumulative intellectual work of historians, literary critics, performance theorists, sociologists, demographers, and scholars from a wide range of disciplines. As a result, Irish Jewish studies not only engages a diverse range of objects of study in Ireland and Northern Ireland—literary texts, dramatic performances, and other cultural artifacts; specific histories, immigration patterns, and much more—but is also attentive to matters of a more global nature: the diasporic communities of North America, Australia, and England, for example, and the always vexed imperatives new arrivals face to assimilate into new cultures, to retain some sense of an antecedent cultural identity, and to interact with each other. And, as in the specific juxtaposition of the Great Famine with the Holocaust, one of many recent and direct comparisons of the experiences of Irish and Jewish people,[5] Irish Jewish studies may have nearly as much to say about European histories as it does about the histories of Ireland and Northern Ireland. At base, then, as its name suggests, Irish Jewish studies endorses the proposition that, for scholars committed to area and ethnic studies or to the study of nationhood and nation building, there is much to gain by working together and much to lose by locating intellectual work narrowly within institutional or disciplinary silos.

The past decade has witnessed the potential of this commitment in such books as Michael Rothberg's *Multidirectional Memory: Remembering the Holocaust in the Age of Decolonization* (2009), George Bornstein's

The Colors of Zion: Blacks, Jews, and Irish from 1845 to 1945 (2011), M. Alison Kibler's *Censoring Racial Ridicule: Irish, Jewish, and African-American Struggles over Race and Representation, 1890–1930* (2015), and, I hope, by my own *"Something Dreadful and Grand": American Literature and the Irish-Jewish Unconscious* (2015). However different these texts are, the last three in particular rely on premises foundational to most examples of Irish Jewish studies. One is a focus on representational "interchangeabilty" or substitution—what performance studies scholar Joseph Roach has theorized as the process of surrogation[6]— where one ethnicity stands in for another in performing putatively "essential" ethnic, racial, or religious qualities. Moreover, Roach's emphasis of the primacy of a "circum-Atlantic" world as opposed to a "transatlantic" one might be modified to benefit Irish Jewish studies. For Roach, the notion of a circum-Atlantic "insists on the centrality of the diasporic and genocidal histories of Africa and the Americas, North and South, in the culture of modernity." Focused primarily on the Americas, he understandably elevates the Caribbean as the center of intercultural exchange and finds in performance the "memory of otherwise forgotten substitutions" that help define American modernity. Revising this perspective slightly, I have suggested that, insofar as Irish Jewish studies are concerned, a circum–*North* Atlantic has existed with particular vitality from the mid-nineteenth century through the present in which a continuous circulation of peoples, cultural forms, and traditions contributed to both Irish and American modernity.[7] And often these forms collided—or were more purposefully conflated—to communicate a message about two or more groups at the same time or in a single text or image.

So, for example, in the "Cyclops" episode of James Joyce's *Ulysses*, when a man sings "If the Man in the Moon Was a Jew, Jew, Jew," Bornstein astutely hears echoes of the ragtime tune "If the Man in the Moon Were a Coon, Coon, Coon." The cultural products of and allusions to multiethnic America resonate across Joyce's Dublin, and with these references come the substitution of one ethnic group for another that underlies Bornstein's reading. The same process of exchange is evident when an apelike Irish peasant perches opposite a grinning black figure in a straw hat on the opposing trays of a scale in a cartoon from an 1876 issue of *Harper's Weekly* with the caption "The Ignorant Vote—Honors Are Easy." The thesis of the unflattering caricature seems clear: because both are equally ignorant, their franchise could be similarly unfortunate to, even corrosive of, American democracy. To be fair, such substitutions, albeit often exploited to advance invidious stereotypes of racial and ethnic otherness, at times performed positive cultural work as well: in nineteenth-century melodrama, for instance, in which Irish and Jewish characters played roles as virtuous heroines or brave defenders of the helpless or imperiled. By midcentury, this practice had become so common on the London stage that it could be parodied, as Henry J. Byron did in *Ivanhoe-An Extravaganza* (1862). By the play's sensational climax, Byron's version of Walter Scott's Rebecca, perhaps the most famous Jewish character of the century in British writing, is referred to as "Kathleen Kavanagh, Eily O'Connor, whichever you like," the former the heroine of Edmund Falconer's popular and contemporary *Peep o' Day* (1862), the latter the heroine of Dion Boucicault's influential Irish drama *The Colleen Bawn* (1860).[8]

In my relating these examples, I must admit to my repetition of a shortcoming of some Irish Jewish studies by ignoring Alison Kibler's admonition that Irish, Jewish, and African American groups are rarely "monolithic or unified"; on the contrary, gender and class affiliation differentiate all of these communities.[9] Much the same might be said, as Shaw's allusion to Nordau as a "remarkable cosmopolitan Jew" in the preface of "The Sanity of Art" confirms, about uses of the adjective *cosmopolitan*, which connotes an impossibly wide variety of characteristics, not all of them flattering or creditable. In the service of identifying discourses such as surrogation that might be useful to Irish Jewish studies, however, I believe Shaw's description of Nordau as "one of those remarkable cosmopolitan Jews who go forth against modern civilization as David went against the Philistines" is worthy of our attention (284). Admittedly, the phrase *remarkable cosmopolitan Jews* might not seem, well, very remarkable, yet the terms *cosmopolitan* and *Jew* reappear in Shaw's preface in ways that suggest how Irish Jewish studies might engage theories of cosmopolitanism, which has already energized Irish studies for some time now, and assess how these theories at times reveal an implicit or unintentional antisemitism.

In the preface to "The Sanity of Art," as I have mentioned, Shaw alludes to Nordau as both a Jew and a cosmopolitan. Early in the preface, Shaw hypothesizes that readers shocked by Nordau's denunciation of Dante Gabriel Rossetti, Richard Wagner, and Henrik Ibsen might have felt that they lacked the experience of a "sufficient variety of culture to contradict the cosmopolitan doctor" (285), hinting at a common connotation of *cosmopolitan* as signifying a sophistication wrought from extensive travel and the cultural opportunities it can afford. It is difficult *not* to infer from Shaw's invocation of the term, in other words, a profound sense of privilege; as Bruce Robbins reminds us, the first entry under *cosmopolitan* in the *Oxford English Dictionary* is John Stuart Mill's linking of the term to capital: "'Capital,' Mill wrote in 1848, 'is becoming more and more cosmopolitan.'" Both capital and cosmopolitanism, Robbins explains, know no boundaries,[10] ideas that are embedded today in such commonly heard, hackneyed expressions as *globe-trotting* and *jet-setting*. So, while Shaw's characterization of Nordau as a David fighting an uphill battle against cultural Philistines seems if not heroic, at least complimentary, the figure of the well-traveled "cosmopolitan doctor" implies the opposite: privilege, money, and the power that accrue from both. But the matter is muddled even further by Shaw's claims that he is both "familiar with all the arts, and as accustomed as any Jew with the revolutionary cosmopolitan climate" (*MCE* 285). Ironies abound here. Paramount among them are Shaw's identification with Jewishness and the cosmopolitan and his almost visceral disgust with Nordau's writerly success (his "cheapest of victories"); moreover, Shaw's collapsing of *revolutionary* and *cosmopolitan* in his description of Nordau creates a kind of paradoxical turbidity that may, in the end, prove useful.

To underscore the considerable irony of this last point, in *Degeneration* Nordau advocates fiercely for tradition, convention, and orthodoxy, hardly desiderata of an aesthetic or any other revolution and certainly not qualities Nordau found in Richard Wagner, someone Shaw admired greatly. For Nordau, too much contemporary culture, like the term *fin de siècle* itself, reveals a "practical emancipation from traditional discipline," leading inexorably to an "unbridled lewdness, the unchaining of the beast in man."[11] Sounding as much like an opponent of deconstruction in the 1970s and 1980s as a puritan startled by the existence and representation of human sexuality, he also deplored what he regarded as the emergence of an incipient intellectual relativism: "Over the earth the shadows creep with deepening gloom . . . in which all certainty is destroyed and any guess seems plausible" (6). For Nordau, Wagner best exemplifies the flight from convention and cultural decline that define the end of the century, as he "is in himself alone charged with a greater abundance of degeneration than all the degenerates put together with whom we have hitherto become acquainted" (171). From these allegations, it seems, others inevitably follow. Wagner's "furious anti-Semitism," Nordau charges, fueled his persecution mania that Jews blocked attempted productions of his operas, which themselves were the product of a "graphomania" that transgressed the most "firmly-established limits" of the "artistic domain" (or genre) to which it belonged (198). Plagued by an "aesthetic delirium," possessed of an "anarchistic acerbity" (180), and given to a "shameless sensuality" in his work (181), Wagner can "do nothing with life" itself. Being both "blind and deaf to it," he can only copy "exciting sketches" and achieve little more—or so Nordau asserts (192).

Shaw, of course, held an entirely different view of Wagner and his *Ring*, as he outlines in "The Perfect Wagnerite" (1898). Shaw's Wagner, a "revolutionist" intimately connected with the society in which he lived, is no "mere musical epicure and political mugwump." Bravely, Shaw asserts, Wagner sided in 1849 with the "right and the poor against the rich and the wrong" at the cost of his own financial ruination (*MCE* 187). And several of his works, *The Rhine Gold* especially, allegorize an analogous politics by exposing the effects of gold's unbridled power to enslave workers, "lashed to their work by the invisible whip of starvation" (*MCE* 173). Wagner's music, moreover, "single and simple," was equally radical in leaving the "adept musician of the old school" bewildered, as *The Ring* contains "not a single bar of classical music" in it (*MCE* 168). Thus, if Nordau *is* a cosmopolitan steeped in a "revolutionary climate," his indictment of Wagner is in some senses both parochial and anticosmopolitan in its privileging of tradition over innovation. By contrast, Shaw valorizes Wagner's emancipation from "devastating tradition" and the "pernicious results" to which they often lead, which is a necessary escape, not a sign that he exhibits "persecution mania," megalomania, mysticism, morbidity, "incoherence," "fugitive ideation," or other deviances found in Nordau's damning and protracted analysis (171).

Shaw's deployments of *cosmopolitan* are thus both complicated and unique. In Irish studies, conversely, *cosmopolitan* typically connotes universality and international affiliation as opposed to national identification, or it calls attention to Ireland's colonial history, hence Irish hybridity. Nels Pearson describes the former resonances in the opening paragraphs of *Irish Cosmopolitanism* (2015) when he acknowledges the paradoxical quality of the phrase *Irish cosmopolitan*: "After all," he asks, "if a 'cosmopolitan' is one who pledges allegiance to humanity at large, rather than to a specific national or ethnic collective, then what is the need, or rationale, for designating an Irish Cosmopolitanism?"[12] A number of answers to this question have presented themselves, as Irish studies has invested seriously in cosmopolitanism and realized rich interpretive dividends. For Joseph Valente, the notion of Irish cosmopolitanism is rooted in colonialism, with the result that "any discourse of native resistance" to colonial hegemony is itself "internally fissured" and "hybridistic"; in other words, the "subaltern identity" of Irishness is "inevitably coinvolved at some point with the idiom of the oppressor." For Rebecca Walkowitz, writing about international modernism, James Joyce does not so much demonstrate these characteristics as cultivate a cosmopolitan "posture" marked by an "insubordinate attention" to the details of narratives, the effect of which is to value "Irish traditions without seeking to codify or sentimentalize them" and to embrace "the impropriety of art as a strategy of social transformation." Somewhat like Shaw's Wagner, Walkowitz's cosmopolitan Joyce emblematized by Stephen Dedalus "chooses intellectual freedom over social conformity by allowing his mind to wander," while Valente's "cosmopolitan sublime" defines not a "view from nowhere" but a "mobile decentered view" enabled by location in a "metropolitan colony" where the "hierarchical and agonistic interdependency of any given identity" might be encapsulated."[13] When speaking of Irish subjectivity, then, cosmopolitanism troubles notions of native authenticity and essentiality; when speaking of an Irish literary modernism, the cosmopolitan conveys senses of experimentation, irreverence, subversion, and the multiple but finally unsatisfactory national belongings of a character like Stephen Dedalus or a writer like Samuel Beckett.

But to return to Shaw's review of *Degeneration*, what is a "cosmopolitan Jew," and what does Shaw convey both by using the term and by repeating variations of it? Or, following the principle of surrogation, can an Irish cosmopolitan like Joyce substitute for a cosmopolitan Jew like Nordau? And what about Shaw himself—is he a kind of cosmopolitan Jew as well? This last question is only partly facetious. Recall that in his epistolary skirmish with Lawrence Langner over the representation of a character called simply the Jew in his controversial 1936 play *Geneva*, Shaw called Langner "the most thoughtless of Sheenies," to which Langner, founder of New York's Theatre Guild and producer of some fourteen of Shaw's plays between 1920 and 1935, responded with a double rejoinder. In September 1938, he claimed, "If I really am one of the most 'thoughtless of Sheenies,' then you are one of the most inconsistent of Micks," and then in a letter a few weeks later, alluding to the shipwreck of Spanish fleets centuries earlier when surviving sailors of Jewish extraction took residence on the west coast of Ireland, he suggested that Shaw might very well be Jewish himself, declaring "Yes, G.B.S. the truth will out. You too are a Sheeny."[14]

This puckish suggestion aside, surely Shaw was more cosmopolitan than Irish, and he was hardly a nationalist; in fact, he inveighed often against nationalism in general and Fenianism in particular. In his "Preface for Politicians" preceding *John Bull's Other Island* (1907), he denigrates nationalism as a "curse" and adds, "Nobody in Ireland of any intelligence likes Nationalism any more than a man with a broken arm likes having it set." Yet, he argued, many Irishmen could think of nothing else, because England had "broken" Ireland's "nationality," and it would "think of nothing else but getting it set again."[15] Somewhat more acerbically, and oddly given the lexicon of psychological terminology in *Degeneration* that Shaw derided, he regarded the patriotism often conjoined with an aggressive nationalism as a "morbid condition which a healthy man must shake off if he is to keep sane." And Fenianism provided Shaw with a prime example. In his magisterial novel *Strumpet City* (1969), which represents the Larkinite labor strikes leading to the tragic Lockout of 1913 that devastated Dublin, James Plunkett includes an amusing aside on this very point when a character reports hearing Shaw speak and answer a question from the audience about Sinn Féin with comic dismissiveness: "I have met only one Sinn Feiner since I returned to Dublin," Shaw is reported to have said. "She is a very nice girl." Shaw regarded his own identity, in fact, as far closer to that of a cosmopolitan than an Irishman and said so in 1921: "I am a tolerably good European in the Nietzschean sense, but a very bad Irishman in the Sinn Fein or Chosen People sense."[16] (In this articulation, is Shaw again betraying the power of surrogation by joining Irish nationalism with a Judaical sense of a "Chosen People"?)

Such a self-identification partially explains Shaw's observation, mentioned earlier, that "being familiar with all the arts," he was "as accustomed as any Jew to the revolutionary cosmopolitan climate" (*MCE* 285), thereby hinting at an Irish Jewishness Shaw negotiated for much of his career. In other words, several layers of complexity, even contradiction, haunt Shaw's allusions to cosmopolitan Jews in both his preface to and text of "The Sanity of Art." Recall, for example, that he charged cosmopolitan Jews with waging a war on modernity, yet he associates the cosmopolitan Jew with life in a "revolutionary" climate, something closer to the subversive innovations Walkowitz finds in Joyce and Nordau despised in such artists as Wagner and Ibsen. To be fair to Nordau, his complaint about Ibsen is quite different from his objection to Wagner, for his criticism of such plays as *Hedda Gabler* and *Ghosts* has more to do with Ibsen's reputation as a "model of realism" than with ideas about widespread cultural decline at that "dusk of nations" known as the fin de siècle. "As a matter of fact," Nordau complains, "since Alexandre Dumas père, author of *The Three Musketeers* and *The Count of Monte Cristo*, no writer has heaped up in his works so many improbabilities as Ibsen" (344). What are we to make of this critique, and how does it impact our thinking about an evolving Irish Jewish studies?

To answer, I might return to Nels Pearson's very good question about the need for an "Irish Cosmopolitan," a question that acknowledges the oxymoronic qualities of the phrase: How can one be both Irish and cosmopolitan at the same time? Certainly, an active socialist like Sean O'Casey, much like his friend Shaw, answered this question emphatically by deriding Cathleen ni Houlihan as a "bitch" sometimes, "an old snarly gob" and an "ignorant one too," implying that the plight of international workers as so heartbreakingly represented in *Strumpet City* superseded the aims of the nationalist project. But it is not just the potentially oxymoronic or discordant quality of phrases such as *Irish Cosmopolitan* or *cosmopolitan Jews* that complicates matters but the varying connotations of the term *cosmopolitan*. Indeed, as Christine Sypnowich observes, *cosmopolitan* can resound with sinister implications as well positive ones, a valence of the term too often obscured by emphases on worldliness, a commitment to international justice, and cultural sophistication. "Genuine tensions" exist, she argues, "between the cosmopolitan aesthetic, on the one hand, and cosmopolitan ethics on the other." While cosmopolitan aesthetes like Nordau and Shaw enjoy—or not, as the case may be—aesthetic and cultural diversity, cosmopolitan ethicists insist on the "priority of justice" and a kind of singular universal standard. And labeling anyone a "cosmopolitan Jew" may violate this standard, as *cosmopolitan* in several historical contexts has conveyed senses of dirtiness, foreignness, and decadence and was often associated with Jews or Bolsheviks in Russia whom "bigots sought to exclude."[17] To call someone a cosmopolitan Jew is thus not to introduce the paradox Pearson identifies in the phrase *Irish Cosmopolitan* but rather in some cases to hurl a double disparagement (as fascists like Adolf Hitler were very well aware): that is, the term intensifies the foreignness, and even bestial quality, of a person—someone like Nordau, perhaps?

Nordau's argument in *Degeneration*, a lengthy and convoluted one, is difficult to summarize, but a greater sense of it beyond his antagonism to Wagner and Ibsen is necessary if we are to add a second discourse to the discussion of cosmopolitanism in the service of Irish Jewish studies, which is the discourse of antisemitism. Here, the work of scholars like Joseph Litvak is especially helpful. Starting from definitions of *antisemitism* advanced by Adorno and Horkheimer in *Dialectic of Enlightenment*, Litvak advances two propositions of relevance to my aims here. The first is the prominence of what he terms *withoutness* in Adorno and Horkheimer's list of supposedly odious Jewish characteristics: "happiness without power, reward without work, a homeland without frontiers"; the second is the preeminence of envy in antisemitism. For Litvak, the "anti-Semiticized masses perform the 'serious work' of envy as group psychopathology." Another way of saying it is that the Jew appears exempt "from the rules with which the 'the ruling powers' keep 'the ruled' in their place." Litvak asks, "What could be more desirable, and what therefore more urgently needs to be refigured as despicable?" Envy constitutes the "secret logic" of antisemitism, Litvak concludes, and, as I hope to show, while the erotic component he detects in Jew envy is absent from Shaw's lambasting of *Degeneration*, the sense of "withoutness" is very much present. Of lesser import in this instance but nonetheless valuable more generally is the same issue Litvak reads in Willa Cather's 1925 novel, *The Professor's House*, namely, the figuring of the Jew as "'repellently' international" and the "avatar of a frankly 'Oriental' extravagance."[18]

That is to say, Shaw's dismissal of Nordau is as much an assault on his character as it is a refutation of *Degeneration*'s polemic against not only fin de siècle artists such as the French symbolists, the decadent movement, and especially Ibsen's "realistic" drama but also the notion of a fin de siècle in the first place. For Nordau, as I have mentioned earlier, the term denotes a "contempt for traditional views of custom and morality" and heralds a "practical emancipation from traditional discipline." The result is a declining society in which the voluptuary reigns and "the beast in man" is unchained (5). In order to please, music like Wagner's must "either counterfeit religious devotion, or agitate the mind by its form" (12); similarly, novels "treating of the relations between the sexes, with no matter how little reserve, seem too dully moral. Elegant titillation only begins where normal sexual relations leave off" (13); and, in more political domains, for Nordau the writing of revolutionists and anarchists also reveals decadence, indicating, much like the degenerate artist, an inability to "adapt himself to existing circumstances" (22). Citing both contemporary psychological studies and the alarming demographies of swollen cities with their rising crime and suicide rates, Nordau detects a devastating exhaustion attributable to modernity itself. And at the heart of his argument resides a human subject beaten down by increased working hours and a burgeoning information age, for in addition to working longer and traveling farther to earn her bread, the urban resident must try to negotiate the frenetic speed of modern life itself: "To speak without metaphor, statistics indicate in what measure the sum of work of civilized humanity has increased. . . . [Humanity] grew fatigued and exhausted, and this fatigue and exhaustion showed themselves . . . under the form of an acquired hysteria. . . . The new aesthetic schools and their success are a form of this general hysteria" (40). For Nordau, Ibsen's plays are symptomatic of this disorder, as the characters featured are not "human beings of flesh and blood, but abstractions such as are evoked by a morbidly-excited brain" (342). One result is that Ibsen's women characters resemble Leopold von Sacher-Masoch's "imperious and triumphant women," thus inverting all "healthy and natural relation[s] between the sexes" (414).

These claims are astounding, to be sure, and one would not expect Shaw to acquiesce to them. But rather than carefully engage Nordau's lengthy and often highly specific readings of Ibsen's *A Doll's House*, *Ghosts*, *Rosmersholm*, *The Pillars of Society*, and others—or refute the despicable caricature of Wagner as the most degenerate figure of the age—Shaw resorts to a kind of counterattack about which one might be wary. That is, in "The Sanity of Art," Shaw anticipates the motif of "withoutness" Litvak identifies as endemic to antisemitism: in this case, Nordau's reaping of financial reward and international acclaim without performing sufficient work to earn either. The "splenetic pamphleteer," as Shaw describes him, has nothing to show for himself but a "bookful of blunders tacked on to a mock scientific theory" (*MCE* 330); more damagingly and seduced by "sham science," Nordau "exposes his sciolism time after time as an authority on the fine arts" (*MCE* 331). Shaw's use of "sciolism" specifies a sense of superficial knowledge underlying his opponent's "sham-scientific vivisection" of modern art, just the opposite of the good doctor's keen acumen in being "shrewd enough to see that is a good opening for a big reactionary book as a relief to the Wagner and Ibsen booms" (*MCE* 313). Thus, while *Degeneration* may be, in Shaw's eyes, a discursive "mess" distinctive for its "occasional putrescence" and "general staleness," it is a successful mess that has made "a very considerable impression" (*MCE* 313). And, because he has not bothered himself with the trouble and hard work of real learning and reflection, Nordau has achieved a notoriety he does not truly deserve. Is it possible that envy, just a tinge or scintilla of it, a mere smithereen, animates the argument of "The Sanity of Art" as much as a handsome payment motivated Shaw's acceptance of the assignment to review the book in the first place?

———

Whatever we might think about Shaw's critique of *Degeneration* in "The Sanity of Art," I hope we might agree that it introduces the possibility that theories of cosmopolitanism and antisemitism might be mobilized to further the intellectual work of Irish Jewish studies. Similarly useful are considerations of surrogation as well, as Shaw's insinuation of Nordau's reward without real work recalls not only one of the premises of antisemitism but also a long-standing derogation of the Irish. Throughout the later 1840s, for example, the *Times* of London endeavored to rationalize the Great Famine for its readership, displacing the blame for human suffering from imperial governance to native failing and indigence. One posting in particular has long drawn my attention for its sneering denigration of relief work that included the distribution of food. In asking "What Next," the *Times* in 1847 offered its own answer: "The corn [given to victims], of course, must be ground: the meal, of course, must be converted into bread or pudding; and then, with something to give it relish, and something else to wash it down, must be inserted leisurely and abundantly into each individual's mouth, just when it suits his own private arrangements."[19] Even relief organizations echoed these insinuations, recommending that when it is "practicable," some "return in work . . . will be required from the individuals relieved."[20]

Work will be required of us as well, as will an intellectual and theoretical openness from which an emergent critical discourse or set of discourses typically benefits. In outlining the ethical promises of cosmopolitanism, Kwame Anthony Appiah reminds us that its distinctive commitments include not only a *pluralism* that acknowledges that "there are many values worth living by and that you cannot live by all of them," but also a *fallibilism* that regards all knowledge as provisional and imperfect, "subject to revision in the face of new evidence."[21] Such, I might add, is the nature of discourse itself, as its etymological roots as a current that runs back and forth, to and fro, suggest. In this light, Irish Jewish studies might not only embrace the discourse of cosmopolitanism but also aspire to interrogate its inherent fallibilism. And all the while it must also be sensitive to the numerous and perhaps novel ways in which antisemitism can be engaged and effectively disabled. At its base, then, and much like cosmopolitanism, Irish Jewish studies as an intellectual and historical enterprise must also insist on an ethics committed to universal standards of justice.

PART FOUR | **Promised Lands**

II

The Historical Revitalization of Hebrew as a Model for the Revitalization of Irish?

MUIRIS Ó LAOIRE

In a sixty-year period that straddled the end of the nineteenth and beginning of the twentieth centuries, Hebrew was revitalized and reintroduced in Palestine, becoming a full-fledged vernacular of some Jews living there. Later it was to become an official language of the State of Israel. While the particular sociolinguistic conditions that surrounded language revitalization in this critical period are no longer observable, the revival of Hebrew represents a rare case of a thriving language revernacularization[1] that often serves as a model in regions and states where energies and resources have been devoted to the promotion of a language spoken by relatively small minorities in demographic terms. This chapter examines the sociolinguistic settings and conditions in the revitalization of Hebrew and offers comparable and contrastive insights to the restoration of Irish (*Gaeilge*) in Ireland during the same historical period. While a burgeoning cultural nationalism spurred the idea of language revitalization in both sociolinguistic contexts, the data on the nativization[2] of Hebrew illustrates salient contrastive differences to the restoration of Irish that will be explored and discussed in this chapter.

The revitalization or the revival of Hebrew as a modern language and vernacular from its foundations and base in biblical and classical

Hebrew has been the subject of much debate and commentary among linguists and historians. The restoration, revival, or revitalization of Hebrew was the result of an ambitious political goal in Palestine that began roughly at the end of the nineteenth century and continued apace in the nascent State of Israel after 1948. A similar timeline demarcates the restoration of Irish as one of the languages of Ireland. Irish, although never without native speakers or a speech community, had contracted but was still extant, to a large extent, in almost all institutional and established social, cultural, political, and educational domains at the end of the nineteenth century. When the Gaelic League (Conradh na Gaeilge) embarked on a campaign of revival and restoration in 1893, the shift to English from Irish was already firmly in place.[3] The restoration of Irish as the spoken vernacular in effect became one of the first projects undertaken by the Irish Free State in 1922. The primary aim was the widespread reversal of the language shift from English to Irish, but the evolution of sociopolitical and sociocultural events and experiences brought about the adoption of lesser aims and ambitions.

The history of the restoration of both languages reveals how state planning for language and the actions and decisions of populations may converge, intermesh, and diverge to produce different outcomes. The restoration of Hebrew as the vernacular of Israel is universally deemed as successful. Today, Modern Israeli Hebrew is widely spoken by the vast majority of the Israeli population. In contrast, the restoration of Irish as the widespread vernacular of Ireland has not occurred to any remarkable degree, and there has been a relative lack of success in intergenerational transmission. In fact, it is not uncommon over the years in the debate and literature on language obsolescence and revival to find Hebrew presented as a good model of revitalization against which Irish is measured and compared unfavorably. Not only is this contrast true of cross-comparisons to Irish, but the revival of Hebrew frequently functions as an example in countries that encourage the revival and support of minority languages.[4]

Restoration, Revival, or Revitalization?

In the literature on the history of languages, the terms *language revival* and *language restoration* tend to be interchangeable. Both terms refer to a situation where a community begins again to use a language that was defunct and extinct. Critically, it alludes to the reuse of the language as the language of the home and, in particular, to speaking it to newborn children. The language through daily use initially in the home gradually extends outward and reclaims language domains previously lost to it: neighborhoods, schools, work, industry, and entertainment. The term *revitalization* is in many ways a more accurate one to describe the phenomenon of a language gradually regaining and restoring its use.

Spolsky argues that the term *revitalization* may be a more apposite term than *revival*, since it refers to the restoration of vitality to a language.[5] *Language revitalization* denotes a reversal of language shift or language loss where new cohorts or sets of speakers, functions, and domains are added to the language. Domains are the sites of language use—for example, home, neighborhood, work, school, and so on. The domain of the home is the most critical site in language revitalization contexts, it being the site where natural language transmission occurs. This renewed use of language in the home depends ultimately on the decision of parents to speak the language on a daily basis to their children.

The crucial decision parents make to transmit a language to their children in the home domain can be influenced by a number of factors, ideological, pragmatic, or instrumental. Producing new native speakers in the home domain is not necessarily a sufficient criterion for an appreciative increase in native speakers. The domains of language use need to extend out of and beyond the home to the domains of neighborhood, school, work, and entertainment. This extension is what happened in the effective revitalization of Hebrew by the first groups of immigrants to Palestine at the end of the nineteenth century.[6] Efforts to add new and native speakers to existing domains in the case of Irish during the same period led to some increase in the number of speakers, but here efforts fell short of what could be considered a successful revitalization.

The Gradual Disuse of Hebrew as a Vernacular

Hebrew ceased to be a spoken language more than two thousand years ago. While the date for the gradual disuse of the language as a vernacular is contested, some scholars such as Chaim Rabin would contend that the last monolingual speaker of Hebrew would have lived on or before the Bar Kokhba Revolt (ca. 120 CE). Scholars point to the gradual shift from Hebrew to Aramaic in the centuries that followed.

The Hebrew language remained in use, nonetheless, as a language to be studied, to be prayed, and to be read. Rabin describes the emergence of an Aramaic-Hebrew diglossia among Jewish populations in the following terms: "It is widely believed that the Hebrew language 'died' some two thousand years ago and was brought to life again in modern times. This is an erroneous idea. The word 'revival' applies . . . only to its use in everyday speech. Hebrew was, at all times, the sole medium of written language of at least part of the Jewish people."[7]

A large volume of literature, religious and secular, was produced in Hebrew from the period of its gradual disuse as a spoken language to its revitalization as a vernacular at the end of the nineteenth century. For this reason, some scholars such as Jack Fellman contend that Hebrew was never really a "dead" language, like Hittite or Akkadian. Haim Blanc in a similar fashion refutes the idea of the death of Hebrew.[8] He points out, nonetheless, that Hebrew throughout these centuries was no one's mother tongue. The language also developed and evolved as a written language. The Mishnah, a collection of Jewish oral traditions surrounding prayer, blessings, laws, sacrifice, and festivals that was redacted at the beginning of the third century CE, was written largely in Hebrew (Mishnaic Hebrew) and revealed an enriched and greatly enlarged vocabulary that dealt with every facet of life—agriculture, economics, civil and criminal law, and ethics—and contained legal and abstract terms.[9] Throughout the centuries when the language was not spoken, an immense corpus of literature was produced in Hebrew, and new terms and coinages were constantly added to the language.

The *Haskala* (Jewish Enlightenment) movement of eighteenth-century Europe witnessed the initial steps toward modernization of Hebrew in its written form. Dramas, novels, and poetry were produced in Hebrew. As well as remaining the language of literature, it appears that, to some limited extent, the language may also have served as a lingua franca between Jews who had no common language,[10] although Benjamin Harshav reminds us that there is no compelling evidence of widespread use as such.[11] There is also some evidence that the language was used for trade and other secular purposes.

Lewis Glinert has uncovered interesting evidence to suggest that the modernization of Hebrew might also have occurred to some extent outside the "canons" of literature.[12] The *Shulkhan Arukh* (Long Table), a collection of Jewish law, was widely consulted and taught in traditional Jewish elementary schools in Europe and in Palestine and contained a lexicon for everyday items and normal aspects of daily life that complemented the ongoing modernization of the language in the domain of literature.

In sum, it is important to bear in mind that Hebrew could never be considered as having been an entirely dead or moribund language. While it had a vibrant and evolving literature, nonetheless, crucially, it still lacked native speakers and vernacular status. This situation was to change at the end of the nineteenth century and at the beginning of the twentieth century.

The Revitalization of Hebrew

The revitalization of Hebrew as a modern spoken language can be dated to the end of the nineteenth century. The restrictive antisemitic atmosphere of Czar Alexander II's Russia and pogroms from 1881 onward witnessed an exodus, a mass emigration of around two million Jews from eastern Europe, mainly to the United States. The rise and spread of nationalistic movements in Europe spurred the idea of a return to Hebrew as the spoken language of Jews. A small number of eastern European Jews emigrated to Palestine. Bernard Spolsky describes the weltanschauung of these emigrants as follows: "Among them were young intellectuals, influenced by European nationalism, and imbued with the notion of building a life in Palestine that was better than and different from the one they had known in Eastern Europe. It was these Jews who started coming to Palestine in the 1880s who brought with them and embraced the notion of using Hebrew as their national language, an all-purpose vernacular that would serve to mark the distinction from life in the Diaspora."[13]

Eliezer Ben-Yehuda (1858–1922), often credited as being the "father of the revival of modern Hebrew," was one of the leading figures in his prolific writings calling for a return to Hebrew as a vernacular of Jews in Palestine. Ben-Yehuda, who wrote about bringing up his own children through Hebrew, lived in Jerusalem but had little impact in securing any appreciable shift by families to the language. Many religious Jews in Jerusalem were Yiddish speakers who continued to see Hebrew as the holy tongue (*lashon kodesh*) and wanted the language to be restricted exclusively to religious functions.[14] Eventually, it was among the second wave (*aliyah*, lit. Ascension) of immigrants (1905–15) in the new Zionist settlements such as Rishon-le Zion that the revitalization of Hebrew more rapidly took place. These new idealistic immigrants were characterized by possessing a mobilizing motivation to make Hebrew the language of the home and interpersonal communication.

The question as to how these new immigrants managed to transform Hebrew from being the language of prayer and literature into a spoken language needs to be asked. How was it possible, in the absence of native speakers and models of the daily language of interpersonal communication?[15] Izre'el correctly claims that this question of the linguistic processes at work in the revernacularization of Hebrew has not always been answered satisfactorily.[16]

Moshe Nahir has proposed a four-stage overlapping model in this process of revernacularization:[17]

1. The children were "instilled" with a mobilizing motivation, a strong ideological commitment, and positive attitudes to the language in the schools.[18]

2. They were presented with grammar, vocabulary, and models of language use during lessons. There are folkloric and anecdotal stories of the first teachers of Hebrew stumblingly speaking the language themselves, while succeeding in transmitting it to children in preschools and primary schools. The direct method of teaching was used. The direct method, also termed the natural method, is where only the target language (Hebrew in this instance) is used and where pupils refrained from using their native languages (more than likely, Yiddish, Russian, German, or Polish in this instance).

3. The third stage is where the children gradually started to speak the language in school and crucially began to use it outside school. Scott B. Saulson states that the kindergartens "opened their doors to living Hebrew in places where Ben-Yehuda and the fighters for the revival of Hebrew could not reach."[19] The following extract by Rabin was included in an RTÉ TV series on the Irish-language *Watch Your Language* in 1970 and explains this process of nativization of the language in schools: "We found that the children, after picking up some Hebrew in school, force their parents to speak Hebrew at home because they are ashamed when their parents cannot speak Hebrew. They are our best apostles." The child, therefore, became the teacher of his or her parents and siblings.[20] Sociolinguistic data on the emergence of Hebrew as a spoken language suggests the nativization of the language first and foremost through and in the domain of education and extending from there to the parents and the home domain.

4. The fourth stage was when these children who were imbued with a love and knowledge of the language at school grew up; they spoke and used Hebrew exclusively as the language of the home with their own children. In this way, the first native speakers of the language were born. Nahir refers to this stage as the "great leap" in the revitalization of the language.

These processes took place roughly between 1906 and 1914. There is evidence to suggest that the progress was initially very slow.[21] By 1916, however, 40 percent of Jews in the new settlements in Palestine reported that Hebrew was their first language, and more than 75 percent of the young population used it as their sole language of communication.[22] The foundations for the revitalization of Hebrew were laid.

From a language-acquisition perspective, the data suggest that the children in the settlements who acquired Hebrew as a second language during the Second Aliyah already spoke Yiddish or other European languages. Izre'el suggests that the emergence of Hebrew as an acquired second language can be compared to the emergence of a creole.[23] Unlike a pidgin language, a creole is a natural stable language that develops and evolves from a mixture of different languages. While this theory had been mooted and argued by some scholars, there was always a claim that Modern Hebrew was not a "mixed" language. The idea was also rejected by creolists as well, since Hebrew was always a written language. This question requires further debate that a corpus of Modern Israeli spoken Hebrew would fuel. Regardless of the nuts and bolts of the characteristics of nascent Hebrew in language acquisition and in pure linguistic terms, it suffices for our purposes here to stress that the force of ideology accounted for the strength of motivation to adopt a new language from within. It was these same ideological forces at work that ensured that Hebrew and not Yiddish, German, or French became the language of the modern state of Israel.[24]

The Revival of Irish Outside the Gaeltacht and the Revitalization of Hebrew

Analogous references to the revival of Hebrew are often present in discourses on the restoration of Irish. Such references date back as early as 1924, when an Irish-language newspaper, *Fáinne an Lae*, considered the revitalization of Hebrew as a paradigm for the revival of the Irish language.[25] *Language revitalization* is not an entirely apposite term to describe efforts to restore Irish as a living language outside the Gaeltacht from the end of the nineteenth century onward; it is nevertheless a very useful one. While Irish revivalist efforts have resulted in an appreciable increase in the number of people who have acquired some knowledge of the language, Irish, unlike Hebrew, always had native speakers. The task that confronted language enthusiasts at the end of the nineteenth century and the state itself after 1922 was to attempt to reverse the progressive and extensive language shift to English that had occurred from the seventeenth century onward. While Irish always had speakers in all language domains in the Gaeltacht regions, new sets of speakers, functions, and domains needed to be added to the language outside these Irish-speaking regions. In sum, revivalist efforts that began at the end of the last century and have been endorsed and subsumed by native governments since 1922 have not led to a revitalization of the type associated with Hebrew.

The Early Revivalists

The early Irish-language revivalists are often termed *conraitheoirí* (Gaelic Leaguers) in Irish, in that most found their way into Conradh na Gaeilge (The Gaelic League), which was founded in Dublin on July 31, 1893, by Douglas Hyde. Initially, the organization was not party political and attracted nationalists of different backgrounds and persuasions and quickly and steadfastly became the leading institution promoting the revival of Irish. Many of the ideas of the early revivalists were to become fundamental principles in the Gaelic League propaganda in the years to come and in the Irish state's planning for the language from 1922 onward. These early revivalists could be described as being exponents of cultural nationalism, and they espoused a restoration of the language as a means of remaining in vital communion with the past and as a way of counteracting assimilation and modernization. They stressed the intrinsic links between language and nationalism, recalling the Herderian notion of the existence of a separate language as proof of nationhood.

The Needs and Imagination of the Masses

Hyde in particular posited the continuation of the Irish tradition as the ideological base for the restoration of the language, even though he vacillated somewhat in his understanding of what exactly would constitute such a restoration.[26] The centrality of transmission of the language was strongly emphasized, which is now recognized as the critical element in achieving language revitalization. Education was to become a very important site for language planning. It is interesting to note, however, that Eoin Mac Neill, who along with Hyde was a founding member of the Gaelic League, did not believe that the revival could be brought about through the sole agency of the school. In an article he wrote in *An Claidheamh Soluis* (*Sword of Light*), the newspaper of the Gaelic League, on November 2, 1900, he stated this belief very clearly: "There can be no greater delusion than to imagine that a language can be kept alive alone by teaching. A language can have no real life unless it lives in the lives of the people." In his blueprint for the restoration of the language *Toghairm agus Gleus chum Oibre* (*A Summons and Call to Work*), Mac Neill emphasized the importance of achieving a linguistic restoration in the home. "A language has never survived, when it has not survived beside the fireplace [at the hearth]. Even though the teaching of Irish is important, it is not the most important thing. The first thing we need to do then is to keep the language alive at the hearth" (my translation). Intergenerational transmission, that is, handing on the language in the home, is critical to achieving language revitalization.[27] The language needs to live in the lives of people. It is argued here, however, that the enterprise of the restoration remained in a large part extrinsic to the lives of the masses at the end of the nineteenth and beginning of the twentieth centuries.

Muiris Ó Laoire has argued that the ideas and rhetoric of the early revivalists, which became the blueprint for the restoration of Irish in the new state, had little in them to engage the motivation and imagination of the masses. It can be averred that cultural nationalism at the end of the nineteenth century was a different type of nationalism from the kind that the Irish had espoused and participated in, en masse, earlier in the century. It has been argued that this type of nationalism was characterized and marked by a strong socioeconomic dimension, particularly with its prospect of agrarian form. Ó Laoire has summarized the difference between how this form of nationalism and cultural nationalism was espoused by the masses: "The cultural nationalism to which De hÍde and revivalists subscribed, on one hand, was neither governed nor motivated by socio-economics and had little to offer the mass of the Irish population, both inside and outside the Gaeltacht. It is not surprising, therefore, that the language and culture-agenda proposed by middle class enthusiasts had little to engage the imagination and needs of the masses."[28]

Engagement in Revitalization

There is no evidence to suggest that the Gaelic League was not a popular movement. Within a short period after its foundation, like the Gaelic Athletic Association that preceded it, the Gaelic League became a successful cultural movement and achieved widespread participation in its educational program. By 1906, thirteen years after its establishment, it is reported that there were 964 branches of the Gaelic League in existence. By 1915, this figure had dropped to 265 but rose again to 819 by 1922. Yet while the Gaelic League was undoubtedly a successful cultural movement, it failed to muster significant support among the working classes,[29] with the main support for its branches coming almost exclusively from middle-income groups. With the foundation of the Free State in 1922, the main thrust of the Irish-language revival ideology remained the same, closely influenced by the cultural nationalism model. Proposals to revive the language, therefore, on the basis of that model were largely unfamiliar to the masses, and they did not engage with it. Tom Garvin refers to the "elite" conviction that derived essentially from the Gaelic League and that was never an authentic or widely held popular belief. The mass assent to the intensive teaching of the language that was spearheaded by the schools was passive and by and large failed to engage the imagination and engagement of people. As Aidan Doyle writes, "Most Irish people, even members of *Sinn Féin*, the nationalist party, were not really serious about replacing English with Irish."[30] The language had to compete with English, which had more attractive socioeconomic appeal, and as such people were unlikely to discard it.

When contrasted with the relatively more effective revitalization of Hebrew in schools and in the settlements during the Second Aliyah, the question becomes one of integrative motivation. The children in the schools not only were intent on changing their language to Hebrew but also taught it to their parents and siblings and in time established it as the language of the home. Where this necessary development occurred, there was no disconnect or disjuncture in ideology. The shift to Hebrew was more achievable, since it was constrained to smaller units of population who shared a common emigration experience, a strong mobilizing ideology, and motivation. They were more than willing to discard their mother tongues that were reminiscent of their preemigration plight in eastern Europe. In this relatively contained and relatively homogeneous social constitution, the revitalization was more effective than it was in the more cosmopolitan setting of Jerusalem. There were circles of families in Dublin and elsewhere who successfully shifted their home language from English to Irish, but this network never extended to more than a handful of converts who invariably came from the middle-class stratum and were not representative of the public as a whole. While the Irish revivalists may have failed to engage public support and imagination, the revivalists of Hebrew engaged and mustered significant support.

In both contexts, education was the site for language revitalization. There are two interesting points of contrast here. The school-home link was not fostered in the case of Ireland. Schools taught the language intensively and in varying contexts, including full immersion (in a minority of schools) without reference to language use in the home and neighborhood domains. Irish remained and still remains to a considerable extent a language taught and used exclusively in school. In the case of Hebrew, during the Second Aliyah in particular, there is clearly contrasting evidence of children using the language outside the school to teach it and speak it to their parents and siblings. In other words, the schools here seem to have taken what could be described as a replacive attitude to the language. Hebrew was taught with the intent of replacing Yiddish and the other languages brought to Palestine by the Second Aliyah immigrants. Irish, too, was seen as a replacive language. The compulsory policy was based on the revivalist philosophy that rejected assimilation and was founded on the assumption that if English had replaced Irish primarily because of an Anglicized educational system, the reverse was possible by teaching it intensively in the schools.

The evolution of the use of the threatened language outside the school situation is a vital ingredient in achieving revitalization and marks the breakthrough from language learning into vernacular use. In this sense, there was never a "great leap" in the revitalization of Irish to any appreciable extent, that is, a "spontaneous process . . . which brought the language outside the school's walls on the lips of young people on the streets and roads and into the mouths of parents in homes."[31] Understanding the reasons this great leap never occurred remains a relevant question in the context of contemporary language planning for the Irish language.

Conclusion

A discussion of Irish-language revitalization outside the Gaeltacht in relation to the revitalization of Hebrew underpins a number of questions about the nature and processes of revitalization itself. First, language revitalization is a process that demands a majority and homogeneous commitment to certain ideologies and behaviors. It is more about individual responses to an ideological call for language replacement than about state policy and planning. The processes of revitalization in Ireland devolved mainly on the educational system. But after decades of intensive teaching, and while some families had changed their home language to Irish, the language remained and still remains largely a cultural symbol outside the Gaeltacht. While state efforts at language planning succeeded in securing a place for Irish in the national consciousness, they have fallen short in bringing about any mass shift to the language.

The revitalization of Irish must not be subjected to any facile and oversimplified comparison with the revitalization of Hebrew that might be resonant of a fallacious rationale ("They managed to do it in Israel. Why can't we?"). Hebrew, nonetheless, offers mainly contrastive insights to the restoration of Irish in Ireland at the end of the nineteenth and the beginning of the twentieth centuries. While a burgeoning cultural nationalism spurred the idea of language revitalization in both sociolinguistic contexts, there were also key differences. In the case of Hebrew, the proportion of activist minority Jewish settlers committed to switching the language of the home initially during the First Aliyah expanded in less than a half century into a widely based majority. In Ireland the intellectual middle-class educated minority was unable to persuade the wider public to follow its agenda.

Second, while the agency of schooling through Irish and Hebrew was targeted in both situations, it was only when the ideological motivations were espoused by leaders, teachers, parents, and children that the school could be a conduit for the production of new speakers.

The revitalization of Hebrew still holds relevance for research into the internal linguistic situation in the homes of a growing number of children who attend all-Irish primary schools (*gaelscoileanna*) and secondary schools (*gaelcholáistí*) outside the Gaeltacht, particularly as to the question of how a family where such children are present would make a conscious effort to replace English with Irish as the home language. We also need to focus in research on the conditions favorable to the use of the language by children and young people outside the school. The contrast between the success of Hebrew and the apparent lack of success of Irish points more to complexities of language planning and the motivations for meaningful language use.

12

"From the Isle of Saints to the Holy Land"

*Irish Encounters with Zionism
in the Palestine Mandate*

SEÁN WILLIAM GANNON

Although Ireland's relationship with the British Empire was irretrievably ruptured by the 1919–21 Irish War of Independence and the consequent creation of the Irish Free State, Irish participation in the British imperial project persisted well into the era of decolonization. That Irishmen continued to swell the ranks of the British army is well known. But a roll call of Britain's ruling caste across most of its colonial possessions between 1922 and the mid-1960s reveals that Irishmen were also well represented in every branch of the colonial service. The Palestine Mandate was a case in point. There Irishmen served at all levels of the civil establishment, the judiciary, and, particularly, the police. The arrival of more than 250 disbanded Irish members of the Royal Irish Constabulary (RIC) in April 1922 with the British Section of the Palestine Gendarmerie inaugurated an Irish involvement in the territory's policing that culminated in the recruitment of approximately five hundred Irishmen into its successor force, the British Section of the Palestine Police (BSPP), in the final three years of the Mandate. For the great majority of these Irishmen, their posting to Palestine constituted their first encounter with Jews or Jewish nationalism (or both). Occasionally friendly, but more frequently fraught, this encounter, in many cases, defined their views of Israel and Zionism for the rest of their lives.

This chapter explores this encounter. Taking as its particular focus the five hundred Irish policemen recruited in the final years of the Mandate, who accounted for almost half of all Irish enlistments in the BSPP, it examines the attitudes of Irishmen serving in the Palestine Mandate toward its Jewish inhabitants and assesses the influence of prior perceptions of Jews and Judaism on their formation. It also examines their views on Jewish nationalism and investigates the extent to which Ireland's historical experience shaped Irish perspectives on the Arab-Zionist conflict and the Zionist insurgency against British rule.[1]

"The Average Englishman Here Is Instinctively Anti-Semitic"

Irish attitudes toward Jews and Jewish nationalism in the Palestine Mandate cannot be properly understood without reference to the general perceptions that prevailed among the British establishment there. Although the great majority of British officials worked to implement the terms of the mandatory instrument's Article 6, many were personally antipathetic to the creation in Palestine of a Jewish "national home."[2] Some believed that it clearly contravened British wartime commitments to the Arabs regarding the country's future. But the objections of others derived from antisemitism, which was commonplace at all levels of British society throughout the Mandate period. During the years of the Occupied Enemy Territory Administration (OETA) (South) when Palestine was governed by its British military garrison, and the first decade of civilian rule inaugurated under High Commissioner Sir Herbert Samuel in July 1920, this antipathy drew on British sociocultural stereotypes of Jews according to which they were "deniers of Christ, clannish and rootless wanderers, or exotic wielders of vast international power as financiers, revolutionaries or both," and was exacerbated by recurrent concerns about the emergence of "Judeo-Bolshevism" in the Yishuv.[3]

But antisemitism was also acquired through the British-Zionist encounter itself: what Joshua Sherman described as the "thrusting, self-confident" manner of many Zionist functionaries intensely irritated British officials accustomed to greater deference from those persons they considered colonial subjects, and their consequent detestation of Zionists sometimes developed into general hostility toward Jews.[4] Even Jewish Britons felt bigotry's chill, with Helen Bentwich (wife of Palestine's attorney general, Norman Bentwich) complaining in 1921 that "the average Englishman here is instinctively anti-Semitic" and that "there are such a lot of English people one can't meet on equal terms because of their anti-Semitism."[5] The situation worsened after Samuel's departure four years later, when, as one British policeman noted, "anti-Semitism was no longer dangerous and official British 'society' was able to do justice to its long-suppressed feelings"; indeed, Samuel's successor, Lord Plumer, could tell his own replacement, Sir John Chancellor, in August 1928 that Jewish complaints about "the lack of cordiality towards them, socially, from British officials were . . . probably true."[6] Chancellor himself held antisemitic views, believing that Jews had throughout history constituted a "disrupting element socially and politically" in the communities among which they lived (Russia being but the most recent example), and he grew quickly to detest the Zionists: "They are very aggressive and demand this and won't accept that, until I asked them who they thought was governing the country, them or me?"[7] Similar was Palestine's director of education Jerome Farrell: in November 1946 he complained in a departmental memorandum that the "inhuman mass selfishness of concentrated Jewry" was "a phenomenon so far . . . without parallel in history" and warned that there was "no common moral and theological ground on which organized Jewry and a Christian civilization [could] stand together in harmony."[8]

Jews also suffered by comparison with Palestine's Arabs, who the British generally (though, by no means universally) romanticized as a race. Writing to her parents from Jerusalem in 1922, Eunice Holliday reported that she liked the Arabs "very much indeed, they seem so much more dignified, refined and well-bred than either Jews or Europeans: somehow they seem so grand, as if they come from a very great people, and yet they are so simple," and Britons continued to be attracted by what they saw as their "pride in their traditions, and above all the exquisite courtesy and generous hospitality that enabled most British individually to enjoy social and official encounters with them."[9] "Whether they whined, or threatened, or cajoled or protested," the Arabs were, British Jewish jurist Horace Samuel complained in 1930, always "picturesque, ingratiating, sympathetic," while the Jews were seen as "clumsy, fussy and aggressive," even when right was seen to be on their side.[10] The same was still true seventeen years later: in his account of his time as a member of the Anglo-American Committee of Inquiry into Jewish immigration into Palestine in 1946, British member of Parliament Richard Crossman stated that "somehow we like the Arabs even though they fight us, and we dislike the Jews even if our interests run together," and he quoted a British official as stating that "there are two societies in Jerusalem, not three. One is Anglo-Arab and the other is Jewish. The two just can't mix."[11]

"Most Constables Regretted What the Jews Did"

Arthur Koestler claimed that "the lower one descended in the hierarchy" of the British Palestine Mandate, "the more noticeable was anti-Jewish feeling, which on the lowest level, that of the Palestine Police, reached scandalous proportions."[12] The force undoubtedly did contain its share of antisemites. However, the great majority of them were created during their BSPP service rather than recruited into the force fully formed. In the early years, recruits were exposed to Judeo-Bolshevik conspiracy theories that, although first raised by British army officers during the OETA (South) period, were most stridently expounded by the then Palestine police chief, Lieutenant Colonel Percy Bramley, for whom they became something of an obsession; in fact, he continued to lobby the Colonial Office on the issue after his retirement in April 1923. And despite being downplayed by the Palestine government and Bramley's successor, Arthur Mavrogordato, the perceived Judeo-Bolshevik threat became a central focus for the Criminal Investigation Department (CID) of the Palestine Police in the 1920s, so much so that the Shaw Commission inquiring into the 1929 anti-Zionist riots blamed the department's preoccupation with the issue for the lapses in intelligence about the upsurge in Arab anti-Jewish feeling that directly led to the carnage that left 133 Jews dead.[13] Antisemitic feeling in the BSPP was exacerbated by the fallout from the riots themselves, particularly the blistering criticism of the police response by Zionist Jews in Palestine and elsewhere.

However, it was the perceived savagery of what Richard Catling, head of the CID's Jewish Affairs section, termed "the Jewish brand of terrorism" during the final years of the Mandate that frequently transformed simmering resentment into outright racial hatred. No single assault on the BSPP equaled in infamy the attacks perpetrated against the British army, such as the April 1946 shooting of seven members of the Sixth Airborne Division in a Tel Aviv parking lot and the hanging of two British sergeants, Mervyn Paice and Clifford Martin, in July 1947. But attacks on the police, whom the Irgun lambasted as the "mercenaries and instruments of [the] regime" and the "Palestine Gestapo," were unremitting throughout the 1946–48 period.[14] Twenty-two BSPP personnel had been killed by Zionist insurgents between 1939 and 1945. But more than four times this number were killed between January 1946 and the termination of the Mandate in May 1948. BSPP constable Frank Jones cited such attacks as the turning point for him in terms of his attitudes toward Palestine's Jews: "I treated them all as Palestinians, they were always equal, until they hanged those army sergeants, and I thought 'what sort of people are these?' They were killing off six British policemen a month; they murdered over 250 of us. . . . That's when I knew what an evil people the Jews were." Similarly, Constable Bertie Braddick cited the attack on the Sixth Airborne Division as his reason for enlisting in the BSPP and was himself almost killed by a Jewish insurgent: "I think generally most constables regretted what the Jews did and thought it was a disgusting way of behaving. . . . I regret what the Jews did and I think they should pay for it. And frankly I would like to see the Arabs wipe them right off the face of the earth. Every single one of them, man, women and child, not only there but everywhere." Such violent antisemitic feeling was fueled by the British belief that the Jews were biting the hand that had recently fed them. As deputy police superintendent Jack

Binsley subsequently put it, the Zionist insurgency represented for the BSPP "the most blatant ingratitude toward a benevolent country who had granted them access to Palestine and then protected them from the Arabs to allow them to create a home in the Holy Land."[15]

The police also directed their outrage at the wider Yishuv. David Cesarani made a case for a "persistent and resilient philo-Semitism" among the British security forces during this period, but there is little evidence of it in the BSPP. Some policemen did admire the Zionists' manifest achievements. But the majority were infuriated by what they viewed as the Yishuv's tacit support for the insurgents. BSPP constable Anthony Wright summed up this feeling in his diary in June 1946: "The terrorist is the 'man-in-the-street' and the worker on the land; the scoutmaster, the teacher, the factory worker and shop-keeper." And this message was reinforced in Arab propaganda pamphlets widely circulated among the police: "The *Yishuv* manned the terrorist groups. The *Yishuv* protected, sheltered and covered the terrorists. The *Yishuv* never cooperated with you in any way to stop [their] cowardly and barbarous deeds. . . . The acts were hailed by all the Jews as acts of Jewish bravery." The stridently antisemitic poem "A Policeman's Lament" proved particularly popular with BSPP personnel. Framed as the last words of a mortally wounded British policeman, it urged the BSPP to take revenge by killing "every damned son of Zion" and make "Hell . . . their National Home."[16]

"It Was Impossible to Feel Impartial"

The attitudes of Irish policemen serving in the later Mandate period toward Palestine's Jewish communities were broadly reflective of the feelings of their British-born colleagues. The Irish Redemptorist writer J. J. W. Murphy, who visited Palestine during this time, later stated that "it was impossible to feel impartial [between Arabs and Jews] when all the hostility came from the Jewish side only," and the great majority of Irish policemen were anti-Jewish in outlook on account of the Zionist insurgency, an insurgency that claimed the lives of nine compatriot colleagues between December 1945 and May 1948. So, despite having "never had any contact" with them during his time as a BSPP constable, Thomas Freeburn from Fermanagh developed a general dislike of Palestine's Jews: "I did not like the Jewish people. . . . I'm not saying [they] were all bad. But it was very difficult to like them, I'll put it like that. Mainly because of what was happening." The views of Martin Moore, who enlisted as a BSPP constable in October 1946, were also defined by what he termed "the Jewish terrorist campaign." While his sympathies prior to deployment were "more pro-Arab . . . but without any real convictions," he was, having grown up in the Little Jerusalem area of Dublin's south city, well disposed toward Judaism and Jewish culture, and he had Jewish friends. However, his experience of policing in Palestine turned him "violently against the Jews" living there. So it was with George Burton from Meath, who enlisted in the BSPP in 1938 and served until the Mandate's end: he "sympathized with the Arabs, and more so as the Jewish terrorists increased in violence," as did Constable Patrick Cawley from North Tipperary, recruited in October 1946: "You wouldn't be able to say one side was worse than the other or one was better than the other; the only thing we could say is that it was the Jewish terrorists that were giving us the agro."[17] Even policemen self-described as pro-Zionist in outlook felt conflicted by the insurgents' campaign: "My sympathies were with the Jews to a certain extent because I was aware of the Holocaust and all the atrocities that went on there. But at the same time . . . it was difficult to have sympathies when you were being shot at as well."[18]

While the personal testimonies of Irish postwar recruits are devoid of the deep-seated racial hatred that their British counterparts sometimes display, a small number do betray a decidedly antisemitic worldview. However, Irish antisemitic policemen were, in common with their British counterparts, usually created in Palestine rather than recruited fully formed: the great majority of Irish policemen had no prejudices or preconceptions about Jews prior to their departure for Palestine or any real knowledge of Jewish nationalism. This absence of antecedent antisemitism among Irish Catholic policemen is somewhat surprising, for antisemitism was commonplace in Irish Catholic culture during the period of the Palestine Mandate and was shared by many Irish Catholics who served there, most notably Sir Michael McDonnell, the territory's chief justice between 1927 and 1936.[19] (According to Sir John Chancellor, "Both he and Lady McDonnell [were] devout Catholics and, like all Latins in Palestine, strongly anti-Semitic," while the head of the Jewish Agency's political department, and future first Israeli foreign minister, Moshe Shertok/Sharett, described McDonnell as an "inveterate Jew-hater.")[20] Moreover, while many in Ireland held a principled objection to the territorial partition on which a Jewish state's creation necessarily depended,[21] Irish anti-Zionism essentially sprang fully formed from Irish Catholic Judeophobia's head, finding its basis in anti-Judaic theology according to which the Roman expulsion of the Jews from Judea in the first and second centuries CE constituted a divine punishment for their deicide and perfidy (their continuing exile a continuing vindication of the Christian revelation) as well as in ancient Christian anxieties about perceived resultant Jewish enmity, which found collective expression in mid-twentieth-century Ireland in the Judeo-Bolshevik myth. According to its Irish version, "atheistic communism" was a Jewish-controlled vehicle for the subversion of the Catholic Church and Catholic social order, and international Jewry's violent attempt to reassert sovereignty over the cradle of Christianity through Zionism was therefore viewed as another front in Judeo-Bolshevism's war on the church already raging in Eastern Europe.

Nonetheless, the majority of Irish Catholic postwar recruits were unaware of Zionism's theological dimension, and the ones who were conversant with their church's position, including the self-described devout, variously dismissed it as "academic," "irrelevant," or "poppycock." In repudiating theological arguments, Irish Catholic policemen stood in marked contrast to some of their non-Catholic colleagues, who saw the Zionist struggle in distinctly eschatological terms. In June 1936 an official of Palestine's Anglican Church noted that for "those who study their Bibles, believing that the prophecies with regard to the Jewish people mean something . . . it seems to be in line with God's inscrutable plans that Palestine is to be the centre of Jewish national life in the future." BSPP constable John Fitzpatrick, a Church of Ireland member from Clare, held a similar attitude, suggesting that Zionism constituted the prophesied "ingathering of exiles" ("As I saw it the Jews were coming home"), while the Derry Presbyterian Constable William Bond saw it as part of the "divine providential plan" for God's "chosen people."[22]

"Zionism and Judaism Differ *Toto Caelo*"?

The indifference of Irish Catholic recruits to theological anti-Zionism was not shared by the Palestine Police Catholic chaplain, Father Eugene Hoade. Born in Galway in 1903, Hoade arrived in Palestine in 1931 as vice principal of Jerusalem's Franciscan Terra Sancta College and was made custodian at the Basilica of Gethsemane in 1937. In September 1938, he was appointed Catholic chaplain to the Palestine Police with the honorary rank of district superintendent. Hoade arrived in Palestine a confirmed anti-Zionist, blaming "Zionism— political and acquisitive"—for destroying the harmonious relations that he believed the territory's communities had, historically, enjoyed. He also believed that the Holy Land was "the inheritance of no particular race but belonged to the world," and he used his considerable influence in Jerusalem to advance the Vatican-supported provision of the November 1947 United Nations' Palestine partition plan to designate the city an internationally administered *corpus separatum*.[23] However, in internationalization's absence Hoade, like the Holy See, considered Arab sovereignty a far more palatable proposition than Zionist jurisdiction, and he vigorously campaigned to prevent Palestine's Christian holy places from being placed under Jewish control. His Irish compatriots among Palestine's Catholic clergy (which included a number of nuns working with the Sisters of Charity and the Sisters of Saint Joseph of the Apparition) took a similar view. Most notably, his Franciscan confrere Father Tarcisius Hand lobbied the Irish government to take a proactive position on the holy places' preservation in the years following Israel's foundation.

Shortly after his arrival in Palestine, Hoade stated his belief that "Zionism and Judaism differ *toto caelo*."[24] Yet his understanding of Zionism was colored by his attitudes toward Jews, attitudes that were very much informed by the theological Judeophobia current in contemporary Catholic thinking. According to Hoade, Jewish nationhood effectively ended "in the infamy of Calvary," and the Jewish dispersal was divinely ordained. ("Everybody must see in the history of the Jewish people the hand of God.") Moreover, drawing on Catholic doctrine about enduring Jewish enmity, he believed that Zionist forces were deliberately destroying Palestine's Christian heritage through the systematic desecration of churches and shrines during the 1947–49 war.[25] However, Hoade's anti-Zionism was also politico-nationalist in nature. According to J. J. W. Murphy, "The pattern of nationalist politics familiar to the Irish [in Palestine] was very little help" when judging the Arab-Zionist conflict, the claims of both sides being "full of the folklore and martyrology of their respective national struggles in the past—the Palestinian equivalents of [17]98 and Easter Week, of Robert Emmett, Michael Dwyer and Kevin Barry." But Hoade, who came from a staunchly Republican background (his mother and three of his brothers took an active role in Ireland's War of Independence), drew clear parallels, viewing the Palestinian Arabs as victims of a Zionist colonialist enterprise of the kind visited on Ireland by Britain.[26] (In fact, so too did Murphy, who believed that "the traditional picture of Cromwell's 'Hell or Connaught' policy in Ireland gives a fair idea of what happened in Palestine during 1948 to the Arabs whose homes then were in what is now Jewish territory.")[27] So strong was Hoade's belief in Zionism's injustice that he actively assisted Jerusalem's Arab militias during the 1947–49 war and continued to involve himself in anti-Zionist intrigue afterward when Gethsemane, situated just east of the Old City, came under Jordanian control. In April 1954, he was prevented by the Israeli authorities from crossing through the Mandelbaum Gate as what the Associated Press described as "a presumably suspect old enemy of Israel," and, indeed, his animosity toward Zionism had continued unconcealed.[28] Mythologist Joseph Campbell, who met Hoade in Jerusalem the same year, noted that he remained "very strong in his feelings for what the Jews had done," declaring, "We are at war . . . six years of it." Hoade was expelled from Jordan in 1956 as "politically suspect" on account of his ongoing pro-Palestinian activism.[29]

"A Certain Sense of Fair Play"

Hoade's view of Zionism as a politically immoral adventure was not unusual among Irish officials in Palestine; in fact, Irishmen had been voicing reservations about the Zionist project since the days of OETA (South). For example, James Pollock, an administrative officer in the military regime, quickly earned a reputation for being anti-Jewish.[30] While Pollock shared in OETA (South)'s endemic antisemitism, he maintained that his "anti-Jewish sentiments [were] the result of a certain sense of fair play" toward Palestine's Arab, who he felt had been the victims of British bad faith. As he wrote his father, "The Arabs say we have betrayed them, that the Arab army fought with the British against the Turk, to free the country of oppression, and now the freedom we offer is the oppression of the Jews, the most intolerant and arrogant people in the world," and Pollock clearly concurred with these sentiments.[31] Sympathy for the Arab case was particularly evident among Palestine's Irish judiciary, and some Irish judges demonstrated partisanship toward the Arabs during the Great Revolt against the Mandatory administration of 1936–39. For example, president of Jerusalem's district court Oliver Plunkett publicly stated that he refused to consider himself bound by the special regulations issued by High Commissioner Sir Arthur Wauchope, setting out mandatory prison sentences for particular offenses, while Sir Michael McDonnell was so strongly sympathetic to the Arab anticolonialist cause that he was effectively dismissed as chief justice in 1936 because, in Wauchope's words, "any judge holding such extreme and partisan views [could not] administer even-handed justice between Arab and Jew."[32] While there is some truth in the charge that McDonnell's anti-Zionism derived "from a fascist, antisemitic point of view," he clearly believed in the justice of the Arab case for self-determination per se and, like Pollock, felt that the Balfour Declaration was a gross betrayal of British promises made to this end.[33] Moreover, McDonnell drew on the Irish historical experience to reject in principle the use of partition and segregation in the resolution of intercommunal conflicts, and he saw rebellions like the one the Arabs were waging as a natural response to continued bad governance.[34]

Irish policemen in the Palestine Mandate were less receptive to the Arab case. This attitude partly derived from their frequent employment as the instruments of Arab nationalism's suppression. The first significant deployment of Irish policemen—the 250 former RIC who, as the "Police Notes" column of the *Irish Times* put it, "transfer[red] from the 'Isle of Saints' to the Holy Land" with the British Section of the Palestine Gendarmerie—took the lead in containing what was essentially an inchoate Arab anti-Zionist insurgency in 1922–23. As Major General Hugh Tudor, the former Irish police chief appointed Palestine's joint general officer commanding and director of public security in February 1922, remarked sourly to Norman Bentwich, these men "had to leave Ireland because of the principle of Irish self-determination, and were sent to Palestine to resist the Arab attempt at self-determination."[35] Furthermore, some 250 Irish policemen were serving in the BSPP in 1936–39 when the force formed the front line against the Arab Revolt, and the killing of policemen was one of the insurgents' tactical constants. (Hundreds of Irishmen also served in British army regiments such as the Royal Ulster Rifles, the Royal Irish Regiment, and the Irish Guards, which were transferred to Palestine to assist in the rebellion's suppression.) Yet a distinct indifference to Arab nationalist arguments was also discernible among Irish policemen who served in the post–Second World War period when the Arabs were essentially on the Mandatory's side.

Some of these men looked down on Palestine's Arabs, believing, like Irish high commissioner Sir Alan Cunningham that they were a hopelessly primitive people.[36] However, the great majority were very well disposed, identifying with elements of Arab culture and discerning in the Arab character a temperament and outlook similar to their own. For example, Patrick Cawley "personally found the Arabs very very like the Irish—very laid back . . . very humble people to deal with . . . very easy to get on with." So too did Michael Burke, a BSPP constable from Sligo recruited in October 1946, who admired the Irish-style "simplicity" of Arab culture, particularly the lifestyle of the bedouins: "They were people who were living and existing and, bearing in mind that I [came] from the west coast of Ireland . . . I had to depend on the sea and on the land to live when I was a child [so] I fitted in quite well normally." The hospitality of Arab village culture struck a particular chord with Irish policemen, particularly those individuals from rural areas of Ireland such as Thomas Freeburn, for whom it evoked memories of home: "If you had to go with them to their home for any reason it would be 'come, come, coffee, sit, sit.' They were very friendly, nice people in comparison to the Jewish people. . . . They reminded me sometimes of good-hearted Irish people, you know, that sort of thing."[37]

This sense of affinity meant that Irish policemen had great sympathy for the Arab situation in the spring of 1948. Freeburn's statement that he was "very very sad . . . as any right-minded person would be" at the outcome of the 1947–49 war is typical of the reaction among Irish (and indeed British) BSPP personnel, and even those Irish such as John Fitzpatrick, who supported the Zionist project, "had a great deal of sympathy for the Arabs" and felt they "were being manipulated by their own people as well as by everybody else."[38] But such pro-Arab sympathies were generally personal rather than political. Contemporary sources indicate that Irish Palestine policemen had little sense of thwarted Arab nationalism in the final years of the Mandate, and charges that the Arabs were denied their right to self-determination by Zionism were leveled in retrospect. The parallels between the Arab and Irish experience that were occasionally articulated in Ireland, particularly after the defeat of the Great Arab Revolt, were seldom drawn by Irish policemen, reflective perhaps of a colonial condescension, even among those individuals most sympathetic to Palestine's Arabs, that viewed them as incapable of the evolved national consciousness that legitimized opposition to imperial rule.

"Ireland 1921—Palestine 1945"

Not so Palestine's Jews. In his 1939 account of his experiences with the Second Irish National Pilgrimage to the Holy Land four years earlier, Edward Doherty noted that "it appears as if the Jews will never form a people here, notwithstanding recent developments, for they are no longer a nation, but a mere assemblage of people coming from different countries and quite incapable of re-annexation."[39] But by the mid-1940s, Zionism's success in forging a Jewish national identity in Palestine was self-evident, leading some Irish policemen to draw parallels between Irish and Jewish nationalism and view Zionism's anti-British campaign as an independence struggle similar to Ireland's own. Although Vladimir Jabotinsky remained ambivalent as to the relevance of the Irish Revolution as a historical model for revisionist Zionism, "understanding and learning from Irish Republicanism" became, in the wake of the 1929 riots, "an integral part of devising a more militant stand."[40] And although the Irish model was ultimately rejected as a blueprint for action (asked whether the Irgun had been "influenced by guerrilla groups in other countries militarily and ideologically," its former leader Menachem Begin simply replied, "We learned from the history of our own people and ourselves"),[41] parallels between the Zionist insurgency and the Irish Revolution continued to be drawn in the postwar period, most passionately by Irgun insurgent Avshalom Haviv at his capital trial in July 1947:

> You will probably remember that in Ireland too you [Britain] seized a small country and captured people by force of arms and deceit in the name of religion and under the cover of "law and order." When the sons of Ireland rose up against you, you tried to drown the rising against tyranny in rivers of blood, you set up gallows, you murdered in the streets, you exiled, you ran amok and believed, in your stupidity, that by dint of persecution, you would break the resistance of the free Irish.[42]

Militant pro-Zionist organizations such as the Irgun front, the American League for a Free Palestine, adopted a similar line (its sloganeering on the subject summed up by an apoplectic James Dillon, then a nonparty Irish parliamentarian, as "Free Ireland—Free Palestine: Support the resistance against the British terror"), as did American publisher and author William Ziff, who frequently drew Ireland-Palestine parallels.[43] Meanwhile, in Palestine, some policemen noted the painting of slogans such as "Ireland 1921—Palestine 1945" and "Eire 1922" on the funnels of Jewish immigrant ships docked in the harbor at Haifa.[44]

BSPP sergeant Patrick McGrath recalled that the immigrant ship slogans angered those Irishmen who saw no similarities between the Jewish campaign for statehood and the Irish Revolution twenty-five years before. But some drew clear parallels. As John Humphreys, a BSPP constable from Limerick recruited in March 1947, explained, "From the aspect of Irishness it was obvious that the Jews deserved a homeland. . . . They had come from a situation where they had been victimized throughout the Western world, from Russia, all over Europe, the Holocaust, the whole damn thing. And they were determined to fight to get a Jewish state as a nation and I thought they were entitled to it, like we were ourselves." Patrick Tynan, a BSPP constable from Galway recruited in March 1947, and Paul MacMahon also cited similarities with "the Irish situation" to argue that "the Jews needed a national home," and they drew a distinction between the Haganah on one side and the Irgun and Lehi/Stern Gang on the other, considering the former a legitimate military force.[45] As John P., a BSPP constable from Tipperary, put it, the Haganah, unlike the Irgun and Lehi, "was fighting a very honest war," and he felt similar to Martin Moore, who drew an ex post facto analogy with Northern Ireland to describe the Haganah as "more or less like the SDLP," the province's constitutional national party, and "the Stern Gang and the Irgun [as] terrorists" equivalent to the Provisional IRA.[46] And while Patrick Cawley condemned the Irgun and Lehi out of hand, he drew on the Irish historical experience to express some sympathy for idealists such as Dov Gruner, the young Irgun operative executed by the British at the Acre jail in April 1947: "He was only a young lad, like Kevin Barry . . . only a teenager. . . . [O]kay, he did atrocities and things like that but like a lot of other youngsters in the days of the old IRA they all joined in thinking they were fighting for Ireland. These fellows thought they were fighting for Jewish Israel."[47]

Most Irish policemen shared their British counterparts' suspicion of the wider Yishuv. Although BSPP sergeant Gerald Murphy noted that "police who studied Hebrew acquired Jewish friends and, in consequence, developed a greater sympathy with the Jewish cause," fewer than 10 percent of Irish policemen elected to do so, the remainder studying Arabic instead. Moreover, those friendships formed were frequently compromised by lack of trust on the Irishmen's part. Murphy recalled his hesitancy to form a relationship with a Jewish female acquaintance, fearing that "her deportment might be the dissimulation of a practiced terrorist decoy," and many other policemen were similarly suspicious. For example, while Paul MacMahon tried to "bear in mind that not all Jews were terrorists" and noted that many were "very friendly," he felt that "a lot of them that were very friendly were still terrorists, friendly to your face." However, the attitudes of some Irish policemen toward the Yishuv were tempered by memories of the Irish Revolution, during which the British security forces tended to regard all civilians as "Shinners." So although John P. felt "absolute hostility" from the Jewish population he policed, he tried "not [to] tar them all with the [terrorist] brush as the British had done to the Irish," while Michael Burke took any hostility he encountered from either side on the chin, as he "understood . . . being an Irishman . . . what the occupation of another person's country meant." And although Patrick McGrath was unforgiving of what he saw as widespread Jewish support for the insurgents, he differentiated between Zionist and non-Zionist Jews: "Mind you, what the Jews did! The Zionists I mean, the old Jewish people who weren't Zionists, I had an affinity for them. I respected them."[48]

Conclusion

Speaking to Israeli writer Hadara Lazar about his years in the Palestine judiciary, Sir Michael Hogan recalled "a saying that anybody coming to Palestine arrived as rather pro-Jewish, but after a while became rather pro-Arab, and generally ended as being pro-British," and his own sympathies shifted in this way.[49] Those attitudes of his compatriot policemen generally did not. Although a small number of those Irish recruited in the Mandate's twilight years arrived with pro-Arab or pro-Jewish sympathies, the great majority had little prior knowledge of the Arab-Zionist conflict and were without sympathies either way. Moreover, the ones who did arrive "pro-Jewish" usually stayed so, despite a feeling that, as one put it, "the Jews went too far." And while most did become "rather pro-Arab," they also "ended" their service this way and remained "pro-Arab" afterward, coming to believe, in Gerald Murphy's words, that "the Arabs were robbed and the robbery legalized."[50] Indeed, Irish BSPP veterans are (in common with the great majority of their British counterparts) today overwhelmingly pro-Palestinian, and several are members of Palestinian support groups and charities for which the Palestine Police Old Comrades' magazine (published thrice annually from 1947 until 2015) carried appeals. And although post-1967 events, particularly the Israeli settlement of the West Bank, are occasionally cited as their reasons for hostility to Israel, most Irish veterans date it to their time in Palestine and the opposition to Zionism in which it resulted. In this sense, these men generally "became" anti-Zionist, "ended" anti-Zionist, and remained anti-Zionist for life.

Epilogue

AIDAN BEATTY AND DAN O'BRIEN

Irish history writing has often suffered from an inward-looking perspective. The twenty-six counties' assumed status as a *sacra insula* postindependence finds an odd analogue in the bulk of the work on that state's history. That events in Ireland might have been profoundly influenced by goings-on further afield has been downplayed in favor of what R. M. Douglas aptly calls, in his contribution to this volume, "an unarticulated *Sonderweg* thesis for modern Ireland." Irish historians reassured themselves "that nothing that happened on the European continent need disturb the tranquility of their scholarly lives." Indeed, much of the literature on the so-called Irish Revolution of 1912–23 has had surprisingly little to say about other contemporaneous revolutions, not the Bolshevism of Russia, Hungary, or Germany or the anticlericalism and land seizures of Mexico or the colonial transfer of power to the Wafd in Egypt. More recently, thankfully, this edifice has shown some cracks. The recent transnational turn in Irish historiography has done much to place Ireland into broader geographies and to show how porous are the borders of that "combination of chemical elements [we are] pleased to call Ireland."[1] Scholars such as Ciaran O'Neill and Enda Delaney have advanced this new subfield of Irish history writing.[2] The often miserly response from an older guard of Irish historians, however—refusing to accept that there was ever an inward-looking problem in the first place—shows a marked resistance to change as well as the truth of Douglas's barbed comments.[3]

The essays in this collection emphasize the value of placing Ireland in broader global currents. R. M. Douglas's contribution shows how a comparative European perspective does much for the study of antisemitism in Ireland, and Sander L. Gilman's essay highlights the structural similarities and shared trajectories of anti-Jewish and anti-Irish rhetoric in the nineteenth century. Dan Lainer-Vos highlights the comparabilities and key differences of Irish and Jewish American political activism and how, in both cases, a diasporic longing for home collided with the American realities of these two prominent white ethnic groups. In almost the same vein, Muiris Ó Laoire's chapter explores how much the revival of the Irish language can be better understood when we compare it to the roughly contemporaneous revival of Hebrew. Seán William Gannon, in his contribution, reveals how large numbers of Irish people continued to operate within transnational British imperial networks well after 1922; Irishmen serving in the Palestine Police in the 1940s drew on both nationalist and imperialist ideas to understand their role as gendarmes in a Jewish Arab society on the verge of civil war. And George Bornstein's chapter, a creative approach to autobiography, is a comparable commentary on how one "Irish" life was lived within transnational frames.

The problem of an inward-looking perspective in Irish history writing has been neatly paralleled by a most unadventurous methodology. Surveying the recent course of revisionist historiography, the dominant mold in Irish academe, Kerby Miller made the biting comment that "much revisionist history—once innovative and stimulating—has become tediously predictable." John Regan has strongly criticized the county histories and local studies favored by many mainstream Irish historians: "In these approaches—local, personal, intimate—the greater political forces at play—abstract, impersonal, universal—too easily can go overlooked. . . . Rather than liberating us this approach may be limiting, even voyeuristic. . . . It also marginalizes ideology as a motivational factor." These criticisms certainly hold water; just as Irish historians have often been unwilling to look further afield for comparative analyses, so too they have ignored new theories, new methodologies, and new approaches. It should be said, though, that Marxist historians and gender historians have a long track record of importing new methods for understanding the Irish past.[4]

The chapters collected here showcase a number of innovative approaches to history writing. Natalie Wynn's survey of the methodology of Irish Jewish history writing demonstrates the limits of previous studies of the Jews of Ireland, Cormac Ó Gráda's *Jewish Ireland in the Age of Joyce* and Dermot Keogh's *Jews in Twentieth Century Ireland* among them. As Wynn brings to light, these works, which have long defined what we think we know about the Irish Jewish community, have shown a marked readiness to accept the central myths of that community rather than engage in a more thorough deconstruction of the meanings of Irish Jewish identity. Wynn's chapter thus sets out a program for future studies of Irish Jewish history. Peter Hession's contribution, part of a number of recent spatially focused works of Irish studies,[5] also shows how much an innovative approach to the past can elucidate what we think we know about Irish Jewish history. Trisha Oakley Kessler's chapter, straddling the boundaries of cultural history and economics, indicates how such a theoretically informed interdisciplinary methodology is needed to fully understand the Irish past in general and the Irish Jewish past in particular.

A smoldering controversy in Irish historiography in recent years has honed in on accusations—and counteraccusations—about possible "ethnic cleansing" of Protestant populations before and after 1922, with communities in West Cork placed at the center of these polemics. Events that may (or may not) have happened in the townland of Dunmanway have been a primary concern, as has the work of the deceased Canadian historian Peter Hart, who first fomented many of these claims. Hart has been posthumously accused, not always unfairly, of simplistic readings of primary sources and, at the outermost limits, of fabricating evidence.[6] The debates have been intense, politically charged, and sometimes verbally violent. They have also quickly turned down a dead-end street. While questions of social tolerance, ethnic violence, and ethnic exclusion, and the imaginary borders a society chooses to draw around itself, are all clearly important, this debate has engaged with none of those issues. Instead, the focus, as with so much else in Irish history writing, has been on the hyper-empirical, on censuses, school records, and endless riffing on demographic minutiae. More profound questions about the nature of the Irish nation, about multiculturalism, and about the multiple meanings of sectarianism and identity have thus been all but ignored. Irish Jewish history provides an escape from this frustrating cul-de-sac.

As Heather Miller Rubens's analysis in this volume shows, many Irish Jews flocked to the cause of Irish nationalism in the crucial years before 1916, yet Jewish support for Irish nationalism was an instant source of controversy. Trisha Oakley Kessler has similarly shown how the de Valera government's willingness to bring Nazi-era Continental Jewish industrialists to Ireland caused a stir among the antisemitic wing of mainstream Irish politics; Jews were seen as too foreign to ever become properly Irish. Abby Bender's chapter shows how Irish identity and Jewishness have had a long and highly complicated history. And Stephen Watt's contribution adeptly explores George Bernard Shaw's investigations of Jewish Questions, in particular the work of the fin-de-siècle pessimist and convert to Zionism Max Nordau. As Watt brings to light, Irishness and Jewishness had their wires crossed in Shaw's vision. Watt's chapter also points to the need for Irish historians to pay greater attention to literature and literary scholars; the parochialism of Irish history writing is thrown into even sharper relief by the cosmopolitanism, interdisciplinarity, and innovative global borrowing of Irish literary theorists.[7] Moreover, Bender, Miller Rubens, Watt, and Oakley Kessler all point to the importance of Jewish studies for Irish studies.

It is not only Irish literary theory but also Irish literature itself that can inform this debate. Ruth Gilligan's novel *Nine Folds Make a Paper Swan* (2016) presents an expansive vision of Jewish-Irish relations that crosses borders of time and space. Divided into three sections, the novel follows a Lithuanian Jewish family who lands in Cork at the turn of the last century. Set fifty years later, the second section shows a traumatized Jewish adolescent navigating an Irish institution for troubled youth. The novel closes with a view of the present day, where a young Irish woman living in Britain contemplates conversion after falling in love with a Jewish Londoner. The novel expertly investigates the intricate analogies between Irish and Jewish culture, laughing, as Joyce did, at much of the supposed correspondences but finding nonetheless (like Joyce also) a foundational commonality in the art of storytelling. Many of Gilligan's characters are storytellers of one kind or another. One, an early Jewish immigrant to Cork, tells a fantastical tale of a group of women who have spent their lives knitting, "until one day they had an argument and tried to pull apart, only to discover that they had knitted themselves together—their clothes, their hair, even their eyelashes, bound into one."[8] This volume is the story of the Irish and Jews, bound together not by wool but by stories. Always multisided, often apocryphal, and rarely straightforward, these knotted yarns of connection are what this collection sets out to unravel.

In the recent essay collection *Kingdom of Olives and Ash* (2017), Irish novelist Colm Tóibín reflects on a visit to Jerusalem in 1992 in the wake of the reelection of Yitzhak Rabin: "It was hard . . . in reading about the early years of Israel, not to be reminded of the revolutionary generation in Ireland in the years leading up to the 1916 rebellion—their idealism, their belief in culture, their sense that they were making a better life for Irish people in the future." He follows this memory with a caveat: "And it was difficult too in thinking about the fate of the Palestinians who suffered in the creation of Israel not to remember the history of dispossession in Ireland, of Irish Catholics in the sixteenth and seventeenth centuries being removed from their land." Like Abby Bender and Elizabeth Cullingford, Tóibín highlights the ultimate futility of drawing stable parallels between ethnic, social, and national groups that are always, inevitably, in flux. The stories a nation tells itself are always open to reinterpretation. Writing in the same book, Tóibín's compatriot Colum McCann records his recent visits to Israel and Palestine. There he met with two men—one Israeli, one Palestinian—who both lost daughters in the ongoing conflict. Their organization, Combatants for Peace, promotes dialogue between the two sides, as, they argue, it is only through the sharing of stories, the building of empathy, and the harnessing of shared sorrow that peace may succeed. As one tells the other, "It's a disaster to discover the humanity and nobility of your enemy—because then he is not your enemy anymore."[9]

The study of the Jews in Ireland and the diasporas of Jews and Irish throughout the world can help readers reflect on today's global issues of increasing immigration and growing intolerance. In "Shalom Park," the Irish Jewish poet Simon Lewis writes of the former center of Jewish Cork:

> As I leave through the Shalom Park gates
> it sounds like a scene from the past,
> the calls and screams of children,
> their mothers shouting in Russian,
> Polish, Czech[10]

The old Jewish quarter has become home to the new Irish and their families. In similar ways, the migratory patterns of the Jews and Irish provide models through which to consider migration today. Though Lewis's poems do not shy away from the bigotry often experienced by Jewish newcomers in Ireland, they are also filled with a tentative optimism, as found in "Landsmanschaft," in which a recently arrived Litvak writes home to his family:

> Though we don't speak their language,
> they tip their hats to us like friends.
> Cousin, I think you'd like it here.[11]

By exploring narratives of arrival, displacement, and belonging, Irish Jewish studies furthers the consideration of Ireland's place in the world and the world's place in Ireland.

Irish Jewish studies is not just the study of actual Jews who happened to live in Ireland (and whose history is often treated as a kind of separate existence in Ireland) but also the history of perceptions of Jews by some of the most important figures and institutions in mainstream Irish life. Irish Jewish studies can and should focus on the core of Irishness, not just on supposed anthropological oddities at the fringes. Studying "Jews" often means studying how particular societies use invented ideas of Jewishness as a means to draw borders around who does belong in society and exclude those individuals who do not. This latter approach, one of the most lively in Jewish studies today, is telegraphed by Bender, Miller Rubens, Watt, and Oakley Kessler.[12] Indeed, all the chapters in this collection are grounded in both Jewish studies and Irish studies and show how much each can inform the other. The Irish and the Jews were two of the classic outliers of Europe, with Irish nationalism and Zionism developing remarkably similar theories about how to end that "Other" status. This collection of essays thus makes a timely and important contribution to both Irish studies and Jewish studies.

Notes | Contributors | Index

Notes

Introduction

1. This point assumes, of course, that the *Annals of Inisfallen* were written contemporaneously; it is far more likely their final composition was completed in the later Middle Ages. This fact greatly complicates our reading of the annals, but this book aims to complicate our understanding of Irish Jewish history.

2. The most recent census in 2016 records the Jewish population in Ireland at 2,557, though Jewish representatives in Ireland suggest that this increase is owed largely to the short-term presence of Israeli specialists in the information technology industry.

3. Guy Beiner, "The Rediscovery of Jewish Ireland," review of *Jewish Ireland in the Age of Joyce* (2006), by Cormac Ó Gráda, *Jewish Culture and History* 15, no. 3 (2014): 259.

4. Derek Penslar, *Shylock's Children: Economics and Jewish Identity in Modern Europe* (Berkeley: Univ. of California Press, 2001), 9.

1. British Israelites, Irish Israelites, and the Ends of an Analogy

1. Thomas Moore, *Moore's Irish Melodies: The Illustrated 1846 Edition* (1846; reprint, Mineola, NY: Dover, 2000), 157; *Joyce's "Ulysses" Notesheets in the British Museum*, ed. Philip F. Herring (Charlottesville: Univ. Press of Virginia, 1972), 82, 53; George Bernard Shaw, *The Drama Observed*, ed. Bernard F. Dukore (University Park: Pennsylvania State Univ. Press, 1993), 100.

2. Mairéad Carew, *Tara and the Ark of the Covenant: A Search for the Ark of the Covenant by British Israelites on the Hill of Tara (1899–1902)* (Dublin: Royal Irish Academy, 1986), 11 (quote), 47, 89.

3. William Butler Yeats, *In the Seven Woods: Being Poems Chiefly of the Irish Heroic Age* (Dundrum: Dun Emer Press, 1903), 1.

4. William Butler Yeats, *Later Articles and Reviews: Uncollected Articles, Reviews, and Radio Broadcasts Written after 1900*, ed. John P. Frayne and Madeleine Marchaterre (New York: Scribner, 2004), 100.

5. John Eglinton, *Anglo-Irish Essays* (1918; reprint, Freeport, NY: Books for Libraries Press, 1968), 35–36.

6. Breandán Ó Buachalla, "James Our True King: The Ideology of Irish Royalism in the Seventeenth Century," in *Political Thought in Ireland since the Seventeenth Century*, ed. D. George Boyce, Robert Eccleshall, and Vincent Geoghegan (London: Routledge, 1993), 26.

7. Raymond Gillespie, "Political Ideas and Their Social Contexts in 17th Century Ireland," in *Political Thought in Seventeenth-Century Ireland*, ed. Jane H. Ohlmeyer, 116. For a discussion of the Bible in Irish, see John Quigley, "The History of the Irish Bible," *Irish Church Quarterly* 10, no. 37 (1917): 49–69.

8. See Abby Bender, *Israelites in Erin: Exodus, Revolution, and the Irish Revival* (Syracuse, NY: Syracuse Univ. Press, 2015), 39.

9. David S. Katz, *God's Last Words: Reading the English Bible from the Reformation to Fundamentalism* (New Haven, CT: Yale Univ. Press, 2004), 41.

10. For more on the English as Israelites, see Tom Claydon and Ian McBride, introduction to *Protestantism and National Identity: Britain and Ireland, c. 1650–c. 1850* (Cambridge: Cambridge Univ. Press, 1998), 11; and Conor Cruise O'Brien, *God Land: Reflections on Religion and Nationalism* (Cambridge, MA: Harvard Univ. Press, 1988), 26.

11. Peter Linebaugh and Marcus Rediker, *The Many-Headed Hydra: Sailors, Slaves, Commoners, and the Hidden History of the Revolutionary Atlantic* (Boston: Beacon, 2000), 290.

12. Tom Garvin, *Mythical Thinking in Political Life: Reflections on Nationalism and Social Science* (Dublin: Maunsel, 2001), 32.

13. Katz, *God's Last Words*, 40; Charles O'Conor, *Dissertations on the Ancient History of Ireland* (Dublin: G. Faulkner, 1753), x, quoted in Colin Kidd, *British Identities before Nationalism* (Cambridge: Cambridge Univ. Press), 34. See also Joep Leerssen, *Remembrance and Imagination: Patterns in the Historical and Literary Representation of Ireland in the Nineteenth Century*, 73; and Joseph Lennon, *Irish Orientalism: A Literary and Intellectual History* (Syracuse, NY: Syracuse Univ. Press, 2004), 2–25 and passim.

14. See Leerssen, *Remembrance and Imagination*, 72; and Lennon, *Irish Orientalism*, 29.

15. William Cooke Taylor and William Sampson, *History of Ireland, from the Anglo-Norman Invasion till the Union of the Country with Great Britain* (New York: Harper, 1841), 299. James Joyce became attached to such theories of the Semitic origin of the Irish language. In "Ireland, Island of Saints and Sages," he writes, "[The Irish] language is oriental in origin, and has been identified by many philologists with the ancient language of the Phoenicians." Joyce, "Ireland, Island of Saints and Sages," in *The Critical Writings*, ed. Ellsworth Mason and Richard Ellmann (Ithaca, NY: Cornell Univ. Press, 1989), 156.

16. The idea that Anglo-Saxons were the descendants of the lost tribes gathered "doctrinal coherence" only in the 1870s and 1880s, just as the century's interest in race was increasing. For more on the racialization of biblical genealogies, see Colin Kidd, *The Forging of Races: Race and Scripture in the Protestant Atlantic World, 1600–2000* (New York: Cambridge Univ. Press, 2006), 209.

17. Ibid., 204; Thomas Rosling Howlett, *Anglo-Israel, the Jewish Problem and Supplement: The Ten Lost Tribes of Israel Found and Identified in the Anglo-Saxon Race* (London: Spangler and Davis, 1892), 90.

18. Edward Hine, *Forty-Seven Identifications of the Anglo Saxons with the Lost Ten Tribes of Israel Founded upon Five Hundred Scripture Proofs* (London: W. H. Guest and S. W Partridge, 1874), 84, 27; Said quoted in Kidd, *Forging of Races*, 213, 82. On Said's comments about the genocidal potential of Exodus, see Bender, *Israelites in Erin*, 8.

19. Theobald Wolfe Tone, *The Writings of Theobald Wolfe Tone, 1763–98*, vol. 2, *America, France and Bantry Bay, August 1795 to December 1796* (Oxford: Oxford Univ. Press, 2001), 301.

20. See Ian McBride, *Scripture Politics: Ulster Presbyterians and Irish Radicalism in the Late Eighteenth Century* (New York: Clarendon Press, 1998).

21. Padraic Colum, ed., *Anthology of Irish Verse* (New York: Boni and Liveright, 1922), 128. This text was first published in the *Irish Penny Journal* on January 16, 1841.

22. Marjorie Howes, "Tears and Blood: Lady Wilde and the Emergence of Irish Cultural Nationalism," in *Ideology and Ireland in the Nineteenth Century*, ed. Tadhg Foley and Sean Ryder (Dublin: Four Courts Press, 1998), 152.

23. Lady Jane Wilde, *Poems*, 2nd ed. (Glasgow: Cameron and Ferguson, ca. 1871), iii.

24. Charles Stewart Parnell, *Field Day Anthology*, 2:310.

25. Cormac Ó Gráda, *Jewish Ireland in the Age of Joyce: A Socioeconomic History* (Princeton, NJ: Princeton Univ. Press, 2006), 10.

26. Elizabeth Cullingford, *Ireland's Others: Ethnicity and Gender in Irish Literature and Popular Culture* (Notre Dame, IN: Univ. of Notre Dame Press in association with Field Day, 2001), 99. See also Aamir Mufti's *Enlightenment in the Colony: The Jewish Question and the Crisis of Postcolonial Culture* (Princeton, NJ: Princeton Univ. Press, 2007); and Brian Cheyette's review of the latter, "The Boy Singer Goes Global," *Times Literary Supplement*, Mar. 21, 2008.

27. Andrew Gibson, *Joyce's Revenge: History, Politics, and Aesthetics in "Ulysses"* (Oxford: Oxford Univ. Press, 2002), 50. It was, unsurprisingly, problematic for nationalists that Irish Jews identified primarily with Unionism—many Jews had family and congregational affiliations in England and felt connected to it. See Ó Gráda, *Jewish Ireland*, 188–89. And as Hasia Diner notes, while the Catholic Irish hated Cromwell, he was "a hero in all renditions of Jewish history, the individual

responsible for bringing to an end the four-century-old Jewish expulsion from England." Hasia Diner, "The Accidental Irish: Jewish Migration to an Unlikely Place," paper presented to the Shelby Cullom Davis Center for Historical Studies, Princeton Univ., Apr. 4, 2003, 53.

28. Ó Gráda suggests that the term *pogrom* is not really appropriate, while Keogh writes that it is. See Ó Gráda, *Jewish Ireland*, 193; and Dermot Keogh, *Jews in Twentieth-Century Ireland: Refugees, Anti-Semitism and the Holocaust* (Cork: Cork Univ. Press, 1998), 26.

29. *United Irishman*, Apr. 23, 1904; Griffith quoted in Dominic Manganiello, *Joyce's Politics* (London: Routledge, 1980), 131.

30. Palmieri was Joyce's voice coach for several lessons that year. See Richard Ellmann, *James Joyce* (Oxford: Oxford Univ. Press, 1959), 151. I am indebted to Paddy Hawe for his generosity in sending me the libretto, concert program, and information on the background of MacDonagh's composition.

31. Johann A. Norstedt, *Thomas MacDonagh: A Critical Biography* (Charlottesville: Univ. Press of Virginia, 1980), 44, 45; Thomas MacDonagh, *The Exodus: A Sacred Cantata* (Dublin: Doremi, 1904), 37; *United Irishman*, June 4, 1904; review quoted in Norstedt, *Thomas MacDonagh*, 46. MacDonagh had certainly observed the connection between the Irish and contemporary Jews, noting that they were alike in their suffering. See D. George Boyce, *Nationalism in Ireland* (London: Routledge, 1995), 310.

32. In *The Resurrection of Hungary: A Parallel for Ireland* (1904), Griffith describes how Count Istvan Széchenyi of Hungary "led his country within sight of the promised Land." Quoted in Gibson, *Joyce's Revenge*, 120.

33. Gibson, *Joyce's Revenge*, 48; O'Grady quoted in Neil R. Davison, *James Joyce, "Ulysses," and the Construction of Jewish Identity* (Cambridge: Cambridge Univ. Press, 1996), 37. Davitt had also written an exposé on the Kishinev pogroms of 1903, a series of articles eventually published as *Within the Pale: The True Story of Anti-Semitic Persecutions in Russia* (London: A. S. Barnes, 1903).

34. Francis Sheehy-Skeffington, *Michael Davitt: Revolutionary, Agitator, and Labour Leader* (London: T. Fisher Unwin, 1908), 268.

35. Fanny Parnell, "Michael Davitt," *Pilot* 43 (Dec. 19, 1880): 1.

36. Michael Davitt, "Ireland and the Jews: A Letter to the Editor," *Freeman's Journal*, July 13, 1893, quoted in Keogh, *Jews in Twentieth-Century Ireland*, 20; Louis Hyman, *The Jews of Ireland from the Earliest Times to the Year 1910* (Shannon: Irish Univ. Press, 1972), 196; Adler quoted in Ira B. Nadel, *Joyce and the Jews* (Iowa City: Univ. of Iowa Press, 1989), 186; O'Connell quoted in Shillman, *Short History*, 75. For the full text of the letter, see Jewish Historical Society of England, *Transactions: The Jewish Historical Society of England* (London: Jewish Historical Society of England, 2009), 4:151.

37. Reverend L. Way, a letter in *The Jewish Expositor and Friend of Israel* (London: B. R. Goakman, 1820), 228 (emphasis in the original).

38. Joyce, *Ulysses* (Paris: Shakespeare, 1922), 36. For identical pagination, see the Oxford World's Classics edition, ed. Jeri Johnson (1993; reprint, Oxford: Oxford Univ. Press, 1993).

39. *United Ireland*, Mar. 9, 1901; Griffith quoted in Carew, *Tara and the Ark of the Covenant*, 80.

40. "There is legend that an emissary of the Anglo-Israelite Society once approached a rich cynic with a demand for a subscription to further his identification of the inhabitants of these isles with the ten Lost Tribes, and that the cynic expressed his readiness to contribute $5 if they would undertake to lose the other two." *Spectator*, May 23, 1914. For analysis of the novel, see Bender, *Israelites in Erin*, 56–59.

2. "Not So Different after All"

1. Significant and welcome exceptions do exist, with the names of Michael C. Coleman, Julia Eichenberg, Bill Kissane, and Shane Nagle featuring on what nonetheless remains a regrettably short list.

2. J. J. Lee, *Ireland, 1912–1985: Politics and Society* (Cambridge: Cambridge Univ. Press, 1987).

3. Cormac Ó Gráda, *Jewish Ireland in the Age of Joyce: A Socioeconomic History* (Princeton, NJ: Princeton Univ. Press, 2006), 191, 201; Eunan O'Halpin, "Politics and the State, 1922–32," in *A New History of Ireland*, ed. J. R. Hill, vol. 7, *Ireland, 1921–84* (Oxford: Oxford Univ. Press, 2003), 105; Lee, *Ireland, 1912–1985*, 78.

4. See, for example, J. Hadler, "Translations of Antisemitism: Jews, the Chinese, and Violence in Colonial and Post-colonial Indonesia," *Indonesia and the Malay World* 32, no. 94 (2004): 291–313; D. G. Goodman and M. Miyazawa, *Jews in the Japanese Mind: The History and Uses of a Cultural Stereotype* (New York: Free Press, 1995); D. Rosenthal, "'The Mythical Jew': Antisemitism, Intellectuals and Democracy in Post-communist Romania," *Nationalities Papers* 29, no. 3 (2001): 419–39; and M. Yegar, "Malaysia: Anti-Semitism without Jews," *Jewish Political Studies Review* 18, nos. 3–4 (2006): 81–97.

5. Quoted in J. Regan, *The Irish Counter-Revolution, 1921–1936: Treatyite Politics and Settlement in Independent Ireland* (New York: St. Martin's Press, 1999), 280.

6. *Irish Times*, Jan. 13, 1942.

7. Maurice Barrès, *Scènes et doctrines du nationalisme* (Paris: Éditions du Trident, 1987), 50.

8. *Connacht Tribune*, Oct. 11, 1941.

9. *Irish Press*, Feb. 15, 1937.

10. See, for example, R. Modras, "Father Coughlin and Anti-Semitism: Fifty Years Later," *Journal of Church and State* 31, no. 2 (1989): 242–43.

11. For discussions of the Fahey oeuvre, see M. C. Athans, *The Coughlin-Fahey Connection: Father Charles E. Coughlin, Father Denis Fahey, C.S.Sp., and Religious Anti-Semitism in the United States, 1938–1954* (New York: Peter Lang, 1991); and E. Delaney, "Political Catholicism in Post-war Ireland: The Revd. Denis Fahey and *Maria Duce*, 1945–54," *Journal of Ecclesiastical History* 52, no. 3 (2001): 487–511.

12. A typical expression of the former is the declaration by Polish primate Cardinal August Hlond in a pastoral letter that the Jews "represent the vanguard of atheism, the Bolshevik movement, and subversive activity. . . . The fact is that the Jews commit fraud, practice usury, and engage in human trafficking. . . . In commercial relations it is good . . . to avoid Jewish shops and Jewish stalls in the markets." *O Katolickie Zasady Moralne*, Feb. 29, 1936, http://patrimonium.chrystusowcy.pl/kandydaci-na-oltarze/sluga-bozy-kard-august-hlond/dziela/1933-1939/List-pasterski-O-Katolickie-zasady-moralne--871#.WBazRmX5rwx.

13. *Irish Independent*, Sept. 21, 1936.

14. *Irish Press*, Feb. 27, 1933.

15. *Connacht Tribune*, Nov. 21, 1936.

16. *Anglo-Celt*, Mar. 19, 1932.

17. John Cooney notes that McQuaid's address was lauded by Dr. Thomas Finegan, bishop of Kilmore. Cooney, *John Charles McQuaid: Ruler of Catholic Ireland* (Syracuse, NY: Syracuse Univ. Press, 2000), 69.

18. *Irish Independent*, Feb. 23, 1937; Vicki Caron, "Catholic Political Mobilisation and Antisemitic Violence in Fin de Siècle France: The Case of the Union Nationale," *Journal of Modern History* 81, no. 2 (2009): 302–3.

19. *Irish Times*, Jan. 12, 2001. See also M. Manning, *The Blueshirts*, 3rd ed. (Dublin: Gill & Macmillan, 2006); Mike Cronin, *The Blueshirts and Irish Politics* (Dublin: Four Courts Press, 1997); and F. McGarry, *Eoin O'Duffy: A Self-Made Hero* (Oxford: Oxford Univ. Press, 2006).

20. R. A. Stradling, *The Irish and the Spanish Civil War, 1936–1939: Crusades in Conflict* (Manchester: Manchester Univ. Press, 1999), 12–14, 35–36; R. M. Douglas, *Architects of the Resurrection: Ailtirí na hAiséirghe and the Fascist "New Order" in Ireland* (Manchester: Manchester Univ. Press, 2009), 22–42.

21. *Aontas Gaedheal Weekly Post*, June 21, 1935; *Connacht Tribune*, Nov. 21, 1936.

22. See, for example, statements of Dr. O'Doherty, bishop of Galway, to the Catholic Young Men's Society annual conference in *Irish Press*, May 21, 1934; and *Irish Independent*, May 21, 1934.

23. L. P. Curtis Jr., "Moral and Physical Force: The Language of Violence in Irish Nationalism," *Journal of British Studies* 27, no. 2 (1988): 150–89.

24. Ronit Lentin notes that a similar stance prevails at present. "Few Irish Jews admit to the existence of antisemitism: better let sleeping demons rest." The long list of antisemitic episodes personally experienced by her, with which she commences

her essay, indicates otherwise. Lentin, "'Who Ever Heard of an Irish Jew?': Racialising the Intersection of 'Irishness' and 'Jewishness,'" in *Racism and Anti-Racism in Ireland*, ed. R. Lentin and R. McVeigh (Belfast: Beyond the Pale, 2002), 164.

25. For Davitt's statement and its context, see A. Bender, *Israelites in Erin: Exodus, Revolution and the Irish Revival* (Syracuse, NY: Syracuse Univ. Press, 2015), 55–56.

26. *Irish Times*, Mar. 29, 1944; *Irish Times*, Sept. 19, 1946; *New York Jewish Week*, Mar. 12, 1978.

27. *Variety*, Nov. 24, 1948; Colonel Dan Bryan to J. P. Walshe, Department of External Affairs, Jan. 6, 1945, Department of External Affairs Records, P. 90, National Archives of Ireland.

28. *Irish Times*, May 12, 1948; *Irish Press*, Feb. 3, 1948; minute by Berry, quoted in *Irish Times*, Jan. 3, 2003.

29. B. Harrison, "Anti-Zionism, Antisemitism, and the Rhetorical Manipulation of Reality," in *Resurgent Antisemitism: Global Perspectives*, ed. A. H. Rosenfeld (Bloomington: Indiana Univ. Press, 2013), 22–23.

30. 336 *Díospóireachtaí Páirliminte—Dáil Éireann*, no. 2, cols. 399, 362, 373, 379 (June 16, 1982).

31. Dr. John Charles McQuaid to Immanuel Jakobovits, May 26, 1949; I. Jakobovits, *Journal of a Rabbi* (1967), quoted in D. Keogh, "'Making *Aliya*': Irish Jews, the Irish State and Israel," in *Ireland in the 1950s: The Lost Decade*, ed. D. Keogh, F. O'Shea, and C. Quinlan (Cork: Mercier, 2004), 260–61; McQuaid to Monsignor Gino Paro, June 13, 1949, quoted ibid., 264.

32. H.-C. Oeser, *Irish Times*, Sept. 25, 1982.

33. The use as an intimidation technique of demands that ethnic or religious minorities publicly sign "loyalty letters" or other attestations repudiating the actions of other members of their supposed communities is a frequent occurrence in the modern era. See, for example, P. Panayi, *The Enemy in Our Midst: Germans in Britain during the First World War* (Oxford: Berg, 1991), 196–97.

34. *Irish Times*, Oct. 20, 1981.

35. *Irish Times*, Apr. 5, 2004.

36. *Irish Times*, Apr. 5, 1994; *People* (London), Feb. 15, 2004; *Belfast Telegraph*, Aug. 29, 2016.

37. *Belfast Telegraph*, May 25, 2005.

38. *Belfast Telegraph*, Aug. 13, 2014.

39. *Belfast Telegraph*, Oct. 3, 2016.

40. *Irish Independent*, May 15, 2008; *Belfast Telegraph*, Aug. 20, 2014.

41. *Irish Independent*, July 21, 2015.

42. *Irish Times*, Jan. 2, 2004.

43. *Irish Daily Mail*, Apr. 3, 2014; *Herald* (Dublin), Nov. 4, 2015; *Limerick Leader*, Nov. 2, 2013.

44. R. Rivlin, *Shalom Ireland: A Social History of Jews in Modern Ireland* (Dublin: Gill & Macmillan, 2003), 238.

45. *Jerusalem Post*, Feb. 9, 2016.

46. E. F. Biagini, "Minorities," in *The Cambridge Social History of Modern Ireland*, ed. E. F. Biagini and M. E. Daly (Cambridge: Cambridge Univ. Press, 2017), 449; *Belfast Telegraph*, July 23, 2014; Oct. 3, 2016.

47. M. Mac Gréil, *Pluralism and Diversity in Ireland: Prejudice and Related Issues in Early 21st Century Ireland* (Dublin: Columba, 2011), 275.

3. "New Jerusalem"

1. Joseph Lennon, *Irish Orientalism: A Literary and Intellectual History* (Syracuse, NY: Syracuse Univ. Press 2008), 11–12, 34; Jerrold Casway, "Gaelic Maccabeanism: The Politics of Reconciliation," in *Political Thought in Seventeenth-Century Ireland*, ed. Jane Ohlmeyer (Cambridge: Cambridge Univ. Press, 2000), 185; Thomas Herron, *Spencer's Irish Work: Poetry, Plantation and Colonial Reform* (London: Routledge, 2007), 55n48. Marc Caball, "Providence and Exile in Early Seventeenth-Century Ireland," *Irish Historical Studies* 29 (1994): 188. For a brief historical overview of the use of the "Chosen People" motif, see Mairead Nic Craith, *Plural Identities—Singular Narratives: The Case of Northern Ireland* (Oxford: Berghahn Books, 2002), 64–68.

2. Sylvester O'Halloran, *A General History of Ireland* (Dublin: Faulkner, Hoey & Wilson, 1778), 1:42; Charles Vallancey, *An Essay on the Antiquity of the Irish Language: Being a Collation of the Irish with the Punic Language* (London: Richard Ryan, 1772); Francis Crawford, "On Hebræo-Celtic Affinities," *Transactions of the Royal Irish Academy* 22 (1849): 371–404. For a later rendering, see the eccentric: P. A. O. Neymo, *Similitudes; or, The Israelites and the Irish* (Galway: Express, n.d.).

3. Kevin B. Nowlan, *Daniel O'Connell: Portrait of a Radical* (Dublin: Appletree Press, 1985), 50n82; D. George Boyce, *Nationalism in Ireland* (Dublin: Routledge, 1995), 18; Shulamit Eliash, *The Harp and the Shield of David: Ireland, Zionism, and the State of Israel* (London: Routledge, 2007), 6; Abby Bender, *Israelites in Erin: Exodus, Revolution, and the Irish Revival* (Syracuse, NY: Syracuse Univ. Press, 2015), 31.

4. For critical acknowledgment of this imagined lineage, see *Irish Nation*, June 1, 1909; and *Sinn Féin*, Sept. 14, 1912.

5. For antisemitism in Ireland, see Conor Morrissey, "Scandal and Anti-Semitism in 1916: Thomas Dickson and 'The Eye-Opener,'" *History Ireland* 24, no. 4 (2016): 30–33; Dermot Keogh and Andrew McCarthy, *Limerick Boycott, 1904: Anti-Semitism in Ireland* (Cork: Mercier Press, 2005); Margaret Daly and Fiona Carmody, "Irish Jews and Anti-Semitism in the Early 20th Century," *Retrospect* 4 (1984): 46–50; Manus O'Riordan, "The Sinn Fein Tradition," in *The Rise and Fall of Irish Anti-Semitism*, ed. Manus O'Riordan (Dublin: Labour History Workshop, 1984),

18–36; and Gerald Moore, "Socio-economic Aspects of Anti-Semitism in Ireland, 1880–1905," *Economic and Social Review* 12, no. 3 (1981): 187–201.

6. Marilyn Reizbaum, *James Joyce's Judaic Other* (Stanford, CA: Stanford Univ. Press), 8, 38–39, 45. See also Andrew Gibson, *Joyce's Revenge: History, Politics, and Aesthetics in "Ulysses"* (Oxford: Oxford Univ. Press, 2005), 50.

7. Marilyn Reizbaum, "A Nightmare of History: Ireland's Jews and Joyce's *Ulysses*," in *Between "Race" and Culture: Representations of "the Jew" in English and American Literature*, ed. Bryan Cheyette (Stanford, CA: Stanford Univ. Press, 1996), 113.

8. See also Ira Bruce Hadel, *Joyce and the Jews: Culture and Texts* (London: Palgrave, 1989), chap. 5.

9. See, for example, Simone Lässig and Miriam Rürup, "What Made a Space 'Jewish'? Reconsidering a Category of Modern German History," in *Space and Spatiality in Modern German-Jewish History*, ed. Simone Lässig and Miriam Rürup (Oxford: Berghahn Books, 2017); Anna Lipphardt, Julia Brauch, and Alexandra Nocke, "Exploring Jewish Space: An Approach," in *Jewish Topographies: Visions of Space, Traditions of Place* (Aldershot: Routledge, 2012), 1–26; Barbara E. Mann, *Space and Place in Jewish Studies* (London: Rutgers Univ. Press, 2012), chap. 7; and Charlotte Elisheva Fonrobert and Vered Shemtov, "Introduction: Jewish Conceptions and Practices of Space," *Jewish Social Studies* 11, no. 3 (2005): 1–8.

10. Sylvie Anne Goldberg, *Clepsydra: Essay on the Plurality of Time in Judaism* (Stanford, CA: Stanford Univ. Press, 2016), 4. See also Gabriel Josipovici, introduction to *The Sirens' Song: Selected Essays of Maurice Blanchot*, ed. Maurice Blanchot and Gabriel Josipovici (Bloomington: Indiana Univ. Press, 1982), 16; Peter Lawson, *Anglo-Jewish Poetry from Isaac Rosenberg to Elaine Feinstein* (London: Vallentine Mitchell, 2006), viii.

11. A. J. Leventhal, "What It Means to Be a Jew," *Bell* 10 (June 1945): 209–10.

12. "The Wandering Jew," *Dublin University Magazine* (Nov. 1876): 584; Frank Pentrill, "The Wandering Jew," *Irish Monthly* 27, no. 309 (1899): 135–38. See also Timothy P. Martin, "Joyce, Wagner, and the Wandering Jew," *Comparative Literature* 42 (1990): 53–54.

13. *Freeman's Journal*, Mar. 29, 1909.

14. For the Palestine Exhibitions, see Stephanie Rains, *Commodity Culture and Social Class in Dublin, 1850–1916* (Dublin: Irish Academic Press, 2010), 225; *Irish Times*, May 21, 22, June 3, 1908; and *Dublin Daily Express*, May 22, 25, June 3, 1908. For theater reviews touching on the portrayal of Jewish characters and Jewishness, see *Evening Herald* (Dublin), Jan. 7, 1893, Nov. 15, 1895; Nov. 1, 1898; Feb. 12, 1901; Apr. 28, May 22, 26, June 27, 1908; Mar. 30, June 19, 1909.

15. Bender, *Israelites in Erin*, chap. 2; Mairéad Carew, *Tara and the Ark of the Covenant: A Search for the Ark of the Covenant by British-Israelites on the Hill of Tara, 1899–1902* (Dublin: Royal Irish Academy, 2003).

16. Cormac O'Grada, *Jewish Ireland in the Age of Joyce: A Socioeconomic History* (Princeton, NJ: Princeton Univ. Press, 2006), 97.

17. For "New Jerusalem," see *Freeman's Journal*, Oct. 8, 1886; June 16, 1891; and *Leader* (Limerick), June 25, 1904. By comparison, I have not been able to find any usage of the term *Little Jerusalem* before 1920.

18. For other "Little Jerusalems," see Suzanne D. Rutland, *The Jews in Australia* (Cambridge: Cambridge Univ. Press, 2005), 33; and Jacob Rader Marcus, *United States Jewry, 1776–1985* (Detroit: Wayne State Univ. Press, 1993), 4:315.

19. O'Grada, *Jewish Ireland*, 102.

20. For the geography of prostitution in Dublin, see Maria Luddy, "'Abandoned Women and Bad Characters': Prostitution in Nineteenth Century Dublin," *Women's History Review* 6, no. 4 (1997): 486–88.

21. *Jewish Chronicle*, Aug. 9, 1889. For efforts to "manage" difference from above, see Jane Burbank and Frederick Cooper, *Empires in World History: Power and the Politics of Difference* (Princeton, NJ: Princeton Univ. Press, 2011), 2.

22. Marion A. Kaplan, *The Making of the Jewish Middle Class: Women, Family, and Identity in Imperial Germany* (New York: Oxford Univ. Press, 1991), 11; Sylvia Barack Fishman, *Jewish Life and American Culture* (New York: SUNY Press, 1999), 83.

23. Natalie Wynn, "The History and Internal Politics of Ireland's Jewish Community in Their International Jewish Context (1881–1914)" (PhD diss., Trinity College Dublin, 2015), 111; *Irishman*, Feb. 4, 1882; *Freeman's Journal*, May 27, 1880.

24. Stamos Papastamou and Gabriel Mugny, "Rigidity and Minority Influence: The Influence of the Social in Social Influence," in *Perspectives on Minority Influence*, ed. Serge Moscovici, Gabriel Mugny, and Eddy van Avermaet (Cambridge: Cambridge Univ. Press, 1985), 124. See, for example, *Freeman's Journal*, Sept. 9, 1880; *Irishman*, Nov. 3, 1883; *Dublin Daily Express*, Apr. 29, 1892; *Weekly Freeman's Journal*, July 9, 1892; and *Freeman's Journal*, Dec. 5, 1892.

25. Chaim Herzog, *Living History: A Memoir* (New York: Pantheon, 1996), 9; Douglas Bartles-Smith and David Gerrard, *Urban Ghetto* (London: Lutterworth Press, 1976), 28.

26. Gerald Y. Goldberg, "'Ireland Is the Only Country . . . ': Joyce and the Jewish Dimension," *Crane Bag* 6, no. 1 (1982): 6.

27. Perrine Simon-Nahum, "French Judaism," in *A History of Private Life: Riddles of Identity in Modern Times* (Cambridge, MA: Belknap Press, 1991), 5:347; Sharon Gillerman, *Germans into Jews: Remaking the Jewish Social Body in the Weimar Republic* (Stanford, CA: Stanford Univ. Press, 2009), 61–62.

28. *Evening Herald* (Dublin), Jan. 23, July 18, 1892.

29. *Freeman's Journal*, Oct. 15, 1886; June 16, 1891.

30. *Dublin Daily Express*, Aug. 25, 1894. See also *Dublin Daily Nation*, Sept. 13, 1899; Aug. 22, 1900.

31. *Warder* (Dublin), Oct. 14, 1899.

32. *Freeman's Journal*, Oct. 15, 1897; *Warder*, June 8, 1901.

33. The distinction was occasionally made by antisemitic commentators. See, for example, *Irish Catholic*, July 22, 1893; and *Evening Herald* (Dublin), July 28, 1900. For depictions of "dirty" versus "white" Jewishness in the context of Joyce's Dublin, see Robert M. Adams, *Surface and Symbol: The Consistency of James Joyce's "Ulysses"* (Oxford: Oxford Univ. Press, 1967), 105–6. For the term in antisemitic discourse more generally, see Alan Dundes, "Why Is the Jew 'Dirty'? A Psychoanalytic Study of Anti-Semitic Folklore," in *From Game to War, and Other Psychoanalytic Essays on Folklore* (Lexington: Univ. Press of Kentucky, 1997), 92; and Robert Michael, *A Concise History of American Antisemitism* (Oxford: Rowman and Littlefield, 2005), 22, 41, 71.

34. For suicides alone, see *Weekly Irish Times*, Mar. 31, 1894; *Dublin Daily Express*, Mar. 27, 1894; and *Evening Herald* (Dublin), Mar. 26, 1894; Aug. 15, 1904; Nov. 7, 1905.

35. *Warder*, June 15, 1901.

36. *Irish Times*, Mar. 2, 1906.

37. *Dublin Daily Express*, Apr. 23, 1887; *Evening Herald* (Dublin), Feb. 18, 1893.

38. Joanna Bourke, "'The Best of All Home Rulers': The Economic Power of Women in Ireland, 1880–1914," *Irish Economic and Social History* 18 (1991): 34–47.

39. *Freeman's Journal*, Oct. 8, 1886; *Dublin Daily Nation*, July 10, 1897.

40. *Dublin Daily Nation*, July 10, 1897.

41. *Freeman's Journal*, Oct. 8, 1886.

42. Douglas Hyde, "The Necessity of Deanglicizing Ireland," in *The Revival of Irish Literature*, ed. Charles Gavan Duffy and George Sigerson (London: T. Fisher Unwin, 1894).

43. *Flag of Ireland*, Jan. 24, 1885.

44. *Freeman's Journal*, Nov. 3, 1885; Mar. 14, 1887; *Dublin Daily Express*, Mar. 11, 1898; *Dublin Daily Nation*, July 10, 1897; Sept. 29, 1898; Sept. 12, 1899; *Dublin Daily Express*, Oct. 27, 1909.

45. The term was used by the chief rabbi of the British Empire, Hermann Adler, in relation to founding a united cemetery in Dublin during 1898. *Jewish World*, May 20, 1898.

46. For the symbolic and social ritual of Jewish burial, see Edith Turner, *Communitas: The Anthropology of Collective Joy* (London: Palgrave Macmillan, 2012), 5, 136, 222; and Barbara Myerhoff, "'Life, Not Death in Venice': Its Second Life," in *Judaism Viewed from within and from Without: Anthropological Studies*, ed. Harvey E. Goldberg (Albany: State Univ. of New York, 1987), 152.

47. *Weekly Irish Times*, May 8, 1880. See also the funeral of the Reverend Israel Leventon, *Warder*, Aug. 19, 1899.

48. National Library of Ireland, MS 24,886, "Newscuttings Concerning the Jewish Cemeteries at Ballybough and Dolphin's Barn, Dublin, c. 1899–1901." Courtesy of the National Library of Ireland.

49. Ibid.; *Irish Times*, Mar. 1, 1904.

50. *Dublin Daily Express*, June 15, 1901.

51. *Freeman's Journal*, Feb. 21, 1900; National Library of Ireland, MS 24,886, "Newscuttings."

52. *Evening Herald* (Dublin), Sept. 5, 1893. For contemporary panics over Jewish emigrant hygiene related to cholera, see also Howard Markel, *Quarantine! East European Jewish Immigrants and the New York City Epidemics of 1892* (Baltimore: Johns Hopkins Univ. Press, 1997), 49.

53. *Dublin Daily Nation*, May 5, 1900; *Evening Herald* (Dublin), June 21, 1899; *Warder*, June 24, 1899; Feb. 24, 1900.

54. *Dublin Daily Nation*, Oct. 2, 1899 (emphasis added).

55. Ibid.

56. National Library of Ireland, MS 22,436, "Record (in Hebrew) of the Chevra Kadisha, Limerick Hebrew Congregation."

57. Diarmuid G. Hiney, "5618 and All That: The Jewish Cemetery Fairview Strand," *Dublin Historical Record* 50, no. 2 (1997): 119. For Dracula, see H. L. Malchow, *Gothic Images of Race in Nineteenth-Century Britain* (Stanford, CA: Stanford Univ. Press, 1996), 153–57. For the "Irish-Jewish" parallel, see also Joseph Valente, *Dracula's Crypt: Bram Stoker, Irishness, and the Question of Blood* (Urbana: Univ. of Illinois Press, 2002), 68.

58. *All Ireland Review*, May 7, 1904; *Times*, Mar. 9, 1888; Moore, "Socio-economic Aspects of Anti-Semitism," 195. See also Lori B. Harrison, "Bloodsucking Bloom: Vampirism as a Representation of Jewishness in *Ulysses*," *James Joyce Quarterly* 36, no. 4 (1999): 782–83; and Ronit Lentin, "Ireland's Other Diaspora: Jewish-Irish within, Irish-Jewish Without," *Golem: European Jewish Magazine* 3, no. 6 (2002): 77.

59. *Dublin Daily Nation*, Sept. 29, 1898. See also *Jewish World*, May 20, 1898; *Jewish Chronicle*, May 28, 1897. The story was later reprinted in *Evening Herald* (Dublin), May 31, 1897.

60. These were St. Kevin's Parade (1883), Oakfield Place (1885), Lennox Street (1887), Heytesbury Street (1891), Camden Street (1892), and Lombard Street (1893). *Jewish Chronicle*, Dec. 4, 1885; Moore, "Socio-economic Aspects of Anti-Semitism," 196.

61. *Evening Herald* (Dublin), Jan. 13, 1897; *Limerick Leader*, Mar. 19, 1902; Wynn, "History and Internal Politics," 270–72.

62. *Jewish Chronicle*, Oct. 20, 1893; *Evening Herald* (Dublin), Nov. 10, 1893; *Daily Express*, Oct. 11, 1893.

63. "Lennox Street Hebrew Congregation Minute Book," June 4, 1893, cited in Wynn, "History and Internal Politics," 209, 226.

64. Mitchell Bryan Hart, *Social Science and the Politics of Modern Jewish Identity* (Stanford, CA: Stanford Univ. Press, 2000), 271. The core text in Jewish "social hygiene" was Alfred Nossig, *Die Sozialhygiene der Juden und des altorientalischen Volkerkreises* (Stuttgart: Deutsche Verlags-Anstalt, 1894). For concerns over the hygiene of Jewish immigrants from within the established community, see also Susan L. Tananbaum, *Jewish Immigrants in London, 1880–1939* (London: Routledge, 2014), 45–48.

65. Colin Holmes, *Anti-Semitism in British Society, 1876–1939* (London: Routledge, 1979), 33; Alan M. Kraut, *Silent Travelers: Germs, Genes, and the Immigrant Menace* (Baltimore: Johns Hopkins Univ. Press, 1994), 65; Maurice Fishberg, *The Jews: A Study in Race and Environment* (New York: Walter Scott, 1911), 280.

66. "Reviews," *Studies: An Irish Quarterly Review* 4 (Dec. 1915): 685–87; "Reviews," *Dublin Journal of Medical Science* 144, no. 551 (1917): 321. See also *Gael*, Mar. 1903.

67. Fishberg, *Jews*, 328, 526. See also Maurice Fishberg, "Health and Sanitation of the Immigrant Jewish Population," *Menorah* 33 (1902): 75–76.

68. Natalie Wynn, "An Accidental Galut? A Critical Reappraisal of Irish Jewish Foundation Myths," in "Immigrants and Minorities" (forthcoming), 5, 7.

69. National Archives of Ireland, Census of Ireland, 1911.

70. Wynn, "Accidental Galut," 13; Lentin, "Ireland's Other Diaspora"; Larry Elyan, "From Zhogger to Cork: An Irish story," *Jewish Chronicle Colour Magazine* (Aug. 1980); Hannah Berman, *Melutovna: A Novel* (London: Arno Press, 1913), chap. 1.

71. Louis Lentin, "Grandpa . . . Speak to Me in Russian," *Translocations* 3, no. 1 (2008): 159. For the Zlotover family narrative of origin in the village of Avaslan, see Hannah Berman and Melisande Zlotover, *Zlotover Story: A Dublin Story with a Difference* (Dublin: Hely Thom, 1966), chap. 2.

72. Barbara E. Mann, *Space and Place in Jewish Studies* (New Brunswick, NJ: Rutgers Univ. Press, 2012), 100.

73. Rory Miller, "The Jews of Ireland: Present and Past," paper delivered at the Jerusalem Centre for Public Affairs, Jerusalem, July 16, 2008, pt. 1, https://www.youtube.com/watch?v=wpi-TqKGo3Y.

74. *Ha-Melitz*, Nov. 18, 1891; *Warder*, July 28, 1900.

75. Wynn, "History and Internal Politics," 210; O'Grada, *Jewish Ireland in the Age of Joyce*, 119.

76. Benjamin Maria Baader, Sharon Gillerman, and Paul Lerner, "Introduction: German Jews, Gender and History," in *Jewish Masculinities: German Jews, Gender, and History* (Bloomington: Indiana Univ. Press, 2012), 9; Rory Miller, "The Look of the Irish: Irish Jews and the Zionist Project, 1900–48," *Transactions of the Jewish Historical Society of England* 43 (2011): 192.

77. Nick Harris, *Dublin's Little Jerusalem* (Dublin: A&A Farmar, 2002), 199, 203; George Mosse, *Confronting the Nation: Jewish and Western Nationalism* (Boston: Brandeis Univ. Press, 1993), 64, 166, 185.

78. *Freeman's Journal*, Oct. 4, 1899.

79. *Warder*, July 6, 1901; Apr. 26, 1902.

80. *Evening Herald* (Dublin), Dec. 6, 1909; Mar. 28, 1910; Sept. 26, 1910.

81. Herzog, *Living History: A Memoir*, 9; *Evening Herald* (Dublin), Aug. 29, 1910.

82. *Evening Herald* (Dublin), Dec. 12, 1910.

83. *Dublin Daily Express*, May 18, 1909.

84. *Irish Times*, May 17, 1909.

85. *Dublin Daily Express*, May 24, 1909.

86. Jessie S. Bloom, "The Old Days in Dublin: Some Girlhood Recollections of the '90s", *Commentary*.(July 1952): 30, 151; *Warder*, May 3, 1902; *Evening Herald* (Dublin), Apr. 23, May 29, Dec. 13, 1909; Harris, *Dublin's Little Jerusalem*, 54–56, 86–88, 94.

87. For a later treatment of the complexities of Irish Zionism, see David Landy, *Jewish Identity and Palestinian Rights: Diaspora Jewish Opposition to Israel* (London: Zed Books, 2011), 41.

88. One did not simply overwrite the other, as suggested in Colum Kenny, "Arthur Griffith: More Zionist than Anti-Semite," *History Ireland* 24, no. 3 (2016): 38–41. For Aodh de Blacam, see *Sinn Féin*, Mar. 16, 1912. For Griffith at the high point of his antisemitic rhetoric during the Limerick Boycott, see, for example, *United Irishman*, Apr. 23, 30, May 28, 1904.

89. A mixture of positive and mildly negative stereotypes was particularly characteristic of discussions of Jewish culture in the Gaelic League press. See, for example, *Fainne an Lae*, June 18, Sept. 3, 1898; *An Claidheamh Soluis*, Feb. 20, Mar. 27, May 8, 1909; Apr. 4, 1914. Here, too, there was some crossover with the principled "anti-antisemitism" on parts of the radical Left. See, for example, *Worker's Republic*, Sept. 24, 1898. And for controversies within advanced nationalism relating to antisemitism, see *United Irishman*, May 28, 1904; and *Irish Peasant*, Mar. 24, 1906.

90. *Dublin Daily Express*, Apr. 26, 1906; *Irish Times*, June 3, 1908.

91. *Freeman's Journal*, Apr. 6, 1899.

92. Homi Bhaba's postcolonial conceptions of cultural hybridity and "unhomeliness" have been analyzed in relation to Irish Jewish writers such as David Marcus and Leslie Deakin. See, in particular, Catherine Hezser, "'Are You Protestant Jews or Roman Catholic Jews?': Literary Representations of Being Jewish in Ireland," *Modern Judaism* 25, no. 2 (2005): 161–78; Hezser, "Post-colonialism and the Irish-Jewish Experience: The Novels of David Marcus and Ronit Lentin," in *Anglophone Jewish Literature*, ed. Axel Stähler (London: Routledge, 2007), 143–60.

4. Irish Representations of Jews and Jewish Responses/Jewish Representations of Jews and Irish Responses

1. On the coining of the term *antisemitism* by populist journalist Wilhelm Marr in 1879, its grounding in now discredited racial theory, and its contribution

to the rise of National Socialism, see, for example, the contributions of Peter Pulzer in Michael Meyer, ed., *German-Jewish History in Modern Times*, vol. 3, *Integration in Dispute, 1871–1918* (New York: Columbia Univ. Press, 1997); and Amos Elon, *The Pity of It All: A Portrait of Jews in Germany, 1743–1933* (London: Penguin Books, 2002). On the ways in which the racial theory of the late eighteenth to early twentieth centuries fed into other forms of anti-Jewish prejudice, culminating in genocide, see George L. Mosse, *Towards the Final Solution: A History of European Racism* (Madison: Univ. of Wisconsin Press, 1985).

2. For this type of "long view," see Robert S. Wistrich, *Antisemitism: The Longest Hatred* (London: Methuen, 1991).

3. For example, see John D. Klier, *Imperial Russia's Jewish Question, 1855–1881* (Cambridge: Cambridge Univ. Press, 1995), xix, 455; and Mosse, *Towards the Final Solution*. Klier notes that *Judeophobia* was the best term he could come up with to describe the nature of negative sentiment toward Jews in late imperial Russia. Nevertheless, Klier felt that the term fell short of encapsulating exactly what he was trying to describe. Both he and Mosse note the chameleon-like ability of anti-Jewish sentiment to defy classification by constantly morphing in response to the ever-changing concerns of society.

4. Zygmunt Bauman, *Life in Fragments: Essays in Postmodern Morality* (Oxford: Blackwell, 1995), 206–22; Bauman, "Allosemitism: Premodern, Modern, Postmodern," in *Modernity, Culture and "the Jew,"* ed. Bryan Cheyette and Laura Marcus (Cambridge: Polity Press, 1998), 143–56; Brian Cheyette, *Constructions of "the Jew" in English Literature and Society: Racial Representations, 1875–1945* (Cambridge: Cambridge Univ. Press, 1993); Walter Laqueur, *The Changing Face of Anti-Semitism* (Oxford: Oxford Univ. Press, 2006), chap. 8; Gavin I. Langmuir, *Toward a Definition of Antisemitism* (Berkeley: Univ. of California Press, 1996), chap. 14; Mícheál Mac Gréil, *Prejudice and Tolerance in Ireland* (Kildare: Leinster Leader, 1977), 333–47; Mac Gréil, *Prejudice in Ireland Revisited* (Kildare: Leinster Leader, 1996), 210–18. Laqueur illustrates how anti-Jewish prejudice can exist in societies where few Jews are to be found, an observation that is borne out by Mac Gréil's findings on Ireland. Langmuir, likewise, notes what he terms the "chimeric" qualities of antisemitism.

5. David Nirenberg, *Anti-Judaism: The History of a Way of Thinking* (London: Head of Zeus, 2013). Compare this basic argument of Mosse, *Towards the Final Solution*, and Langmuir, *Toward a Definition of Antisemitism*, with Wistrich, *Antisemitism: The Longest Hatred*.

6. For example, see Hans Rogger, "Conclusion and Overview," in *Pogroms: Anti-Jewish Violence in Modern Russian History*, ed. John D. Klier and Shlomo Lambroza (Cambridge: Cambridge Univ. Press, 1992), 314–15. Although Rogger's pioneering work has completely transformed the field of Russian Jewish historiography, he and

other experts note the persistence of popular misapprehensions (in this case regarding pogroms) even in scholarly literature.

7. *Jewish Chronicle*, Oct. 28, 1870; Sept. 27, 1872; Feb. 13, 1874; Jan. 29, 1875; Oct. 27, 1876. During the 1870s the *Jewish Chronicle* repeatedly referred to or hinted at the steady decline of Dublin's Jewish community without expressing any expectation of a change in circumstances.

8. For an assessment of why many young Jews have left Ireland in recent years, see Ronit Lentin, "Ireland's Other Diaspora: Jewish-Irish Within/Irish Jewish Without," *Golem* 3 (2002), http://www.hagalil.com/golem/diaspora/ireland-e.htm.

9. Natalie Wynn, "Jews, Anti-Semitism and Irish Politics: A Tale of Two Narratives," *PaRDeS: Zeitschrift der Vereinigung für Jüdische Studien e.V.* 18 (2012): 51–66. For a detailed consideration of these claims, compare with Wynn, "The History and Internal Politics of Ireland's Jewish Community in Their International Jewish Context, 1881–1914" (PhD diss., Trinity College Dublin, 2015), chap. 2.

10. Wynn, "History and Internal Politics," 109–11. This myth may have originated in nineteenth-century Irish nationalist circles that periodically championed Jewish rights, having been propounded by leading figures such as Daniel O'Connell and Michael Davitt. It was later taken up by Anglo-Jewish establishment figures such as Chief Rabbi Nathan Adler and his son, Hermann, and has become a cornerstone of Irish Jewish communal narrative. Ironically, the same myth can be found in parts of Britain and, perhaps, elsewhere.

11. Louis Hyman, *The Jews of Ireland: From Earliest Times to the Year 1910* (Shannon: Irish Univ. Press, 1972), 217; Joe Briscoe cited in Ray Rivlin, *Shalom Ireland: A Social History of Jews in Modern Ireland* (Dublin: Gill & Macmillan, 2003), 32. Assessments such as the ones by Hyman and Briscoe take advantage of the fact that the architect of the boycott, Redemptorist priest Father John Creagh, was educated in France, where, it is claimed, he imbibed the anti-Jewish prejudice that was prevalent in his order (see *Jewish Chronicle*, Apr. 15, 1904).

12. For example, compare with Wynn, "History and Internal Politics," appx. 1.

13. Dermot Keogh, *Jews in Twentieth Century Ireland: Refugees, Anti-Semitism and the Holocaust* (Cork: Cork Univ. Press, 1998), 54–83 (Jews and militant Irish nationalism); Asher Benson, *Jewish Dublin: Portraits of Life by the Liffey* (Dublin: A&A Farmer, 2007); Rivlin, *Shalom Ireland*; Keogh, *Jews in Twentieth Century Ireland*, 238–41; and Brian Fallon, *An Age of Innocence: Irish Culture, 1930–1960* (Dublin: Gill & Macmillan, 1999), 222–23 (Jewish contribution to Irish public life); compare with Wynn, "History and Internal Politics," chap. 2; and Natalie Wynn, "Creating Jewish 'Space' in Irish History: Jews and the 1916 Rising," special issue, "Between History and Popular Culture," *Kulturna Popularna* (forthcoming). The actions of a handful of prominent Jewish nationalists are widely claimed to have been representative of the communal majority, when in fact the weight of evidence implies that most Jews

followed the Irish political mainstream in being loyal British patriots who also favored constitutional nationalism. This "tame" form of nationalism did not threaten Irish political stability or, by extension, the position of Jews within Irish society.

14. Cormac Ó Gráda, *Jewish Ireland in the Age of Joyce: A Socioeconomic History* (Princeton, NJ: Princeton Univ. Press, 2006), 191.

15. Wynn, "Jews, Anti-Semitism and Irish Politics"; Wynn, "History and Internal Politics," chap. 2. In contrast to the mainstream communal narrative, anecdotal evidence indicates that relations between Jews and the Irish majority have frequently been strained. The reflections of various individuals on their sense of belonging in Ireland often display a high degree of self-censorship that, when read against the grain, makes their accounts inherently contradictory.

16. Lentin, "Ireland's Other Diaspora."

17. Derek J. Penslar, *Shylock's Children: Economics and Jewish Identity in Modern Europe* (Berkeley: Univ. of California Press, 2001), 12.

18. Adam Sutcliffe, "Jewish Money and Jewish Politics," and Gideon Reuveni, "Market Economy and Emancipation: From Ellis Rivkin to Moses Mendelssohn," papers presented at the "Paupers and Bankers: Modern Representation of Jews and Money" symposium, Pears Institute for the Study of Antisemitism, London, June 9, 2015. This event as a whole highlighted the complexities involved in this field of research.

19. Penslar, *Shylock's Children*, 122ff.

20. Ernest W. Harris to S. H. Douglas, General Prisons Board, Aug. 29, 1910, and A. Gudansky, Aug. 29, 1910, in Dublin Hebrew Congregation, Correspondence Book no. 2; Minutes of the Dublin Hebrew Congregation, May 8, 1905, and Nov. 9, 1913. That formal arrangements existed with the state authorities regarding Jewish prison inmates indicates that Ireland's immigrant community had its share of shady characters, like Jewish communities the world over. The little evidence that survives in communal records suggests that their crimes were related primarily to dishonest business practices.

21. Mark Duffy, "A Socio-economic Analysis of Dublin's Jewish Community, 1880–1911" (master's thesis, Univ. College Dublin, 1985), 76–77; Rivlin, *Shalom Ireland*, 96–98.

22. Myer Joel Wigoder, *My Life*, ed. Samuel Abel, trans. Louis E. Wigoder (Leeds: J. Porton & Sons, 1935), 66–67, cited as a straightforward critique of immigrant materialism by Duffy, "Socio-economic Analysis," 76–77; and Rivlin, *Shalom Ireland*, 96–98.

23. Wigoder, *My Life*, 96–97, 101, 52–56; compare with Duffy, "Socio-economic Analysis," 76–77. Wigoder in fact describes Bradlaw as "one of the most respected leaders of the Dublin community." Duffy seems to have missed the connection, as Wigoder always refers to Bradlaw by his Hebrew name, Reuben.

24. Rivlin is equally judgmental regarding what she interprets as a degree of communal laxity (as opposed to pragmatism) toward the Jewish dietary laws. She sums up the Irish Jewish community in the early twentieth century as "traditional" rather than "totally Observant." Rivlin, *Shalom Ireland*, 4–6, 59.

25. *Jewish Chronicle*, Dec. 4, 1885. Leventon's claim that Bradlaw was involved in money lending was denied by his son Henry and cannot definitively be proved from later census records.

26. Bill Williams, *The Making of Manchester Jewry, 1740–1875* (Manchester: Manchester Univ. Press, 1976). For an alternative interpretation of Williams's model, with specific relation to the Irish setting, see Wynn, "History and Internal Politics," 199ff.

27. Ó Gráda, *Jewish Ireland*, chap. 3; David Lenten, "1901 Census Ireland" and "Census 1911" (Excel spreadsheets); with thanks to David Lenten.

28. Ó Gráda, *Jewish Ireland*, 66–68; compare with *Jewish Chronicle*, Oct. 20, 1893 (Great Synagogue); Feb. 15, 1895 (Mendelsohn).

29. *Jewish Chronicle*, Feb. 24, 1899 (remark attributed to "Mr. M. E. S—n," presumably M. E. Solomons), and Aug. 24, 1900 (on Mendelsohn's popularity).

30. *Jewish Chronicle*, May 20, 1898.

31. For an overview of how these disputes were covered by the local press, see Des Ryan, "Jewish Immigrants in Limerick: A Divided Community," in *Remembering Limerick: Historical Essays Celebrating the 800th Anniversary of Limerick's First Charter Granted in 1197*, ed. David Lee (Limerick: Limerick Civic Trust, 1997), 166–74; and Ryan, "The Limerick Jews," *Old Limerick Journal* 17 (Winter 1984): 29.

32. *Jewish Chronicle*, Mar. 14 (Adams), 21 (Goldberg), 1902. Goldberg quoted from Deuteronomy 32:15, "Jeshurun waxed fat and kicked," a reference to the purported complacency and ingratitude of the Israelites that the biblical author believed to have given rise to idolatry. Adams cautioned local Jews regarding the injudiciousness of publicly airing their feuds, with regard to both individual well-being and the communal reputation.

33. *Jewish Chronicle*, June 10 (Jaffe), Feb. 5, 26, May 13 (negative assumptions regarding local Jewish behavior), 1904.

34. Harris to Joseph Prag, May 24, 1904; Harris to chief rabbi, Feb. 4, 1904.

35. Joseph Edelstein, author's comment in *The Moneylender* (Dublin: Dollard, 1908).

36. Benson, *Jewish Dublin*, 18. Marleen Wynn, born in 1935, remembers Edelstein from her youth as one of a number of well-known communal eccentrics. Recent research by Barry Montgomery has revealed a number of reports in Irish newspapers concerning Edelstein's antics over the years. Montgomery, "Shylocks and Gombeens: Joseph Edelstein's *The Moneylender* (1908) and the Usury Narratives of Irish Literature," paper presented at the workshop "Reimagining the Jews of Ireland:

Historiography, Identity and Representation," Trinity Long Room Hub, Dublin, June 20–21, 2017.

37. Despite its grandiose aspirations (see *Jewish Chronicle*, Sept. 25, 1908), the association rapidly slid into obscurity, and its stormy inaugural (and probably only) meeting was subsequently described as nothing more than "a Jewish meeting in favour of Home Rule" (*Jewish Chronicle*, May 2, 1913). In this respect, it is also possible that *The Moneylender* was a polemical response to the community's lack of support for the Judæo-Irish Home Rule Association, which may have been interpreted by Edelstein as a lack of Irish patriotism. (With thanks to Aidan Beatty for his suggestion of a [Jewish] nationalist critique of the Irish Jewish community, which prompted me to reconsider the novel's purpose from a nationalist perspective.)

38. Mac Gréil, *Prejudice and Tolerance*, 334; Mac Gréil, *Prejudice in Ireland Revisited*, 210–11.

5. From Richard Lalor Sheil to Leon Pinsker

1. Augustus Bozzi Granville, *The Great London Question of the Day; or, Can Thames Sewage Be Converted into Gold?* (London: Edward Stanford, 1865), 76.

2. 96 Parl. Deb., H.C. (1848), 219–20.

3. Cormac Ó Gráda, *Black '47 and Beyond: The Great Irish Famine in History, Economy, and Memory* (Princeton, NJ: Princeton Univ. Press, 2000).

4. Claire Mitchell, *Religion, Identity and Politics in Northern Ireland: Boundaries of Belonging and Belief* (Burlington, VT: Ashgate, 2006), 74. See also Anne Kane, *Constructing Irish National Identity: Discourse and Ritual during the Land War, 1879–1882* (New York: Palgrave Macmillan, 2012).

5. David Francis Kessler, "The Rothschilds and Disraeli in Buckinghamshire," *Jewish Historical Studies* 29 (1988): 231–52.

6. E. Llewellyn Woodward, *The Age of Reform, 1815–1870*, Oxford History of England (Oxford: Oxford Univ. Press, 1962), 95.

7. James Walsh, "Richard Lalor Sheil," *Decies* 62 (2006): 95–117. For the general background, see George Bornstein, *The Colors of Zion: Blacks, Jews, and Irish from 1845 to 1945* (Cambridge, MA: Harvard Univ. Press, 2011); Matthew Frye Jacobsen, *Special Sorrows: The Diasporic Imagination of Irish, Polish and Jewish Immigrants in the United States* (Berkeley: Univ. of California Press, 2002); Rory Miller, *Ireland and the Palestine Question* (Dublin: Irish Academic Press, 2005); and Cormac Ó Gráda, *Jewish Ireland in the Age of Joyce: A Socioeconomic History* (Princeton, NJ: Princeton Univ. Press, 2006).

8. *A Collection of Speeches Spoken by Daniel O'Connell, Esq. and Richard Sheil, Esq. on Subjects Connected with the Catholic Question* (Dublin: John Cumming, 1828).

9. "The most significant Irish contribution to the legitimate drama came from Richard Lalor Sheil (1791–1851). It is possible to connect Sheil to a wider European

impulse to reinvent the resources of tragic drama for a range of national cultures: writers from Germany, Italy, France, Poland and of course England all sought, as Jeffrey N. Cox puts it, 'to redefine the tragic and renew the stage.'" Claire Connolly, "Irish Romanticism, 1800–1839," in *Cambridge History of Irish Literature*, ed. Margaret Kelleher and Philip O'Leary (Cambridge: Cambridge Univ. Press, 2006), 1:407–48.

10. Maurice Frederick Fitzhardinge Berkeley to Charles Hyett, June 25, 1831, Glos. RO, Hyett mss D6/F32/13, quoted from "Sheil, Richard Lelor (1791–1851), of Long Orchard, Co. Tipperary," in *The History of Parliament*, http://www.historyof parliamentonline.org/volume/1820-1832/member/sheil-richard-1791-1851#footnote1 _pm8fpo6; Gladstone quote in Justin McCarthy, *History of Our Own Times* (New York: Harper Brothers, 1901), 1:34–35; G. W. E. Russell, *Collections & Recollections*, rev. ed. (London: Smith Elder, 1899), 133. See also W. T. McCullagh, *Memoirs of the Rt. Hon. R. L Sheil*, 2 vols. (London: H. Colburn, 1855).

11. "Disraeli's Maiden Speech," *Jewish Messenger* (New York), Aug. 30, 1901, 7.

12. By the end of the nineteenth century, it was widely anthologized, as in Chauncey Mitchell Depew, ed., *The Library of Oratory, Ancient and Modern: With Critical Studies of the World's Great Orators by Eminent Essayists* (London: A. L. Fowle, 1902), 5:439–45; and William Jennings Bryan, ed., *Masterpieces of Eloquence: Famous Orations of Great World Leaders from Early Greece to the Present Time* (New York: P. F. Collier & Son, 1905), 12:4949–55. Ironically, it was not included in *The Speeches of the Right Honorable Richard Lalor Sheil, M.P. with a Memoir, &c.*, ed. Thomas MacNevin (London: H. G. Bohn, 1847).

13. Oliver P. Rafferty, introduction to *Irish Catholic Identities* (Manchester: Manchester Univ. Press, 2013), 11.

14. All references are to 96 Parl. Deb., H.C. (1848) 220–83, here cols. 272–78.

15. There are many accounts. One of the most interesting, given the visual nature of British cultural antisemitism at the time, is Sharrona Pearl, *About Faces: Physiognomy in Nineteenth-Century Britain* (Cambridge, MA: Harvard Univ. Press, 2010), 140–43.

16. Werner Schneiders, *Aufklärung und Vorurteilskritik: Studien zur Geschichte der Vorurteilskritik* (Stuttgart: Frommann, 1983), 263–323.

17. See, for example, Richard D. Hoblyn and L. M. Griffiths, *A Dictionary of Terms Used in Medicine and the Collateral Sciences* (London: Whittaker, 1849).

18. *Columbian Magazine; or, Monthly Miscellany* 110, no. 1 (1786), quoted in *Oxford English Dictionary Online*, s.v. "phobia."

19. *Times* (Nov. 20, 1855): "Baron Prokesch is . . . an 'Anglophobe'; so that it may safely be predicted that he and the British Ambassador will soon be on the very worst possible terms." Quoted from *Oxford English Dictionary Online*, s.v. "Anglophobe."

20. Ernest Cashmore, *Dictionary of Race and Ethnic Relations* (London: Routledge, 1996), 182.

21. The next appearance of this term is in 1890 when, in a communication from Russia, the anonymous *Times* correspondent comments on "the first faint signs of Hebrewphobia [that] showed themselves in the Russian Press" in response to the public outcry of intellectuals headed by Leo Tolstoy against the "persecution of the Jews." The essay labels this response as "anti-Semitism." *Times*, Nov. 18, 1890, 5.

22. Leon Pinsker, *Auto-Emancipation*, trans. D. S. Blondheim (New York: Maccabean, 1906), 6.

23. Ibid., 3.

24. Ibid., 4.

25. Alex Bein, *The Jewish Question: Biography of a World Problem*, trans. Harry Zohn (Rutherford, NJ: Fairleigh Dickinson Univ. Press, 1990), 594.

26. Moshe Zimmermann, *Wilhelm Marr: The Patriarch of Anti-Semitism* (New York: Oxford Univ. Press, 1986), 38ff.

27. Pinsker, *Auto-Emancipation*, 5, 12.

28. Friedrich Nietzsche, "An Spinoza," in *Nachgelassene Fragmente 1884–1885, Herbst 1884,* 28 [49], *Kritische Studienausgabe,* ed. Giorgio Colli and Mazzino Montinari (Munich: dtv Verlagsgesellschaft, 1988), 11:319; Andreas Sommer, "Nietzsche's Readings on Spinoza: A Contextualist Study, Particularly on the Reception of Kuno Fischer," *Journal of Nietzsche Studies* 43 (2012): 156–84.

29. Pinsker, *Auto-Emancipation*, 4, 13.

30. Jacques Kornberg, *Theodor Herzl: From Assimilation to Zionism* (Bloomington: Indiana Univ. Press, 1993), 164.

31. Theodor Herzl, *Zionist Writings: Essays and Addresses*, vol. 1, *January, 1896–June, 1898*, trans. Harry Zohn (New York: Herzl Press, 1973), 166–67.

32. Max Nordau, *Degeneration* (London: William Heinemann, 1898), 243; Nordau quoted in Meir Ben-Horin, *Max Nordau: Philosopher of Human Solidarity* (New York: Conference of Jewish Social Studies, 1956), 180.

33. On the question of comparative Irish and Zionist nationalisms, looking at Pinsker, see Aidan Beatty, "Zionism and Irish Nationalism: Ideology and Identity on the Borders of Europe," *Journal of Imperial and Commonwealth History* 45 (2017): 315–38. Beatty argues for a greater symmetry, given that his comparative text to Pinsker's *Auto-Emancipation* (1882) is Terence MacSwiney's *Principles of Freedom*, written between 1912 and 1916. Sheil's contribution is clearly antecedent to this late-nineteenth-century debate about Zionist and Irish nationalism recuperating Jewish and Irish degeneration. Sheil in spite of his evocation of a form of medical discourse refutes a biological argument with one of civil rights.

6. Rebellious Jews on the Edge of Empire

1. "Judaeo-Irish Home Rule Association: Meeting in the Mansion House; Letters from Mr. John Redmond, M.P. and Mr. John Dillon, M.P.," *Freeman's Journal,*

Sept. 11, 1908, 10; "Week by Week—Jews and Home Rule," *Jewish Chronicle*, Sept. 18, 1908, 7–8; "Provincial Jewry: Dublin," *Jewish World*, Sept. 18, 1908, 22–23.

2. "Judaeo-Irish Home Rule Association," 10.

3. "'Jews and Home Rule': To the Editor of the *Jewish Chronicle*," *Jewish Chronicle*, Sept. 18, 1908, 21; "Correspondence: 'Jews and Politics'—'To the Editor of the *Jewish World*,'" *Jewish World*, Sept. 18, 1908, 16.

4. "Leading Notes: Jews and Politics," *Jewish World*, Sept. 18, 1908, 7; "Week by Week," 7–8.

5. Halitvack [pseud.], "The Dublin Jews from Within," *Jewish World*, Jan. 11, 1907, 33; "The Week—Israel in Erin," *Jewish World*, Jan. 11, 1907, 24.

7. Rethinking Irish Protectionism

1. Michael Kitson and Solomos Solomou, *Protectionism and Economic Revival: The British Interwar Economy* (Cambridge: Cambridge Univ. Press, 1990).

2. Eamon de Valera, "Economic Policy," *Dáil Éireann*, July 12–13, 1928; de Valera, "The Unemployed," *Dáil Éireann*, Apr. 29, 1932, in *Speeches and Statements by Eamon de Valera, 1917–1973*, ed. Maurice Moynihan (Dublin: Gill & Macmillan, 1980), 153–62, 203–9.

3. Scholarship on Irish protectionism has primarily concentrated on the economic impact of such a policy on industrial growth. A. K. Kennedy, T. Giblin, and D. McHugh, *The Economic Development of Ireland in the Twentieth Century* (London: Routledge, 1988); Cormac Ó Gráda, *Economic Development of Ireland since 1870* (Aldershot: E. Elgar, 1994).

4. Dermot Keogh estimates the number to be as few as sixty during the war years. Katrina Goldstone uses a source from the Department of Justice to show that from 1939 to 1947, the Irish Coordinating Committee for the Relief of Christian Refugees, established in December 1938, admitted forty-two refugees through the Jewish subcommittee and ninety-eight non-Aryan refugees. Keogh, *Jews in Twentieth Century Ireland: Refugees, Anti-Semitism and the Holocaust* (Cork: Cork Univ. Press, 1998), 115–98; Goldstone, "'Benevolent Helpfulness'? Ireland and the International Reaction to Jewish Refugees, 1933–9," in *Irish Foreign Policy, 1919–1966: From Independence to Internationalism*, ed. Michael Kennedy and Joseph Morrison Skelly (Dublin: Four Courts Press, 2000), 116–36.

5. This chapter is based in part on material that appears in "In Search of Jewish Footprints in the West of Ireland," in *Jewish Culture and History: Jews in the Celtic Lands*, Taylor and Francis Online, spring 2018.

6. Paul Durcan gave voice to this moment in "The Hat Factory," in *A Snail in My Prime* (London: Harvill Press, 1993), 18. Thanks also to Guy Beiner for his lectures on these factories as examples of social amnesia and to Ernie Sweeney, Castlebar.

7. Like many refugees from Germany and Austria, Thea may not have identified herself as Jewish but was classified as such under the Nuremberg Laws of 1935.

8. Correspondence between Victor Böhm, Brussels, and Thea Dziwietnik, Galway, Nov. 30, 1938, Bruder Böhm Company Collection, 1910–1979, Series II: Business, Leo Baeck Institute Archives, https://archive.org/details/bruederboehm.

9. Kristallnacht (Night of Broken Glass) was an anti-Jewish pogrom in Germany, Austria, and the Sudetenland during November 9–10, 1938, in which two hundred synagogues were destroyed, seventy-five hundred Jewish shops looted, and thirty thousand males Jews sent to concentration camps at Dachau, Buchenwald, and Sashsenhausen.

10. Martin Dean, *Robbing the Jews: The Confiscation of Jewish Property in the Holocaust, 1933–1945* (Cambridge: Cambridge Univ. Press, 2008).

11. *Connaught Telegraph*, May 22, 1937.

12. The importation of ladies' hats was prohibited, save under license, in November 1937. *Irish Press*, Nov. 11, 1937.

13. Rachel Levy-Philipson, interview with the author, Montreal, Oct. 2015. Rachel is the daughter of Serge Philipson, general manager of Les Modes Modernes, Galway.

14. Both Orbach and Goldberg were called back to France, from Ireland, to join the army in 1939. Rachel Levy Archives, Montreal Holocaust Memorial Centre, 2002.08.51–2002.08.100.

15. Visas were extended for Orbach and Philipson, thanks to the continued pressure from Serge Philipson and Senator John McEllin, but both struggled to leave France.

16. Anny Giersh, daughter of Karl Polaisie, a refugee worker at Western Hats, interview with the author, Feb. 20, 2012, http://www.iajgsjewishcemeteryproject.org/czech-republic/chomutov.html.

17. George Clare, *Last Waltz in Vienna: The Destruction of a Family, 1842–1942* (London: Macmillan, 1982), 205.

18. Richard P. Davies, *Arthur Griffith and Non-violent Sinn Fein* (Tralee: Kerryman, 1974), 127–44; Alice Stopford Green, "Arthur Griffith," *Studies: An Irish Quarterly Review* 11, no. 43 (1922): 338–45.

19. Eamon de Valera, "League of Nations: The Testing-Time," in *Speeches and Statements*, ed. Moynihan, 222.

20. de Valera, "Economic Policy," 158.

21. Detailed information on employment numbers formed part of Fianna Fáil's electoral campaign. *Mayo News*, Feb. 13, 1932; *Southern Star*, Feb. 13, 1932.

22. Eamon de Valera, "We Cannot Have It Both Ways," in *Speeches and Statements*, ed. Moynihan, 251–53.

23. *Irish Trade Journal*, Dec. 1933, 143; correspondence between O'Gorman and the Department of Industry and Commerce, NAI,INDC/IND.7/114.

24. Cormac Ó Gráda, *Ireland: A New Economic History* (Oxford: Clarendon Press, 1994), 411; Jon Press, *The Footwear Industry in Ireland, 1922–1973* (Dublin: Irish Academic Press, 1999), 50.

25. Matthew Butler, secretary of the Federation of Saorstat Industries, "Can Industry Cure Unemployment?," *Longford Leader*, Aug. 8, 1936, and *Meath Chronicle*, Aug. 8, 1936.

26. *Meath Chronicle*, Oct. 5, 1935; *Connacht Tribune*, Dec. 3, 1935; *Irish Independent*, Jan. 15, 1937.

27. Herbert Strauss, "Nazi Persecution of the Jews and Emigration," in *Hostages of Modernization: Studies on Modern Antisemitism, 1870–1933/39* (Berlin: W. de Gruyter, 1993), 237–68.

28. United States Holocaust Memorial Museum (USHMM) Archives, DFA/2: pre 100 Series 2/994.

29. This consideration was an important one, as one of the main arguments used by many countries, including Ireland, to refuse settlement was the presence of high unemployment. See Goldstone, "'Benevolent Helpfulness'?," 116–36.

30. Herbert Loebl, "Refugees from the Third Reich and Industry in the Depressed Areas of Britain," in *Second Chance: Two Centuries of German-Speaking Jews in the United Kingdom*, ed. Werner E. Mosse et al. (Tübingen: J. C. B. Mohr, 1991), 384. See also Herbert Loebl, "Government-Financed Factories and the Establishment of Industries by Refugees in the Special Area of the North of England, 1937–1961" (master's thesis, Durham Univ., 1978); Antony Glaser, "Jewish Refugees and Jewish Refugee Industries," in *The Jews of South Wales: Historical Studies*, ed. Ursula Q. Henriques (Cardiff: Univ. of Wales Press, 1993), 177–201.

31. Loebl, "Refugees from the Third Reich," 381.

32. Dean, *Robbing the Jews*, 84–97.

33. USHMM Archives, DFA/2: pre 100 Series 2/994 (emphasis added).

34. Correspondence between Leo McCauley, chargé d'affaires, Paris, and Joseph Walshe, secretary of the Department of External Affairs, Apr. 7, 1933, USHMM Archives, DFA/3/102/9.

35. USHMM Archives, DFA/3/102/9.

36. Siobhan O'Connor, "Policy and Public Opinion towards German-Speaking Exiles in Ireland, 1933–1945" (PhD diss., Univ. of Limerick, 2009), 40.

37. Goldstone, "'Benevolent Helpfulness'?," 119.

38. Mary E. Daly, "Cultural and Economic Protection and Xenophobia in Independent Ireland, 1920s–1970s," in *Facing the Other*, ed. Borbála Faragó et al. (Newcastle: Cambridge Scholars, 2008), 9.

39. In 1938 Ireland received many applications from Jewish industrialists hoping to start clothing and knitting industries. See National Archives of Ireland, Dublin (NAI), DFA/102/571, DFA/102/593, DFA/102/558; and Mary Daly, "An Irish-Ireland for Business? The Control of Manufactures Acts, 1932 and 1934," *Irish Historical Studies* 24, no. 94 (1984): 260.

40. J. J. Lee, *Ireland, 1912–1985: Politics and Society* (Cambridge: Cambridge Univ. Press, 1989), 203.

41. Rachel Phillipson-Levy, *Memoir: An Odyssey Revisited* (Montreal: Montreal Institute for Genocide and Human Rights Studies, Concordia Univ., 2001), http://migs.concordia.ca/memoirs/levy/levy.html. The people of Newport petitioned Senator McEllin to bring work to the town. *Connaught Telegraph*, Mar. 16, 1935.

42. Correspondence between Marcus Witztum and Dr. Koffler, c/o La Tirette, 27 Avenue de Belgique, Antwerp, May 1, 1940, Military Archives, Ireland, G2/2631.

43. Correspondence between Joseph Walshe at the Department of External Affairs and Liam Archer at the Department of Defense, July 23, 1940, Military Archives, Ireland, G2/2631.

44. A proposal to make cut-glass ware in Ireland in partnership with Mr. Frantisek Herman, Bohemia, and Messrs. Brown and Son, Grafton Street, Dublin, NAI/DFA/202/241.

45. Correspondence between the Department of Industry and Commerce and the Comité International pour le Placement des Intellectuels Réfugiés, Dec. 7, 1936, USHMM Archives, DFA/3/102/597.

46. *Irish Independent*, May 16, 1939.

47. *Connaught Telegraph*, July 15, 1939; *Ballina Herald*, July 29, 1939.

48. This number also includes individual refugees who came over as specialist workers in Irish industry. See Gisela Holfter and Horst Dickel, *An Irish Sanctuary: German-Speaking Refugees in Ireland, 1933–1945* (Berlin: Walter de Gruyter, 2017).

49. Correspondence between the Department of Justice and the Department of Industry and Commerce regarding W. Konigsberger, a German National (J) Passport arriving in Ireland to work as a general manager at a glove factory in Tipperary. NAI/DFA/202/452.

50. Correspondence between John Leydon and Joseph Walshe, Sept. 30, 1938, NAI/DFA/102/480.

51. Correspondence between Serge Philipson and Goldie Steuer, USA, July 1941, regarding his difficulties in finding any help for his parents still in Poland who were ill and had no money or food. Levy Archives, 2002.08.85–2002.08.100. The parents of Marcel Goldberg, director of Les Modes Modernes, were denied visas to enter Ireland from France. Goldberg spent the war years hiding in France. NAI/DFA/202/285.

52. NAI/DFA/102/622; Correspondence between the Department of Justice and the Department of External Affairs, Jan. 4, 1939. According to Holfter and Dickel, a man by the name of Siegfried Dziewientnik managed to enter Ireland in April 1939 with the help of the Central Jewish Refugee Aid Committee. It is not clear if this man is a different brother, as the file is currently closed. Holfter and Dickel, *Irish Sanctuary*, 356.

53. Correspondence between the Department of Industry and Commerce and the Association of Old Cumann na mBan, Nov. 30, 1939, USHMM Archives, DFA/243/9; letter received from 1916 Veterans Association, USHMM Archives, DFA/3/102/568; memorandum from the Federation of Irish Industries to the minister for industry and commerce, Mar. 1933, NAI/TID/1207/178. Kilkenny mill workers complained against "Jewish elements pulling strings with the Department of Industry and Commerce." *Kilkenny People*, Oct. 9, 1937.

54. USHMM Archives, IDFA/2: pre 100 Series 2/994. The minister refers to the Department of Justice.

55. Mike Cronin, *The Blueshirts and Irish Politics* (Dublin: Four Courts Press, 1997), 115, 135–67.

56. Ó Gráda, *Economic Development of Ireland*, 412–16; Lee, *Ireland, 1912–1985*, 178.

57. *Parliamentary Debates*, Dáil Éireann Official Report (PDDE), written reports, Nov. 30, 1932, 45.

58. Mary E. Daly, *Industrial Development and Irish National Identity, 1922–1939* (Syracuse, NY: Syracuse Univ. Press, 1992), 122–23.

59. Mary E. Daly, *The Slow Failure: Population Decline and Independent Ireland, 1922–1973* (Madison: Univ. of Wisconsin Press, 2006), 45–46.

60. Fearghal McGarry, *Eoin O'Duffy: A Self-Made Hero* (Oxford: Oxford Univ. Press, 2007), 202.

61. Martin Gilbert, *The Holocaust: The Jewish Tragedy* (London: Fontana Press, 1987), 23.

62. PDDE, July 14, 1933. McGilligan had served as the minister for industry and commerce for the Cumann na nGaedhael party, 1924–32.

63. PDDE, Nov. 22, 1933; May 24, 1934.

64. Daly, "Cultural and Economic Protection and Xenophobia," 11–12.

65. PDDE, Nov. 29, 1933.

66. PDDE, Dec. 19, 1934.

67. PDDE, Nov. 29, 1933; May 29, 1934.

68. Jerry Z. Muller, *Capitalism and the Jews* (Princeton, NJ: Princeton Univ. Press, 2010), 15–71.

69. Accusations of exploitative economic practices by Redemptorist priest Father Creagh led to a boycott of Jews in Limerick in 1904. Father Creagh's actions

found support from voices across Ireland. *Dundalk Democrat*, Jan. 30, 1904; *Kerry Evening Post*, Jan. 13, 1904; *Evening Herald* (Dublin), Jan. 13, 1904; *Freeman's Journal*, Jan. 23, 1904.

70. *Irish Press*, June 13, 1938.

71. *Irish Times*, Mar. 31, 1938; *Irish Press*, Apr. 4, 1938. See also Commission on Vocational Organization, Feb. 15, 1940, evidence of the Drapers' Chamber of Trade (Eire), National Library of Ireland.

72. Daly, "Irish–Ireland," 258.

73. The Alien Name License Regulation required all potential name changers to apply for a license, which provided the government with a means to monitor change. *Irish Press*, Apr. 2, 1936; O'Connor, "Policy and Public Opinion," 88.

74. Daly, "Irish–Ireland," 263–65, 258. A delegation from Les Modes Modernes was summoned to apologize to Bishop Browne for keeping him waiting at the official opening of the factory. Galway Diocesan Archives, Bishop Browne Papers, B/1/20, Diocesan Office, Galway. Irish directors welcomed Eamon de Valera to Western Hats, Castlebar, November 1940. *Connaught Telegraph*, Nov. 16, 1940.

75. *Irish Press*, July 19, 1938.

76. *Irish Press*, Mar. 14, 1941; *Irish Independent*, Mar. 10, 1941; *Longford Leader*, July 22, 1939.

77. Hugh Campbell, "Modern Architecture and National Identity in Ireland," in *The Cambridge Companion to Modern Irish Culture*, ed. Joe Cleary et al. (Cambridge: Cambridge Univ. Press, 2005), 285.

78. *Connacht Tribune*, July 23, 1938.

79. *Irish Press*, Mar. 14, 1941. These factories were known colloquially as "daylight factories." See Amy E. Slaton, *Reinforced Concrete and the Modernization of American Building* (Baltimore: John Hopkins Univ. Press, 2001).

80. *Irish Press*, Mar. 14, 1941.

81. Daly, *Slow Failure*, 26–31.

82. *Irish Press*, Jan. 10, 1935.

83. *Irish Press*, Nov. 13, 1937.

84. *Irish Press*, Sept. 3, 1937.

85. *Connacht Tribune*, Dec. 11, 1937.

86. *Connacht Tribune*, Dec. 11, 1937.

8. Irish, Jewish, or Both

1. James Joyce, *Ulysses*, ed. Hans Gabler et al. (New York: Random House, 1986), 30. Further references will be to this edition and cited parenthetically in the text.

2. Stanley Price, *Somewhere to Hang My Hat: An Irish-Jewish Journey* (Dublin: New Island, 2002), 21. Further references are to this edition and cited parenthetically in the text.

3. David Marcus, *Who Ever Heard of an Irish Jew? and Other Stories* (New York: Bantam Press, 1988). Other observations on Jews and Ireland in this paragraph come mostly from Price, *Somewhere to Hang My Hat*, 21 and passim.

4. Cornel West, *Beyond Eurocentrism and Multiculturalism*, vol. 1, *Prophetic Thought in Postmodern Times* (Monroe, ME: Common Courage Press, 1993), 4; Armstrong quoted in George Bornstein, *The Colors of Zion: Blacks, Jews, and Irish from 1845 to 1945* (Cambridge, MA: Harvard University Press, 2011), 134.

5. David Marcus, *Oughtobiography: Leaves from the Diary of a Hyphenated Jew* (Dublin: Gill & Macmillan, 2001). Further references are to this edition and cited parenthetically in the text.

6. Geoffrey Chaucer, *The Canterbury Tales*, trans. Nevill Coghill (Penguin: Baltimore, 1952), 120.

7. David Marcus, *A Land Not Theirs* (London: Bantam, 1986).

8. John M. Synge, *The Complete Plays* (New York: Vintage Books, 1960), 66.

9. Quoted in Bornstein, *Colors of Zion*, 102.

10. Calvin Trillin, *Messages from my Father* (New York: Farrar, Straus, and Giroux, 1996), 101–2.

11. *The Works of Geoffrey Chaucer*, ed. F. N. Robinson, 2nd ed. (Boston: Houghton Mifflin, 1961), 117.

12. See Sean O'Casey, *Autobiographies* (New York: Carroll and Graf, 1984), 1:511–17.

13. For several amusing fictional takes on the result, see Roddy Doyle's collection *The Deportees, and Other Stories* (New York: Viking Penguin, 2007).

9. The Irish Victory Fund and the United Jewish Appeal as Nation-Building Projects

1. *Gaelic American*, Apr. 12, 1919.

2. Central Zionist Archives, Jerusalem, KH7/303.

3. As Rogers Brubaker notes, social scientists, even professed social constructionists, unwittingly engage in groupism, that is, "the tendency to treat ethnic groups, nations and races as substantial entities to which interest and agency can be attributed." Instead, Brubaker suggests analyzing ethnicity, nationalism, and race as a type of cognition or mode of interpretation and studying the social processes that encourage actors to view the world in such terms. Roger Brubaker, *Ethnicity without Groups* (Cambridge, MA: Harvard Univ. Press, 2004), 164.

4. Benedict Anderson, *Imagined Communities: Reflections on the Origin and Spread of Nationalism* (New York: Verso, 1983), 7.

5. See Kerby A. Miller, *Emigrants and Exiles: Ireland and the Irish Exodus to North America* (New York: Oxford Univ. Press, 1985).

6. See Joel Perlmann, *Ethnic Differences: Schooling and Social Structure among the Irish, Italians, Jews and Blacks in an American City, 1880–1935* (New York: Cambridge Univ. Press, 1988).

7. See Jeffrey Haydu, "Making Use of the Past: Time Periods as Cases to Compare and as Sequences of Problem Solving," *American Journal of Sociology* 104, no. 2 (1998): 339–71; and Haydu, "Reversals of Fortunes: Path Dependency, Problem Solving, and Temporal Cases," *Theory and Society* 39, no. 1 (2010): 25–48.

8. See Bronisław Malinowski, "Kula: The Circulating Exchange of Valuables in the Archipelagoes of Eastern New Guinea," *Man* 20 (1920): 97–105; Alvin Ward Gouldner, "The Norm of Reciprocity: A Preliminary Statement," *American Sociological Review* 25 (1960): 161–78; Marcel Mauss, *The Gift: Forms and Functions of Exchange in Archaic Societies* (New York: Norton, 1967); and Claude Lévi-Strauss, *The Elementary Structures of Kinship* (Boston: Beacon Press, 1969).

9. Mauss, *Gift*. See also Marshall D. Sahlins, "Poor Man, Rich Man, Big-Man, Chief: Political Types in Melanesia and Polynesia," *Comparative Studies in Society and History* 5 (1963): 285–303.

10. See David J. Cheal, *The Gift Economy* (New York: Routledge, 1988).

11. Julie Peteet, "Icons and Militants: Mothering in the Danger Zone," *Signs* 23 (1997): 103–29; Nira Yuval-Davis, *Gender and the Nation* (London: Sage, 1997); Nina Bandelj, "Relevance of Nationality in Cross-border Economic Transactions," *Nationalities Papers* 39 (2011): 963–76.

12. On giving as an organizational challenge, see Kieran Healy, "Altruism as an Organizational Problem: The Case of Organ Procurement," *American Sociological Review* 69 (2004): 387–404.

13. Iddo Tavory, *Summoned: Identification and Religious Life in a Jewish Neighborhood* (Chicago: Univ. of Chicago Press, 2016); Louis Althusser, *Lenin and Philosophy, and Other Essays* (New York: Monthly Review, 1971).

14. See Healy, "Altruism as an Organizational Problem."

15. R. K. Merton, "Three Fragments from a Sociologist's Notebooks: Establishing the Phenomenon, Specified Ignorance, and Strategic Research Materials," *Annual Review of Sociology* 13 (1987): 1–29.

16. Michael Doorley, *Irish-American Diaspora Nationalism: The Friends of Irish Freedom, 1916–1935* (Dublin: Four Courts, 2005).

17. Diarmuid Lynch and Florence O'Donoghue, *The I.R.B. and the 1916 Insurrection: A Record of the Preparations for the Rising* (Boulder: Mercier Press, 1957).

18. *Gaelic American*, Apr. 12, 1919.

19. See *Gaelic American*, Apr. 19, 1919.

20. P&B Associations, the Irish corollary of the better-studied Jewish *landsmanshaftn*, were immigrant social clubs grouped on the basis of county of origins.

In addition to providing a setting for sociable interaction, P&B Associations (the better-organized ones at least) provided basic social support and burial services.

21. *Irish Advocate*, May 24, 1919.

22. *Gaelic American*, Aug. 23, 1919.

23. Lynch to FOIF members, May 1, 1919, AIHS/FOIF Papers/4/1, American Irish Historical Society, New York.

24. *Gaelic American*, July 12, 19, 1919

25. Ernest Stock, *Partners & Pursestrings: A History of the United Israel Appeal* (Lanham, MD: Univ. Press of America, 1987).

26. Jewish Federations were umbrella organizations that typically collected funds for Jewish social needs within particular localities.

27. Stock, *Partners & Pursestrings*.

28. For more on these struggles, see Dan Lainer-Vos, *Sinews of the Nation: Constructing Irish and Zionist Bonds in the United States* (London: Polity Press, 2013).

29. S. Halperin, *The Political World of American Zionism* (Detroit: Wayne State Univ. Press, 1985), 201; Stock, *Partners & Pursestrings*, 101.

30. United Jewish Appeal, *Inquiry of the United Jewish Appeal: Report to the Allotment Committee of the United Jewish Appeal for Refugees and Overseas Needs* (New York: United Jewish Appeal, 1941).

31. Robert Herman to National Field Representatives, Jan. 14, 15, 1943, Central Zionist Archives, CZA/A371/31; Feb. 9, 1944, CZA/A371/21.

32. See *Handbook for Speakers, 1947* (New York: United Jewish Appeal of Greater New York, 1947), CZA/KH7/320.

33. Marc Lee Raphael, *A History of the United Jewish Appeal, 1939–1982* (Chino, CA: Scholars Press, 1982), 41–42.

34. Interview with Henry Montor, 34b(128)/OHD, Central Zionist Archives, Jerusalem; Herman to National Field Representatives, Dec. 4, 1941 (CZA/A371/30).

35. A letter from the 1939 campaign, CZA/A371/516.

36. CZA/KH7/319.

37. See "Collection Manual, 1939," CZA/KH7/305; "Collection Manual, 1942," CZA/A371/24.

38. Herman to National Field Representatives, Nov. 24, 1943, CZA/A371/31.

39. Francis M. Carroll, *American Public Opinion and the Irish Question, 1910–1923: A Study in Opinion and Policy* (Dublin: Gill & Macmillan, 1978); Francis M. Carroll, *Money for Ireland: Finance, Diplomacy, Politics, and the First Dail Eireann Loans, 1919–1936* (Westport, CT: Praeger, 2002); Raphael, *History of the United Jewish Appeal*; Stock, *Partners & Pursestrings*; Michael Doorley, "The Friends of Irish Freedom: A Study of an Irish-American Diaspora Nationalism" (PhD diss., Univ. of Illinois at Chicago, 1995); J. S. Woocher, *Sacred Survival: The Civil Religion of American Jews* (Bloomington: Indiana Univ. Press, 1986).

40. The guilt-ridden debate among Jewish Americans over the proper response that should have been taken to the Holocaust overlooks the role of the UJA in funneling community efforts toward fund-raising.

41. Michael F. Funchion, *Irish American Voluntary Organizations* (Westport, CT: Greenwood Press, 1983).

42. *Gaelic American*, Apr. 12, 1919.

43. CZA\KH7\305; Brubaker, *Ethnicity without Groups*.

44. Only toward the end of 1919 in the Irish case and the mid-1940s in the Jews' case was it that the IVF and UJA, respectively, began to import speakers from Ireland, DP camps, and Palestine. Even then, the selection of speakers and the organization of fund-raising events guarded the interaction so that these representatives would not spoil the images that the IVF and UJA crafted. On the orchestration of these encounters, see Dan Lainer-Vos, "Masculinities in Interaction: The Construction of Israeli and Jewish American Men in Philanthropic Fundraising Events," *Men and Masculinities* 17, no. 1 (2014): 43–66.

45. Shaul Kelner, *Tours That Bind: Diaspora, Pilgrimage, and Israeli Birthright Tourism* (New York: New York Univ. Press, 2013).

46. *Gaelic American*, Apr. 12, 1919

47. CZA\KH7\319. *Yishuv*, literally meaning "settlement," was the term used to describe the Zionist colonies in Palestine during the prestate era.

48. Anderson, *Imagined Communities*, 6–7 (emphasis added).

49. Uri Ben-Eliezer, "A Nation-in-Arms: State, Nation, and Militarism in Israel's First Years," *Comparative Studies in Society and History* 37 (1995): 264–85; http://humphrysfamilytree.com/OMara/republican.loan.html.

10. The Discourses of Irish Jewish Studies

1. Bernard Shaw, preface (1907) to "The Sanity of Art: An Exposure of the Current Nonsense about Artists Being Degenerate," in *Major Critical Essays* (London: Constable, 1932), 286. Further quotations from this preface and from "The Perfect Wagnerite" come from this edition, abbreviated *MCE*, and will be cited parenthetically in the text.

2. Declan Kiberd, *The Irish Writer and the World* (Cambridge: Cambridge Univ. Press, 2005), 273. In fairness, Shaw's writing for money is far more complicated than this formulation would suggest. And the complications have little to do with the thesis that, unlike many enunciations of European modernism, the Irish Revival "did not proclaim the need for eternal antagonism between bohemian and bourgeois" (ibid.). In *Shaw Shadows: Rereading the Texts of Bernard Shaw* (Gainesville: Univ. Press of Florida, 2004), for example, Peter Gahan engages Shaw's most significant reviews between 1885 and 1898, noting that after his resignation from the *World* in August 1894, he soon "missed the regular income from reviewing" and soon thereafter

began a three-year stint as a drama critic. Gahan, *Shaw Shadows: Rereading the Texts of Bernard Shaw* (Gainesville: Univ. Press of Florida, 47). And he also undertook such tasks as writing a review of Nordau. His agreement to undertake such tasks also has a genesis more complicated than mere avarice. As I argue in "Unashamed: Negative Affect and Shaw's Psychology of Money," *SHAW* 36, no. 1 (2016): 53–73, poverty and the need to budget his funds preoccupied both the young Shaw and such characters as the eighteen-year-old Robert Smith, the highly autobiographical protagonist of *Immaturity* (1930). Shaw's relationship to money is thus intimately tied to a larger nexus of psychical relationships than Kiberd's observation implies.

3. See Aidan Joseph Beatty, "The Life That God Desires: Masculinity and Power in Irish Nationalism, 1884–1938" (PhD diss., Univ. of Chicago, 2015), 57–103. Beatty develops a persuasive case that Zionism's "project of muscular self-fashioning" and, in particular, its use of sport and "names drawn from the ancient past" in this project parallel a similar strategy in the discourse of Irish nationalism (89, 90).

4. Paul A. Bové, "Discourse," in *Critical Terms for Literary Study*, ed. Frank Lentricchia and Thomas McLaughlin (Chicago: Univ. of Chicago Press, 1990), 50–65.

5. Direct comparisons of these human catastrophes have been made with increasing frequency. See, for example, Tim Pat Coogan, *The Famine Plot: England's Role in Ireland's Greatest Tragedy* (New York: Palgrave Macmillan, 2012), 3.

6. See Joseph Roach, *Cities of the Dead: Circum-Atlantic Performance* (New York: Columbia Univ. Press, 1996), esp. 4–26.

7. Ibid., 4 (quote), 5. See also Stephen Watt, *"Something Dreadful and Grand": American Literature and the Irish-Jewish Unconscious* (New York: Oxford Univ. Press, 2015), 7–8.

8. George Bornstein, *The Colors of Zion: Blacks, Jews, and Irish from 1845 to 1945* (Cambridge, MA: Harvard Univ. Press, 2011), 58 (song), 35 (caption); Henry J. Byron, *Ivanhoe: An Extravaganza* (London: Thomas Hailes Lacy, 1862), 45.

9. M. Alison Kibler, *Censoring Racial Ridicule: Irish, Jewish, and African American Struggles over Race and Representation, 1890–1930* (Chapel Hill: Univ. of North Carolina Press, 2015), 8. Factors of differentiation also include, in the case of Jewish immigrants, one's country of origin, as one of Shaw's greatest admirers, American playwright Elmer Rice, recalls in his autobiography, *Minority Report* (1964), that in his New York City neighborhood, German Jews often expressed their superiority to and difference from recent arrivals from Eastern Europe.

10. Bruce Robbins, "Comparative Cosmopolitans," in *Cosmopolitics: Thinking and Feeling beyond the Nation*, ed. Pheng Cheah and Robbins (Minneapolis: Univ. of Minnesota Press, 1998), 248.

11. Max Nordau, *Degeneration*, English translation (London: William Heinemann, 1898), 5. Further quotations will be cited parenthetically in the text.

12. Nels Pearson, *Irish Cosmopolitanism: Location and Dislocation in James Joyce, Elizabeth Bowen, Samuel Beckett* (Gainesville: Univ. Press of Florida, 2015), 1. Indeed, during the early years of the Irish Revival, the term *Irish cosmopolitanism*, as Declan Kiberd outlines in *Inventing Ireland: The Literature of the Modern Nation* (Cambridge, MA: Harvard Univ. Press, 1995), approached the oppositional tension of an oxymoron. The issue for W. B. Yeats, John Eglinton, Edward Dowden, and others was the language in which Irish literature would be written: in Irish or in English. In this debate, literary cosmopolitanism was almost inevitably connected to imperialism and, variously, with provincialism. See Kiberd, *Irish Writer and the World*, 155–65.

13. Joseph Valente, "James Joyce and the Cosmopolitan Sublime," in *Joyce and the Subject of History*, ed. Mark A. Wollaeger, Victor Luftig, and Robert Spoo (Ann Arbor: Univ. of Michigan Press, 1996), 60; Rebecca L. Walkowitz, *Cosmopolitan Style: Modernism beyond the Nation* (New York: Columbia Univ. Press, 2006), 61, 64; Valente, "Joyce and the Cosmopolitan Sublime," 63.

14. These remarks come from letters appended to the back matter of Lawrence Langner, *The Magic Curtain: The Story of My Life in Two Fields, Theatre and Invention, by the Founder of the Theatre Guild* (New York: E. P. Dutton, 1951), 454–58.

15. Bernard Shaw, *Complete Plays with Prefaces*, 6 vols. (New York: Dodd, Mead, 1963), 2:471.

16. Bernard Shaw, "A Note on Aggressive Nationalism," *New Statesman*, July 12, 1913, reprinted in *The Matter with Ireland*, ed. David H. Greene and Dan H. Laurence (London: Rupert Hart-Davis, 1962), 81, 11; James Plunkett, *Strumpet City* (1969; reprint, Dublin: Gill & Macmillan, 2013), 317.

17. Sean O'Casey, *Inisfallen, Fare Thee Well* (1949), in *Autobiographies 2* (London: Pan Books, 1980), 150; Christine Sypnowich, "Cosmopolitans, Cosmopolitanism, and Human Flourishing," in *The Political Philosophy of Cosmopolitanism*, ed. Gillian Brock and Harry Brighouse (Cambridge: Cambridge Univ. Press, 2005), 56.

18. Joseph Litvak, "Jew Envy," *Women's Studies Quarterly* 34, nos. 3–4 (2006): 83, 94.

19. Quoted in Julia Williams and Stephen Watt, "Representing a 'Great Distress': Melodrama, Gender, and the Irish Famine," in *Melodrama: The Cultural Emergence of a Genre*, ed. Michael Hays and Anastasia Nikolopoulou (New York: St. Martin's Press, 1996), 249. See also James Vernon, *Hunger: A Modern History* (Cambridge, MA: Belknap Press of Harvard Univ. Press, 2007). Vernon explains that not so long ago, the hungry "commanded little attention and no sympathy"; indeed, at the time of the Famine, hunger was considered either a "natural condition or an inevitable one." Worse, the hungry "were considered not fully human; despite often being the objects of Christian charity, they were figures of opprobrium and disgust, not sympathy," which was largely because their condition was regarded as evidence of their "lack of industry and moral fiber" (2).

20. Williams and Watt, "Representing a 'Great Distress,'" 249.

21. Kwame Anthony Appiah, *Cosmopolitanism: Ethics in a World of Strangers* (New York: W. W. Norton, 2006), 144.

11. The Historical Revitalization of Hebrew as a Model for the Revitalization of Irish?

1. Bernard Spolsky, "Conditions for Language Revitalization: A Comparison of the Cases of Hebrew and Maori," in *Language and the State*, ed. S. Wright (Clevedon: Multilingual Matters, 1995), 5–29.

2. Shlomo Izre'el, "The Emergence of Spoken Israeli Hebrew," in *Corpus Linguistics and Modern Hebrew: Towards the Compilation of the Corpus of Spoken Israeli Hebrew (CoSIH)*, ed. B. H. Hary (Tel Aviv: Chaim Rosenberg School of Jewish Studies, 2003), 85–104.

3. Reg Hindley, *The Death of the Irish Language* (London: Routledge, 1990).

4. See, for example, Ghil'ad Zuckermann and Michael Walsh, "Stop, Revive, Survive: Lessons from the Hebrew Revival Applicable to the Reclamation, Maintenance and Empowerment of Aboriginal Languages and Cultures," *Australian Journal of Linguistics* 31, no. 1 (2011): 111–27. See also Christina Eira, "'One Size Fits All'? A Response to Zuckermann and Walsh, 'Stop, Revive, Survive: Lessons from the Hebrew Revival Applicable to the Reclamation, Maintenance and Empowerment of Aboriginal Languages and Cultures,'" *Australian Journal of Linguistics* 31, no. 1 (2011): 129–36.

5. Spolsky, "Conditions for Language Revitalization."

6. Zohar Shavit in a recent study partially sums up the revitalization of Hebrew as follows: "The complex image of the multilingual reality in Eretz-Israel during the British Mandate teaches us not of any failure of the Hebraization project, but of the immense difficulties it confronted. Yet in hindsight the project, despite these difficulties, was ultimately an undeniable success—one of the most important Zionist undertakings, rightfully depicted as a flagship project of Zionism and as a great achievement of the Yishuv." Shavit, "'Can It Be That Our Dormant Language Has Been Wholly Revived?': Vision, Propaganda, and Linguistic Reality in the Yishuv under the British Mandate," *Israel Studies* 22, no. 1 (2017): 132.

7. Chaim Rabin, "The Revival of Hebrew," in *The Rebirth of Israel*, ed. Israel Cohel (London: Goldston, 1952), 108–19.

8. Jack Fellman, *The Revival of a Classical Tongue: Eliezer Ben Yehuda and the Modern Hebrew Language* (The Hague: Mouton, 1974); Haim Blanc, "The Israeli Koine as an Emergent National Standard," in *Language Problems of Developing Nations*, ed. J. Fishman et al. (New York: Wiley, 1968), 237–51.

9. M. Waxman, "The Story of Hebrew," *Jewish Affairs* 3, no. 2 (1949): 3–33.

10. An important consideration here is the role of Hebrew as a lingua franca and as a tool in nation building in the context of the ingathering from the 1920s onward. In this context, William Safran refers to Hebrew slowly emerging as the popular language, a compromise between the Yiddish spoken by Eastern European immigrants and the Arabic or Ladino current among many Middle Eastern Jews. Safran, "Language and Nation-Building in Israel: Hebrew and Its Rivals," *Nations and Nationalism* 11, no. 1 (2005): 43–63.

11. Benjamin Harshav, *Language in the Time of Revolution* (Berkeley: Univ. of California Press, 1993).

12. Lewis Glinert, "Hebrew-Yiddish Diglossia: Type and Stereotype Implications of the Language of Ganfried Kitzur," *International Journal of the Sociology of Language*, no. 67 (1987): 39–56.

13. Spolsky, "Conditions for Language Revitalization."

14. See Arieh Bruce Saposnik's comprehensive discussion of the state of Hebrew in the Yishuv prior to the *aliyot* in chapter 4 of *Becoming Hebrew: The Creation of a Jewish National Culture in Ottoman Palestine* (Oxford: Oxford Univ. Press, 2008), 65–93.

15. It is apposite here to refer to Revival linguistics as posited by Ghilad Zuckermann in *Language Contact and Lexical Enrichment in Israeli Hebrew* (London: Palgrave Macmillan, 2003). Zukermann's concept of Revival linguistics is modeled on "contact linguistics" and explores the universal constraints and mechanisms involved in language reclamation, renewal, and revitalization.

16. Izre'el, "Emergence of Spoken Israeli Hebrew."

17. Moshe Nahir, "Language Planning and Language Acquisition: The 'Great Leap' in the Hebrew Revival," in *International Handbook of Bilingualism and Bilingual Education*, ed. C. P. Paulston (New York: Greenwood Press, 1988), 275–95.

18. For an interesting account of the crucial role of the schools, see Nirit Reichel, "The First 'Hebrew' Teachers in Eretz Yisrael: Characteristics, Difficulties and Coping Methods (1881–1914)," *History of Education* 38, no. 1 (2009): 9–28.

19. Scott B. Saulson, *Institutionalized Language Planning: Documents and Analysis of the Revival of Hebrew* (The Hague: Mouton, 1979).

20. Fellman, *Revival of a Classical Tongue.*

21. Harshav, *Language in the Time of Revolution.*

22. Roberto Bachi, "A Statistical Analysis of the Revival of Hebrew in Israel," *Scripta Hierosolymitana*, no. 2 (1956): 179–247.

23. Izre'el, "Emergence of Spoken Israeli Hebrew."

24. For a discussion, see Harshav, *Language in the Time of Revolution*; and Spolsky, "Conditions for Language Revitalization."

25. For an interesting reference to this newspaper and the Hebrew revivalist publication *HaShachar* (the Dawn), see Aidan Beatty, "Zionism and Irish Nationalism:

Ideology and Identity on the Borders of Europe," *Journal of Commonwealth History* 45, no. 2 (2017): 315–38.

26. Muiris Ó Laoire, "An Historical Perspective on the Revival of Irish Outside the Gaeltacht, 1880–1930, with Reference to the Revitalization of Hebrew," in *Language and the State*, ed. Wright, 51–64.

27. Joshua Fishman, *Reversing Language Shift* (Clevedon: Multilingual Matters, 1991).

28. Muiris Ó Laoire, *Athbheochan na hEabhraise: Ceacht don Ghaeilge? (The Hebrew Revival: A Lesson for Irish?)* (Dublin: An Clóchomhar, 1999), 56.

29. John Macnamara, "Successes and Failures in the Movement for the Restoration of Irish," in *Can Language Be Planned? Sociolinguistic Theory and Practice for Developing Nations*, ed. Joan Rubin and Björn H. Jernudd (Honolulu: Univ. of Hawaii Press, 1971).

30. Tom Garvin, *Preventing the Future: Why Was Ireland So Poor for So Long?* (Dublin: Gill & Macmillan, 2006), 18; Aidan Doyle, *A History of the Irish Language* (Oxford: Oxford Univ. Press, 2015), 211.

31. See Ó Laoire, *Athbheochan na hEabhraise*, 61.

12. "From the Isle of Saints to the Holy Land"

1. This exploration of the views of Irish BSPP personnel in the postwar period is based largely on personal testimonies, including personal interviews provided by nineteen Irish BSPP veterans (sixteen of them to this author), and detailed correspondence with a further three; interviews and correspondence with, and documentary material supplied by, the families of twenty-two others now deceased; personal correspondence in BSPP personnel files formerly held at the Commonwealth and Empire Museum in Bristol; and published biography and memoir.

2. Article 6 obligated the Mandatory to "facilitate Jewish immigration under suitable conditions" and "encourage . . . close settlement by Jews on the land." http://avalon.law.yale.edu/20th_century/palmanda.asp.

3. A. J. Sherman, *Mandate Days: British Lives in Palestine, 1918–1948* (London: Thames & Hudson, 1997), 26, 28–29.

4. Ibid., 27.

5. Jenifer Glynn, ed., *Tidings from Zion: Helen Bentwich's Letters from Jerusalem, 1919–1931* (London: I. B. Tauris, 2000), 67 (quote), 70 (quote), 42, 190. See also Norman Bentwich and Helen Bentwich, *Mandate Memories, 1918–1948* (London: Hogarth Press, 1965), 133.

6. Samuel was Jewish and an ardent Zionist. Douglas Duff, *Sword for Hire: The Saga of a Modern Free-Companion* (London: John Murray, 1934), 155–56; Pinhas Ofer, "The Role of the High Commissioner in British Policy in Palestine: Sir John

Chancellor, 1928–1931" (PhD diss., Univ. of London, 1971), 49. See also Duff, *Palestine Unveiled* (London: Blackie & Son, 1938), 69, 107.

7. Chancellor also believed "a large element" of Palestine's Jews to be "communist Bolshevik." Chancellor to Passfield, Nov. 2, 11, 1930, and Chancellor to Headlam, Mar. 16, 1930, John Chancellor Papers, MSS.Brit.Emp.s.284, 20/17, Bodleian Library, Oxford.

8. Farrell, "Notes on Jewish Education and the McNair Report," Nov. 30, 1946, British National Archives (TNA), Colonial Office files (CO), CO/733/456/2/21. For further examples of antisemitism among British officials in Mandated Palestine, see Evyatar Friesel, "Through a Peculiar Lens: Zionism and Palestine in British Diaries, 1927–31," *Middle Eastern Studies* 29 (1993): 419–44; Bernard Wasserstein, *The British in Palestine: The Mandatory Government and the Arab-Jewish Conflict, 1917–1929* (Oxford: Oxford Univ. Press, 1991), 11–12, 22, 26, 66–67; Christopher Hammond, "Ideology and Consensus: The Policing of the Palestine Mandate, 1920–1936" (PhD diss., Univ. of London, 1991), 60–61, 100–102; and C. R. Ashbee, *A Palestine Notebook, 1918–1923* (London: Heinemann, 1923). On early British anti-Zionism, see Wasserstein, *British in Palestine*, 34–57; John McTague, *British Policy in Palestine, 1917–1922* (London: Univ. Press of America, 1983), 112–18, 180–86; Tom Segev, *One Palestine, Complete: Jews and Arabs under the British Mandate* (London: Abacus, 2000), 92–97; and Horace Samuel, *Unholy Memories of the Holy Land* (London: Hogarth Press, 1930), 58–64.

9. John C. Holliday, ed., *Eunice Holliday: Letters from Jerusalem during the Palestine Mandate* (London: Radcliffe Press, 1997), 14; Sherman, *Mandate Days*, 25. Eunice was the wife of Cliff Holliday, an architect and town planner with the Palestine government.

10. Samuel, *Unholy Memories*, 35–37.

11. Richard Crossman, *Palestine Mission: A Personal Record* (New York: Harper & Brothers, 1947), 130 (quote), 3 (quote), 123, 131.

12. Arthur Koestler, *Promise and Fulfilment: Palestine, 1917–1949*, 2nd ed. (London: Papermac, 1983), 15.

13. The danger posed by Bolshevism was also downplayed by Eugene Quigley, the Sligo-born officer who created Palestine Police CID in 1919–20. Shortly after leaving the department on promotion in February 1922, Quigley told the Colonial Office that, "periodic scares" notwithstanding, "there [would] be no serious menace of Bolshevism" in Palestine, and, indeed, it was only after his departure that the department began to fixate on the issue. TNA, CO/733/39/357.

14. Saul Zadka, *Blood in Zion: How the Jewish Guerrillas Drove the British Out of Palestine* (London: Brassey's, 1995), 106.

15. Frank Jones, interview by Nick Kardahji, Mar. 16, 2006, Jones Collection, GB165-0389, Middle East Centre Archive, St. Antony's College, Oxford (MECA);

Bertie Braddick, interview by William Ward, May 7, 2006, Braddick Collection, GB165-0394, MECA; Jack Binsley, *The Palestine Police Service* (London: Minerva Press, 1997), 128–29.

16. David Cesarani, "'Oh, You Can't Help Feeling for Them': The British Security Forces and the Jews in Palestine, 1945–48," in *Rethinking History, Dictatorship and War: New Approaches and Interpretations*, ed. Claus-Christian W. Szejnmann (London: Bloomsbury, 2009), 191–210; Anthony Wright, *One Man in His Time: The Diary of a Palestine Policeman, 1946–1948*, ed. Michael Lang (Lewes: Book Guild, 1997), 16–17; A. M. O., "British Soldiers! British Policemen! British Civilians," n.d., ca. spring 1948, 23, copy in Desmond Morton Collection, GB165-0405, MECA; A. M. O., "A Policeman's Lament," Mar. 3, 1948, copy in Eugene Hoade Papers (EHP), Irish Franciscan Archives, Killiney, Co. Dublin, box 1, file 8.

17. J. W. W. Murphy, "Irishmen in Palestine, 1946–1948," *Studies: An Irish Quarterly Review* 40 (1951): 84; Thomas Freeburn, interview with the author, Essex, June 12, 2011; Martin Moore, interview with the author, Dublin, Sept. 8, 2009. As a former member of the British armed forces, Cawley was, like Jack Binsley, angered by what he saw as Jewish ingratitude for Britain's role in Nazism's defeat: "My attitude was 'well why are [the Jews] attacking us?' We've just been involved in a war to sort of, not to save them, but they were saved from further humiliation by us taking part in it. So why were they behaving like this?" David Hewitt and Jean Hewitt, *George Burton: A Study in Contradictions* (London: Hodder & Stoughton, 1969), 38; Patrick Cawley, interview with the author, Lancashire, Oct. 10, 2011.

18. Alexander McClements, interview with the author, Cheltenham, July 29, 2014. McClements, a clerk from Coleraine in Derry, enlisted as a BSPP constable in April 1946.

19. Born in London to Irish parents, McDonnell self-identified as Irish and actively supported Irish causes. In 1908 he published a book criticizing British policy in Ireland and calling for Home Rule. Michael F. J. McDonnell, *Ireland and the Home Rule Movement* (Dublin: Maunsel, 1908).

20. Chancellor quoted in Wasserstein, *British in Palestine*, 214; Shertok/Sharett quoted in Tom Bowden, *The Breakdown of Public Security: The Case of Ireland, 1916–1921, and Palestine, 1936–1939* (London: Sage, 1977), 224.

21. "No Nation," the *Irish Independent* newspaper declared in 1947, "has better reason than our own to realise the evil effects that flow from the partition of a country." *Irish Independent*, Dec. 9, 1947.

22. Cawley, interview; Freeburn, interview; Moore, interview; "The Situation in Palestine," unsigned typescript, June 9, 1936, Jerusalem & East Mission Collection, GB165-016, 61/1, MECA; John Fitzpatrick, interview with the author, Longford, June 18, 2012; William Bond, Derry, correspondence with the author, May 2, 2013.

23. *Crusader*, Feb. 1, 1931. So vocal did Hoade become on the issue that he was placed on a short list of candidates to head up the city's proposed international regime.

24. Ibid.

25. Hoade held such views all his life. He treated with skepticism the Second Vatican Council's "watery" revision of replacement theology and continued to see the Israelis as "outwardly . . . very anti-Christian." "Notes on Jewish History," n.d., ca. late 1960s, EHP, 1/8.

26. Murphy, "Irishmen in Palestine," 81, 83; *Connacht Tribune*, Dec. 9, 1939. Hoade was himself frequently described in press reports as a former Irish rebel, but there is no evidence to support this assertion.

27. J. J. W. Murphy, "Britain and Palestine: The First Five Years," *Irish Ecclesiastical Record* 74 (1950): 126.

28. Undated press clippings, EHP, 1/7; *Irish Independent*, Apr. 17, 1954.

29. Joseph Campbell, *Baksheesh and Brahman: Asian Journals—India* (Novato: New World Library, 1995), 2; *Al-Jihad* (Jordan), Dec. 5, 1956.

30. Pollock, from Ballymoney, County Antrim, transferred to Palestine's civilian administration in July 1920 as deputy governor in Ramallah, serving until 1923, when he was appointed an administrative officer in Nigeria. He returned in 1930 to Palestine, where he served in senior positions until the Mandate's termination.

31. Pollock to father, Dec. 21, 1919, and May 28, 1920, James Pollock Papers, 2/5, Public Records Office of Northern Ireland, D1581, Belfast. Courtesy of the Deputy Keeper of the Records.

32. Quoted in Bowden, *Breakdown of Public Security*, 224–25.

33. Wasserstein, *British in Palestine*, 214. For McDonnell's statements of his views, see *Weekly Review*, Feb. 9, 16, 1939; and *Patriot*, June 1, 1939.

34. See, for example, McDonnell, *Ireland and the Home Rule Movement*, 227–28.

35. Bentwich and Bentwich, *Mandate Memories, 1918–1948*, 87.

36. Born in Dublin in 1887, Cunningham served as Palestine's high commissioner from November 1945 until the Mandate's end. For an insight into his view of the Arabs, see Cunningham to Hall, Oct. 14, 1946, Sir Alan Cunningham Collection, GB165-0072, 1/1/184, MECA.

37. Cawley, interview; Michael Burke interview, Feb. 20, 1988, Imperial War Museum, London, sound archive no. 10125; Freeburn, interview.

38. Fitzpatrick, interview.

39. Doherty was a convinced antisemite. For him, Vespasian, who spearheaded the Roman defeat of the Jewish Revolt of 66–70 CE that culminated in Jerusalem's destruction, "ought to appear [to Christian believers] as that Messenger who God ordained was not to leave a stone upon a stone in the city within whose walls the Son of Man endured His Passion and Death," and he wrote of Jews who "quit their

malodorous quarters" every Friday to "grieve over a real woe, while expiating the greatest of all crimes . . . the sense of their punishment quite overwhelming." Edward Doherty, *Here and There in Palestine* (Dublin: Fitzpatrick, 1939), 10, 18–19.

40. Colin Schindler, *The Triumph of Military Zionism: Nationalism and the Origins of the Israeli Right* (London: I. B. Tauris, 2006), 145.

41. Zadka, *Blood in Zion*, 195.

42. Ibid., 110.

43. Dáil Debates, June 20, 1947, vol. 106, no. 9, c2335-7, http://oireachtasdebates .oireachtas.ie. For examples of Ziff's Ireland-Palestine parallels, see *Irish Times*, Jan. 11, 1947; and *New York Journal-American*, Feb. 28, 1947.

44. Cawley, interview; McGrath, interview.

45. John Humphreys, interview with the author, West Sussex, Sept. 26, 2011; Patrick Tynan, interview with the author, Hampshire, Aug. 27, 2012; Paul Mac-Mahon interview, June 13, 1996, Imperial War Museum, sound archive no. 16689. See also Burke, interview.

46. John P., interview with the author, Waterford, Sept. 7, 2003; Moore, interview. This view of the Haganah was not unique to the Irish. See, for example, Francis Mark Russell, interview by Eugene Rogan, May 16, 2006, Russell Collection, GB165-0396, MECA; and Cesarani, "'Oh, You Can't Help Feeling for Them,'" 209.

47. Cawley, interview. Gruner was in fact twenty-five years old. The *Irish Times* also noted "a fairly close analogy between the case of Kevin Barry and that of Dov Gruner," in that, while their executions were "within [Britain's] legal rights," they were politically unwise. *Irish Times*, Apr. 17, 1947.

48. Murphy, from Banteer in Clare, enlisted in April 1947. Gerald Murphy, *Copper Mandarin: A Memoir* (London: Regency Press, 1984), 29, 28; MacMahon, interview; John P., interview; Burke, interview; McGrath, interview.

49. Hadara Lazar, *Out of Palestine: The Making of Modern Israel* (New York: Atlas, 2011), 67. Born in Dublin in 1908, Hogan was posted to Palestine in 1936 as chief magistrate and was subsequently appointed crown counsel. He transferred to Aden as attorney general in 1946, before returning to Palestine in 1947 as solicitor general.

50. Humphreys, interview; Murphy, *Copper Mandarin: A Memoir*, 34.

Epilogue

1. James Connolly, "The Coming Generation," *Workers Republic*, July 15, 1900.

2. Ciaran O'Neill, *Catholics of Consequence: Transnational Education, Social Mobility and the Irish Catholic Elite, 1850–1900* (Oxford: Oxford Univ. Press, 2014); Enda Delaney, *Irish Emigration since 1921* (Dublin: Economic and Social History Society of Ireland, 2002). See also the collection of essays O'Neill and Delaney edited in "Beyond the Nation: Transnational Ireland," Éire-Ireland 51, nos. 1–2 (2016).

3. David Fitzpatrick counters accusations of a historiographic insularity—"One of the boldest academic deceptions of our time"—with the claim that an undefined "great proportion of Irish historians" have always had a transnational approach. Fitzpatrick, "We Are All Transnationalists Now," *Irish Historical Studies* 41 (2017).

4. Kerby Miller, *Ireland and Irish America: Culture, Class and Transatlantic Migration* (Dublin: Field Day, 2008), 371; John Regan, *Myth and the Irish State* (Dublin: Irish Academic Press, 2013), 210–11; Raymond Crotty, *Ireland in Crisis: A Study in Capitalist Colonial Underdevelopment* (Dingle: Brandon, 1986); Denis O'Hearn, *The Atlantic Economy: Britain, the US and Ireland* (Manchester: Manchester Univ. Press, 2001); Maurice Coakley, *Ireland in the World Order: A History of Uneven Development* (London: Pluto Press, 2012); Margaret Ward, *Unmanageable Revolutionaries: Women and Irish Nationalism* (London: Pluto Press, 1995); Louise Ryan and Margaret Ward, eds., *Irish Women and Nationalism: Soldiers, New Women and Wicked Hags* (Dublin: Irish Academic Press, 2004); Maria Luddy, *Prostitution and Irish Society, 1800–1940* (Cambridge: Cambridge Univ., Press, 2008).

5. Marti D. Lee and Ed Madden, eds., *Irish Studies: Geographies and Genders* (Cambridge: Cambridge Scholars Press, 2008); Caitriona Ó Torna, *Cruthú na Gaeltachta, 1893–1922: Samhlú agus buanú chonstráid na Gaeltachta i rith na hAthbheochana* [The Creation of the Gaeltacht, 1893–1922: Imagining and Perpetuating the Gaeltacht Construct during the Gaelic Revival] (Dublin: Cois Life, 2005); Aidan Beatty, *Masculinity and Power in Irish Nationalism* (London: Palgrave, 2016), chap. 4.

6. Peter Hart, *The IRA and Its Enemies: Violence and Community in Cork, 1916–1923* (Oxford: Oxford Univ. Press, 2000). John Regan's criticisms of Hart are accumulated in *Myth and the Irish State*. See also David Fitzpatrick, "Dr Regan and Mr Snide," *History Ireland*, no. 3 (2012); and Eve Morrison, "Kilmichael Revisited: Tom Barry and the 'False Surrender,'" in *Terror in Ireland*, ed. David Fitzpatrick (Dublin: Lilliput, 2012).

7. Sharae Deckard, "World Ecology and Ireland: The Neoliberal Ecological Regime," *Journal of World-Systems Research* 22, no. 1 (2016): 145–76; Declan Kiberd, *Inventing Ireland: The Literature of the Modern Nation* (Cambridge, MA: Harvard Univ. Press, 1996); Brian Ó Conchubhair, *Fin de Siècle na Gaeilge: Darwin, An Athbheochan agus Smaointearacht na hEorpa* [Irish Language Fin de Siècle: Darwin, the Gaelic Revival and European Intellectual Thought] (Cló Iar-Chonnachta: Indreabhán, 2009); Maureen O'Connor, *The Female and the Species: The Animal in Irish Women's Writing* (Oxford: Peter Lang, 2010).

8. Ruth Gilligan, *Nine Folds Make a Paper Swan* (London: Atlantic, 2016), 20.

9. Colm Tóibín, "Imagining Jericho," in *Kingdom of Olives and Ash: Writers Confront the Occupation*, ed. Michael Chabon and Ayelet Waldman (London: Fourth Estate, 2017), 226; Colum McCann, "Two Stories, So Many Stories," ibid., 399.

10. Simon Lewis, "Shalom Park," in *Jewtown* (Galway: Doire Press, 2016), 67.

11. Simon Lewis, "Landsmanschaft," ibid., 17.

12. Daniel Boyarin, *Border Lines: The Partition of Judeao-Christianity* (Philadelphia: Univ. of Pennsylvania Press, 2004); Jeremy Cohen, *Living Letters of the Law: Ideas of the Jew in Medieval Christianity* (Berkley: Univ. of California Press, 1999); Jay Gellar, *The Other Jewish Question: Identifying the Jew and Making Sense of Modernity* (New York: Fordham Univ. Press, 2011); David Nirenberg, *Anti-Judaism: The Western Tradition* (New York: W. W. Norton, 2013).

Contributors

Aidan Beatty is the author of *Masculinity and Power in Irish Nationalism, 1884–1938*, awarded the American Conference for Irish Studies prize for best book in history and social sciences in 2017. His work has also appeared in *Israel Studies*, the *Journal of Jewish Studies*, and the *Journal of Imperial and Commonwealth History*. He has a PhD from the University of Chicago and has held postdoctoral fellowships at Concordia University, Montreal, and Trinity College, Dublin. He currently teaches in the Gender, Sexuality, and Women's Studies Program at Wayne State University, Detroit.

Abby Bender is the author of *Israelites in Erin: Exodus, Revolution, and the Irish Revival* (Syracuse University Press, 2015). She is the assistant director of the HEOP Opportunity Program and assistant professor of the practice in English at the College of Mount Saint Vincent. Her new book project looks at representations of breast-feeding in Irish literature and culture.

George Bornstein is C. A. Patrides Professor of Literature, Emeritus, at the University of Michigan, Ann Arbor. Among his books are *The Colors of Zion: Blacks, Jews, and Irish, 1845–1945* (2011) as well as studies and editions of W. B. Yeats and other modernist poets.

R. M. Douglas is the Russell Colgate Distinguished University Professor of History at Colgate University, New York, and the author, among other books, of *Architects of the Resurrection: Ailtirí na hAiséirghe and the Fascist "New Order" in Ireland* (2009).

Seán William Gannon is Irish Research Council Postdoctoral Research Fellow at the Centre for Contemporary Irish History, Trinity College, Dublin. His doctoral thesis explored Irish involvement in colonial policing in the twentieth century through a case study of the policing of the British Palestine Mandate, and his postdoctoral research is focused on the wider issue of Irish participation in the British imperial project after Irish independence in 1922. His other research interests include the fate of the "losers" in the Irish Revolution (particularly the Royal Irish Constabulary), police counterinsurgency, Irish Jewish history, and the history of Zionism and the Israeli state.

Sander L. Gilman is a distinguished professor of the liberal arts and sciences as well as a professor of psychiatry at Emory University. A cultural and literary historian, he is the author or editor of more than ninety books. His *Are Racists Crazy? How Prejudice, Racism, and Antisemitism Became Markers of Insanity* was published in 2016; his most recent edited volume is a double issue of the *European Review of History/Revue européenne d'histoire* titled *Jews on the Move: Particularist Universality in Modern Cosmopolitanist Thought,* also published in 2016. He has been a visiting professor at numerous universities in North America, South Africa, the United Kingdom, Germany, Israel, China, and New Zealand. He was made a fellow of the American Academy of Arts and Sciences in 2016.

Peter Hession received a BA in history from Trinity College, Dublin, before completing a master's in philosophy and a PhD at the University of Cambridge. His dissertation investigated the relationship between social authority and the urban environment in nineteenth-century Ireland and is currently being converted into a monograph. Since graduating, he has been a visiting fellow at the Irish College, Paris, and lectured at the Universities of Cambridge and Leicester. He currently teaches modern Irish history at University College Dublin.

Trisha Oakley Kessler is a PhD candidate at the School of History, University College Dublin. Her research explores how Fianna Fáil's economic nationalism shaped Irish society through the prism of Jewish refugee industries in provincial Ireland. She teaches on a special subject paper in the history faculty at Cambridge University, "An Alternative History of Ireland: Religious Minorities and Identity in the 26 Counties, 1900–1959," and is a convener of the Modern Irish History Seminar. Trisha is also a research associate at the Woolf Institute, Cambridge.

Dan Lainer-Vos is an adjunct assistant professor in the Department of Sociology at the University of California, Los Angeles. He uses insights from economic sociology and science and technology to study nation building in a transnational context. Dan's first book, *Sinews of the Nation: Constructing Irish and Zionist Bonds in the United States*, recipient of an honorable mention for the Viviana Zelizer Book Award, examines how the Irish and Zionist national movements reached out and enrolled their respective compatriots in the United States. His current book project examines the formation of the Israel lobby in Washington during the 1950s and 1960s.

Heather Miller Rubens is the executive director and Roman Catholic scholar of the Institute for Islamic, Christian, and Jewish Studies in Baltimore. She holds degrees from Georgetown University, the Oxford Centre for Hebrew and Jewish Studies, and the University of Chicago and is currently a member of the Committee on Ethics, Religion, and the Holocaust at the United States Holocaust Memorial Museum. Some of her recent publications include "Something Has Gone Wrong: The JFS Case and Defining Jewish Identity in the Courtroom," *Maryland Journal of International Law* (2014).

Dan O'Brien is an Irish Research Council Postdoctoral Fellow at University College Dublin, where he is completing a monograph on the intertwining fiction of Philip Roth and Edna O'Brien. He is the coeditor of the collection *New Voices: Contemporary American Literature* (2018) and has published reviews and articles in *Breac, Philip Roth Studies*, and the *Dublin Review of Books*.

Muiris Ó Laoire is the author of several articles, chapters, and books on language revitalization, language teaching, language policy, and multilingualism. His PhD at the National University of Ireland, Maynooth (1996), explored comparative aspects of language revitalization in Israel and Ireland from 1800 to 1920. He was appointed full professor at the International Centre for Language Revitalization Studies at the Auckland University of Technology, New Zealand, in 2013. He currently works in the Department of Early Childhood and Education in the School of Health and Social Sciences at the Institute of Technology, Tralee, Ireland.

Stephen Watt is Provost Professor of English at Indiana University, where he teaches a variety of courses in Irish studies. His most recent books include *Beckett and Contemporary Irish Writing* (2009) and *"Something Dreadful and*

Grand": American Literature and the Irish Jewish Unconscious (2015). He is completing a book on Bernard Shaw's fiction, psychoanalysis, and affect.

Natalie Wynn is a postdoctoral researcher affiliated with the Herzog Centre for Jewish and Near Eastern Religions and Culture, Trinity College, Dublin, specializing in Irish Jewish history in the nineteenth and early twentieth centuries.

Index